Lecture Notes of the Institute for Computer Sciences, Social Informatics and Telecommunications Engineering 493

The LNICST series publishes ICST's conferences, symposia and workshops.

LNICST reports state-of-the-art results in areas related to the scope of the Institute. The type of material published includes

- Proceedings (published in time for the respective event)
- Other edited monographs (such as project reports or invited volumes)

LNICST topics span the following areas:

- General Computer Science
- E-Economy
- E-Medicine
- Knowledge Management
- Multimedia
- Operations, Management and Policy
- Social Informatics
- Systems

Eva Brooks · Jeanette Sjöberg ·
Anders Kalsgaard Møller · Emma Edstrand
Editors

Design, Learning, and Innovation

7th EAI International Conference, DLI 2022
Faro, Portugal, November 21–22, 2022
Proceedings

 Springer

Editors
Eva Brooks ⓘD
Aalborg University
Aalborg, Denmark

Jeanette Sjöberg ⓘD
Halmstad University
Halmstad, Sweden

Anders Kalsgaard Møller ⓘD
Aalborg University
Aalborg, Denmark

Emma Edstrand
Halmstad University
Halmstad, Sweden

ISSN 1867-8211 ISSN 1867-822X (electronic)
Lecture Notes of the Institute for Computer Sciences, Social Informatics
and Telecommunications Engineering
ISBN 978-3-031-31391-2 ISBN 978-3-031-31392-9 (eBook)
https://doi.org/10.1007/978-3-031-31392-9

This Springer imprint is published by the registered company Springer Nature Switzerland AG
The registered company address is: Gewerbestrasse 11, 6330 Cham, Switzerland

Preface

We are delighted to introduce the proceedings of the seventh edition of the European Alliance for Innovation (EAI) International Conference on Design, Learning & Innovation (DLI 2022). This conference, held in Faro, Portugal and online, November 21–22, 2022, brought together researchers and practitioners around the world to share their latest research findings in relation to development, use, and learning with digital and emergent technology. The theme for DLI 2022 was *Design and learning for a digitalized society*. The conference presentations revealed that rapid development of new technology and digitalization can reshape the ways in which we work with design, providing novel opportunities for innovations in both formal and informal learning environments.

The technical programme of DLI 2022 consisted of 13 papers were selected from 45 submissions each paper secured at least three double-blind reviews, arranged in three conference sessions. The conference sessions were: Session 1 – Digital Environments and Design Processes Fostering Learning and Interaction; Session 2 – Designs for Innovative Learning with Digital Technology; Session 3 – Digital Approaches Shaping Educational Practices. The three tracks were chaired by Jeanette Sjöberg, Camilla Finsterbach Kaup, and Anders Kalsgaard Møller respectively. Their contribution to the discussion related to the sessions was productive and created fruitful and engaged dialogues.

Tuula Nousiainen, from the Department of Teacher Education, University of Jyväskylä, Finland, gave an inspirational keynote presentation titled *Perspectives to Meaningful Learning Experiences in Digital Environments*, which was grounded in her experiences from several years of research on elements of meaningful technology-enhanced learning and how this relates to learner and teacher competencies. She discussed the topic in light of key concepts such as playfulness and gamification, participation and agency, creative production, and interaction. These themes were illustrated with concrete examples ranging from her early research on children's participation in technology design to her ongoing work related to interaction and collaboration in digital learning environments in teacher education.

The paper presentations addressed new dimensions and key challenges and provided critical and innovative perspectives on employing digital technologies and games to develop and implement future design, learning, and innovation. This was reflected, among others, by the paper which received the Best Paper Award of EAI DLI 2022, titled *Learning Management Systems in Flexible Learning Environments – A Study of Teachers' Experiences* by Joel Holzberg, Michel Thomsen, and Maria Åkesson from Halmstad University in Sweden – Congratulations on the award!

The collaboration between the General Co-chairs, Jeanette Sjöberg and Eva Brooks, and the Technical Programme Committee Co-chairs, Emma Edstrand and Anders Kalsgaard Møller, was essential for the successful planning and performance of the conference. We sincerely appreciated the coordination with Radka Vasileiadis, team leader of the European Alliance of Innovation (EAI) conference department, and Veronika Kissova, conference manager at the EAI, as well as with the steering chair

Imrich Chlamtac. We are genuinely thankful for the organising committee team's support: Emma Edstrand and Anders Kalsgaard Møller (Technical Programme Committee Co-chairs), João Martinho Moura (Web Chair), Kristina Wollentz (Publicity and Social Media Chairs), Patrik Lilja Skånberg (Workshop and Symposium Chair), Jenny Engström (Sponsorship and Exhibit Chair), Kristina Wollentz (Poster Chair), Camilla Finsterbach Kaup (Work in Progress Chair), and Jenny Engström (Local Chair).

We also acknowledge the outstanding work by the Technical Programme Committee Members. Last, but not least, we are grateful to all the authors who submitted their papers to the DLI 2022 conference.

The conference took place in the wonderful city of Faro in Portugal, and we thus want to direct our sincere thanks to the local host of the conference, namely the Center for Research in Arts and Communication / Centro de Investigação em Artes e Comunicação (CIAC) at the University of the Algarve, whose personnel gave their time to work with us towards realizing these two days of conference presentation. We also thank the host venue's staff at Eva Senses Hotel in Faro and all local volunteers. As DLI 2022 was collocated with the 11th EAI International Conference on ArtsIT, Interactivity & Game Creation, we want to express our genuine gratitude to the ArtsIT general chair Jorge Carrega and the general co-chair Anthony Lewis Brooks; thank you for a great collaboration.

To conclude, we strongly believe that the DLI conference provides a fruitful forum for researchers, designers, educators, and practitioners to discuss the cross-disciplinary field of digital technology and its implications on design, learning, and innovation. We also expect that future DLI conferences will provide a fruitful arena for knowledge exchange, as indicated by the contributions presented in this volume. We are looking forward to seeing you all in Aalborg, Denmark for DLI 2023 – most welcome!

Eva Brooks
Jeanette Sjöberg
Anders Kalsgaard Møller
Emma Edstrand

Organization

Steering Committee

Imrich Chlamtac   University of Trento, Italy
Eva Brooks   Aalborg University, Denmark

Organizing Committee

General Co-chairs

Eva Brooks   Aalborg University, Denmark
Jeanette Sjöberg   Halmstad University, Sweden

TPC Chair and Co-chairs

Emma Edstrand   Halmstad University, Sweden
Anders Kalsgaard Møller   Aalborg University, Denmark

Sponsorship and Exhibit Chair

Jenny Engström   Halmstad University, Sweden

Local Chair

Jenny Engström   Halmstad University, Sweden

Workshops Chair

Patrik Lilja Skånberg   Halmstad University, Sweden

Publicity and Social Media Chair

Kristina Wollentz   Halmstad University, Sweden

Publications Chairs

Eva Brooks   Aalborg University, Denmark
Jeanette Sjöberg   Halmstad University, Sweden

Web Chair

João Martinho Moura   Polytechnic Institute of Cávado and Ave, Portugal

Posters Chair

Kristina Wollentz   Halmstad University, Sweden

Work in Progress Chair

Camilla Finsterbach Kaup   Aalborg University, Sweden

Technical Program Committee

S. R. Balasundaram   National Institute of Technology Tiruchirappalli,
                                     India
Pedro Beça   University of Aveiro, Portugal
Thomas Bjørner   Aalborg University, Denmark
Anthony Lewis Brooks   Aalborg University, Denmark
Eva Brooks   Aalborg University, Denmark
Ana Amélia Carvalho   University of Coimbra, Portugal
Martin Cooney   Halmstad University, Sweden
Susanne Dau   University College of Northern Denmark,
                                     Denmark
Emma Edstrand   Halmstad University, Sweden
Taciana Pontual da Rocha Falcão   Universidade Federal Rural de Pernambuco,
                                     Brazil
Dorina Gnaur   Aalborg University, Denmark
Lena Hylving   Halmstad University, Sweden
Henrik Kasch   University College of Southern Denmark,
                                     Denmark
Camilla Finsterbach Kaup   Aalborg University, Denmark
Susanne Lindberg   Halmstad University, Sweden

Anders Kalsgaard Møller	Aalborg University, Denmark
Stamatis Papadakis	University of Crete, Greece
Maja Højslet Schurer	Aalborg University, Denmark
Jeanette Sjöberg	Halmstad University, Sweden
Michele Della Ventura	Music Academy "Studio Musica", Italy

Contents

Digital Approaches Shaping Educational Practices

Digital Environments and Design Processes Fostering Learning and Interaction

Learning Management Systems in Flexible Learning Environments - A Study of Teachers' Experiences

Joel Holtzberg, Michel Thomsen, and Maria Åkesson[✉]

Halmstad University, Halmstad, Sweden
maria.akesson@hh.se

Abstract. Digital transformation in education is expected to progress teaching and learning. To meet this expectation, new types of classrooms called flexible learning environments are designed where digital resources such as learning management systems (LMS) are integrated. This raises the question of how LMS are experienced by teachers in flexible learning environments and how their teaching practice and competence development is supported by the LMS. In this study, ten teachers working in flexible working environments have been interviewed about their experiences with LMS. The study resulted in four themes of experiences (1) Lack of adoption, (2) Control within the system, (3) Collaboration and competence development, (4) Direct feedback and interactions. The insights of the study contributes with implications for choosing and integrating LMS in flexible learning environments.

Keywords: Learning Management System · User Experience · Flexible Learning Environments · Digital Competence

1 Introduction

The Swedish National Agency for Education states that to increase the quality of education, schools need to put emphasis on digitalization (Skolverket, 2022). In Sweden, students in lower and middle school have access to a wide arrangement of digital resources. Schools, in turn, implement LMS and flexible learning environments to support teachers' daily operations and facilitate learning. This transformation challenges teachers and educational design, i.e., how to efficiently use digital resources. Recently, digital resources and physical resources (classrooms, furniture, etc.) have been combined into flexible learning environments where teaching resources are movable and arranged to support teachers, students' needs and innovative teaching (Neill & Etheridge 2008). Research shows (see e.g. Kariippanon et al., 2018) that flexible learning environments give students more control over their learning, promote student-centered pedagogy, allow for better interactions, and that pupils students find such environments comfortable.

Digitalization within education has faced different challenges over time. Early digitalization initiatives often suffered from complicated user-interfaces, while today's

E. Brooks et al. (Eds.): DLI 2022, LNICST 493, pp. 3–21, 2023.
https://doi.org/10.1007/978-3-031-31392-9_1

school leaders and teachers struggle with how best to implement digital resources to support their teaching (Engen, 2019). To put it short, educational institutions can have a hard time implementing digital resources that substantially supports teaching (see e.g. Rasheed et al., 2020). In addition, there is a societal demand onto teachers to be digitally competent and find innovative ways of implementing technology in teaching and learning (Instefjord & Munthe, 2017). One example of the latter is the integration of LMS and flexible learning environments. In Sweden, teachers are often obliged to use a LMS to administrate teaching, distribute information, support pupils and learning activities, etc. Teachers are the main contributors of material on a LMS. They adapt the systems to their teaching to help students understand and achieve their course objectives. The integration of LMS and flexible learning environments inevitably forms a complex learning environment that has not previously been studied.

According to Gudmundsdottir and Hatlevik (2018) newly graduated teachers have mixed experiences with digital resources in teaching. The authors also note the importance of unveiling and understanding negative aspects of digitalization and teachers' experiences. Previous research (see e.g. Al-Fudail & Mellar, 2008) show that when implementing digital resources, stress may occur as a result of a disconnect between the environment and the teacher's skills of using the technology. This raises the question of how teachers experience LMS in flexible learning environments? This paper examines that question to better understand teachers' daily operations in such environments. The aim is to provide insights of value when choosing and integrating LMS in flexible learning environments.

In this study, data was collected from 10 interviews with teachers and analyzed with a thematic analysis which resulted in four themes of experiences (1) Lack of adoption, (2) Control within the system, (3) Collaboration and competence development, (4) Direct feedback and interactions. The insights from the study are presented as four implications when choosing an LMS to be integrated in a flexible learning environment.

2   Related Literature

The literature search was done to investigate previous research to provide an overview of related research. The literature search was based on a systematic search approach (see e.g. Webster & Watson 2002). This resulted in a systematic search that included backwards searching in relevant articles. The search ended when no new concepts were identified. A review of literature is often ready when the articles do not present any new concepts (Webster & Watson 2002). The searches were done in databases such as Scopus and Google scholar. The point of departure for the search words were inspired from the research question itself. The search words that were used included for example: "Flexible learning environments", "Digital learning platforms", "Learning management system", "Digital competence". The search words were used in combination with each other. This resulted in articles about LMS, Schools using technology within flexible learning environments and digital competence development. Additionally, literature was identified to highlight challenges with implementation of technology in teaching. The result is an overview of previous research that served as guidance for the interviews.

The related literature concerns three areas of relevance for this study; The flexible learning environment, learning management systems and digital competence. The literature section also covers challenges related to integrating learning management systems in flexible learning environments.

2.1 The Flexible Learning Environment

Classrooms are traditionally designed with a set arrangement which offers a static one-way of teaching (Neill & Etheridge 2008). Designers are now encouraged by the ministry of education to create futuristic learning environments with more dynamic features (Wells et al., 2018). In flexible learning environments the traditional set of arrangements are replaced with modifiable rooms where the furniture is no longer static (Kariippanon et al., 2018). The change of the classroom structure allows teachers to work collaboratively due to the breakout from the traditional structure (Niemi, 2021). With no frontal teaching students tend to work in smaller groups and teachers can help students with one-to-one learning (Niemi, 2021). Flexible learning environments are designed to support different learning activities facilitated by teachers, both in the physical room and in digital spaces. These activities can be simultaneous interactive. Therefore, both the physical room and the digital spaces such as LMS are open and flexible to support various types of activities. The environment is flexible in terms of being reconfigurable depending on needs. Wood (2018) argues that the concept of flexibility within a space is a cohesive connection between the space, actors and resources and people are often forgotten in the equation of what makes it flexible.

Teaching in flexible learning environments where the classroom barriers has been removed makes it visible and public for teachers to adopt strong teaching practices; moreover, this means that teachers can learn from each other and exchange materials and resources with colleagues (Niemi, 2021). In order to improve the collaboration and the way of working within these environments, educational software is frequently used to support both teaching and learning (Kariippanon et al., 2018). Students' freedom to use digital resources can sometimes result in misuse such as playing games. However, when students use digital resources as intended it allows for individualistic engagement but also collaborative work between students (Cleveland, 2018). The overlap of physical and digital resources further strengthens the abilities for students to learn from home (Cleveland, 2018). The development of technological progress allows for blended learning which uses technology to facilitate content outside of the classroom (Strayer, 2012). Blended learning is a combination of personal interactions and digital instructions (Rasheed et al., 2020). Previous research on blended learning is primarily focused on students' challenges with the online component and less attention is focused on teachers' challenges (Rasheed et al., 2020). Teachers are challenged when using technology in their teaching due to their perception and negative attitudes for using it; the educational institution on the other hand have issues distributing the correct technology to support its teachers (Rasheed et al., 2020).

2.2 Learning Management Systems

Digital resources such as LMS (learning management systems) come from a variety of stakeholders such as private actors that now show an interest in the monetizable value of digital educational resources (Godhe & Hashemi, 2019; Player-Koro et al., 2018). The implementation of LMS can result in outside actors impacting the curriculum and get partial influence on how the school is to be digitized (Godhe & Hashemi, 2019). Private digital services that are used within a governmental setting leads to schools and state education authorities having problems regulating them (Player-Koro et al., 2018). Big tech companies now provide LMS solutions for schools. These providers offer their services with the selling point that they want what's best for the education system; however, even if the use of these services is free, the teachers and students pay with their data and activity from the service (Godhe & Hashemi, 2019). Companies are taking advantage of education technology now being commodified and utilize it for profit-gains (Player-Koro et al., 2018). There might be a presence of stress associated with integration of digital resources within a classroom, the reasoning being a disconnect between the environment and the teachers' individual skill using the digital resources (Al-Fudail & Mellar, 2008). Workload created by technology can be another way of how technostress occurs (Ayyagari et al., 2011). Teachers require digital confidence when using digital resources in order to be a good role model for its students (Krumsvik, 2008). Ertmer and Ottenbreit-Leftwich (2010) explain that one of the most efficient ways for teachers to increase their confidence is by allowing them to have their own successful personal experiences with the technology.

2.3 Digital Competence

Concepts to describe digital skills and abilities can vary depending on geographic positioning (Skolverket, 2019). However, Skolverket (2019) explains that the Swedish curriculum is now adjusted to only use the concept of "Digital Competence". Spante et al. (2018) explain that when digital competence is used in publications it orients towards technology used in a professional setting with an underlying political intent. Skolverket (2019) further pose four points that are included in the definition of digital competence in the context of education.

1. Understanding the social impact of digitalization
2. An understanding of digital resources and the usage of them
3. A critical approach to technology
4. Creatively solve problems with digital resources

Digitalization creates a societal demand on teachers to be digitally competent; and further requires them to create new ways of implementing technology within the classroom (Instefjord & Munthe, 2017). Engen (2019) explains professional digital competence as adapting skills with digital resources to specific situations and being able to apply it to different subjects. Educators of teachers wield responsibility in the form of possessing the skills to use digital resources in their teaching, but they should also help teachers develop their professional digital competence (Instefjord & Munthe, 2017).

There is an expectation that professional teachers will possess digital skills that are adaptable within teaching to help the students with their development of digital competence (Engen, 2019). One argument for why newly graduated teachers are not ready for using digital resources within their teaching is the lack of preparation in their teacher training (Gudmundsdottir & Hatlevik, 2018; Fernández-Cruz & Fernández-Díaz, 2016). Newly graduated teachers' experiences with digital resources in teaching varies, and there is call for future research to understand why teachers develop negative feelings towards such implementation (Gudmundsdottir & Hatlevik, 2018). According to Godhe and Hashemi (2019) there are no explicit guidelines on what teacher students' digital competence should involve due to decision making on a local level.

From this literature overview we summarize the challenges of integrating LMS in flexible learning environments in Table 1.

Table 1. Summary of challenges from the literature section.

Identified challenges	Authors
1. Teacher's attitude and the implementation of the correct technology	Rasheed et al., 2020
2. People are often forgotten in the equation of flexible environments	Wood, 2018
3. Implementation of LMS can result in outside actors impacting the curriculum	Godhe & Hashemi, 2019
4. Stress when there is a disconnect between the environment and the teachers' skills with digital resources	Al-Fudail & Mellar, 2008
5. Digitalization creates a societal demand on teachers to be digitally competent. (And this requires them to create new ways of implementing technology within the classroom)	Instefjord & Munthe, 2017
6. Workload by technology can create stress	Ayyagari et al., 2011

3 Method

This study was conducted in the context of a research project in Sweden named Digi-FLEX. The aim of the project is to study how flexible learning environments and digital frameworks affect teaching and learning. This study was conducted in the context of this project and the teachers informing this study are active in flexible learning environments related to this project.

This study is a qualitative interview study (see e.g. Rienecker & Jørgensen, 2018) with teachers engaged in flexible learning environments. The data collection is based on semi structured interviews. The interviews captured teacher's experiences of using LMS in flexible learning environments. The literature study guided the data collection, and the material was analyzed with a thematic analysis approach (see e.g. Brown & Clarke 2006). The data collection and analysis were done by the first author under guidance by the second and third author.

3.1 Interviews

Semi structured interviews were conducted to collect data from teachers using LMS in their teaching practice in order to capture their experiences with working in lower and middle schools with flexible learning environments. The selection criteria for the teachers in the interview study were that they:

- use any type of LMS in their teaching (e.g. Google Classroom or Loops).
- work within a flexible learning environment.
- teach in lower or middle school.

The selection resulted in 10 teachers from three different schools (see Table 2).

Table 2. Overview of participants in the study.

Participant ID	Gender	Age	School ID	Length of interview
T1	Male	34	A	54 min
T2	Female	40	A	37 min
T3	Male	37	A	44 min
T4	Female	29	B	40 min
T5	Female	54	B	38 min
T6	Female	46	C	56 min
T7	Female	52	C	45 min
T8	Female	42	C	41 min
T9	Female	37	C	49 min
T10	Female	45	C	46 min

The teachers were between 29 and 54, and there were eight female and two male teachers. The length of the interviews varied between 37 and 54 min. All interviews were conducted online and recorded with Zoom. The reason for doing online interviews were for the interviews taking place at schools all over Sweden. This allowed not to be limited to a geographic position. The interview questions concerned the experiences of the teachers relating to the areas and topics in the literature (see Sect. 2). To keep the conversation on track and to cover the same topics between interviews, an interview guide was used. However, relevant follow-up questions were formulated in situ. All interviews were transcribed.

The teachers worked at three different flexible learning environments and the LMS differed between the schools. Only Google Classroom was mentioned by all teachers as a system that they used. Table 3 shows which school uses what LMS.

Table 3. More information about the schools and LMS in the study.

School ID	Description	LMS
A	A school with a flexible learning environment in Göteborg	Loops Education Binogi Google Classroom
B	A school with a flexible learning environment Ängelholm	Fronter Google Classroom
C	A school with a flexible learning environment in Lidköping	PING PONG Google Classroom

3.2 Data Analysis

The data analysis was an inductive thematic analysis and followed the process as described by Braun and Clarke (2006).

1. **Transcribing:** To interpret the interviews, they were transcribed by ear to get familiar with the material. The symbol (*) was used when noticing something that happened during the interview. This allowed for marking the underlying tone of the conversation when revisiting the transcriptions later *(e.g. *laughter or *imitating the person referenced)*. By marking expressions of emotions with an asterisk, it created a nuance in the data that was helpful for the later stages of the analysis.
2. **Coding:** The coding process of the transcriptions had an overlap with the previous step. During the transcription, notes were taken in the corner of the document to highlight quotes that were deemed to be interesting for the study or when recurring statements were present in the dialog *(e.g. T3 is expressing similar concerns as T2)*. Braun and Clarke (2006) state the importance of being immersed in the data, and during the first phase only to make notes that will be returned to at the later phases. When revisiting the text of the transcription it was helpful to have some notes that were written during the transcription phase. To streamline the process, Miro was used as a tool to write digital sticky notes. The sticky notes made it possible to get an overview of the data and helped the process to find resembling experiences. Each sticky note contained the following: participant ID, a quote from the participant, and a code of an experience associated with the quote. The sticky notes were assigned with a specific color depending on participant ID to keep track of the different participants when the sticky notes were placed in different themes.
3. **Identifying themes:** With all codes now on sticky notes, they were organized after loose themes that were interpreted from the codes. Finally, the codes were represented in four themes of teachers' experiences with LMS in flexible learning environments
4. **Reviewing themes:** The themes were reviewed, and the data associated with each theme was revisited to considered whether the data supported the theme, and if the themes were relevant considering the whole data material.
5. **Finalizing the themes for the study:** The outcome of the analysis was four themes of experiences that are used for the study. (1) Lack of adoption, (2) Control within

the system, (3) Collaboration and competence development, (4) Direct feedback and interactions (see Table 4).

Table 4. Examples of codes organized into the themes.

Themes	Codes
Lack of adaption	Lack of inspiration LMS designed for higher education Mobile versions are limited The LMS are not designed with the Swedish curriculum in mind
Control within the system	Lack of control Limitations of system Guardian Control LMS collects material Network issues
Collaboration and competence development	Importance of Colleagues/collaboration Learn by mistakes Many learning management systems LMS enables distance teaching The environment is well thought out
Direct feedback and interaction	Direct feedback Constant access to documents No need for uploading files Freedom with responsibility

3.3 Ethical Considerations

The participating teachers as well as the name of the schools are anonymized by changing or not including information that ties the participant to a specific school. In order to clarify the purpose and confidentiality for the teachers in interviews the following measures were taken in line with the requirements by the Swedish Research Council (2002):

- All were informed about the purpose of the study prior to the interview
- Consent was acquired from each teacher
- All material is treated with confidentiality

All interviews were conducted and transcribed from Swedish. For the findings section the quotes are translated to English.

4 Empirical Findings

The thematic analysis resulted in four themes of teachers' experiences with the LMS in flexible learning environments (1) Lack of adoption, (2) Control within the system, (3) Collaboration and competence development, (4) Direct feedback and interactions.

4.1 Theme: Lack of Adaption

The first theme concerns that the LMS not being adapted to the way the teachers prefer to work in the flexible learning environment. Some teachers mentioned their experiences with the LMS not being aesthetically pleasing or enabling the creativity that the teachers express that they would prefer, as exemplified with the following quotes.

Other services can be very nice for presentations. If you do presentations on the LMS, it is not as professional as a tool. (T7)

We thought it was boring and not so inspiring. In the old LMS there were no pictures, boring and small text and boring information, and a bit confusing. (T5)

One teacher mentioned that there were restrictions in using other platforms to upload video clips and that they were obliged to use the LMS that the school had implemented. The participant expressed this as an issue due the restrictions on the LMS.

We used YouTube to upload ...Tango can't have longer audio clips or movie clips if it is too large. We have just received guidelines from the municipality not using YouTube because it is external, and we have no agreement with them. It affects my teaching a lot. (T10)

Some teachers mentioned that even though one LMS is easier to use, it still lacks the creativity that the teacher expressed that they wanted.

*Google Classroom is easier to use than Tango... so I can say *laughs* it's more user friendly. What we miss sometimes is that it's not quite as creative.* (T6)

The thing that is boring with Google is that it is not aesthetically very multimodal. These functions that I want to work with which are in example keynote where I want to connect audio and video. It does not work in Google because it is a cloud service. (T9)

Three of the teachers expressed an issue with the LMS not being suited for lower and middle school education. T2 gave an example of how students can download applications to their devices; However, there were no limits within that platform allowing students in the lower classes to download applications that are suited for an older demographic.

It is adapted to preschool all the way to high school, so there is YouTube. Something that you use a lot in older classrooms, so there maybe should be a limit. As some apps should lock depending on which year you go to. (T2)

This mismatch of the demographic was also mentioned by teachers 10 and 4 where they expressed that some LMS were used in higher education.

This LMS is also used during university education, I do not know about the target group or if the platform is used outside of teaching. (T10)

Then it may be that it fits in higher education, that when you submit, you are done as well. (T4)

T6 and T10 mentioned that there is a mobile version of one of the LMS. However, it lacks some of the features that the web version offers.

It has almost all functions but not really all, so, it works in a way. Then we have a web version that has all functions. I cannot see assessment matrices via the app. (T6)

It's a bit messy. There is an app that also belongs to the LMS. So, there is both a web version and app. They look so different, and sometimes the app messes up and then you must go out in the web version instead. It's a little unclear. (T10)

T1 explained that functions for grading and scoring were present in the LMS, however expresses the mismatch with how the grading system is implemented in connection to the Swedish curriculum.

There are functionalities for grading and scoring, but it is according to a very American standard, and it is not made according to a Swedish curriculum connection (…) It's less based on the needs I have and more based on what they think globally about the school world. (T1)

T7 however had a different experience due to the LMS that she used had the connection to the Swedish curriculum. As the school is in a transition to a new LMS she did not know if the new LMS had the same connection.

It is adapted to the Swedish curriculum because the assessment requirements are there so everything is ready. But now we will change the LMS, and I do not know what it looks like. (T7)

T10 expressed that there was no option to change the names of certain categories in the user interface. This made T10 adapt to the limitations that the LMS have.

Some of the functions that are in the LMS we may not use in school; we may want to call it something else, so it suits our business better. We have for example a function called discuss and the function itself suitable to upload our protocols from meetings. But it is not so logical to upload protocols to something that is called discuss *laughs* so it is something we have learned over the years that this is how we do it. (T10)

4.2 Theme: Control Within the System

Three of the teachers mentioned that within the LMS students were given privileges that allowed them to delete assignments from the LMS. T4 and T10 mentioned that they knew how to restore assignments if they were removed. However, T2 was not aware that there was a way to restore the deleted material.

I have students who have figured out that if I have added a task they should do, and they think the task is boring for some reason. Then they can delete it and say that they have not received it. (T2)

The students can actually delete assigned documents. But if you are a little technical you know that the document is still on the drive and then you can look it up, it is very stupid, it is a disadvantage. (T4)

I had a student today who claimed that the answers had disappeared from the homework. Then I just said you know I can go back and see the history of what was in the document? Then the student said okay. I did not do it. (T10)

Three teachers mentioned that parents have an account on one of the LMS. However, when teachers use Google Classroom the parents need to access material from the student's credentials.

Only if they go into the students' accounts… but they have no own login. (T2)

The only thing parents do not have access to is Google Classroom. I wish they could, though. (T4)

On Google they actually do not have access to the material. No parental login when we link to Google classroom the students have to login for them. (T5)

Three teachers expressed that the LMS are used to collect course material and assignments for the students. The teachers expressed this as something helpful.

I have 150 students, so the LMS facilitates something incredible. Partly because the text and the practical work they do is collected. (T7)

I usually build the teaching on the LMS with the help of material, very cooperative structures where students can learn with the help of others. (T9)

It is a gathering place where I link to the resources. (T5)

Two teachers mentioned how some LMS serve as self-correcting systems and expressed how it helped them with workload.

It is very easy when you must correct. It takes less time to correct in the LMS compared to correct 100 paper booklets. I think it works well. (T3)

It facilitates self-correcting material so it's good. (T9)

The teachers in this study work in a highly digitalized environment where they are dependent on connection to the internet to do most of their teaching with the help of the LMS. During the interviews the participants expressed concerns with how vulnerable the situation can be when the internet connection is not working or it's in an unstable state.

We had a lesson a month ago when we were going to work and then the whole network was down in the city. And then you think, how do I do now? If you do not come up with something fast it will be chaos in the classroom. (T4)

It has been a bit difficult right now. We have had a day when the network was down and then it was a bit difficult. (T3)

I think that only having digital teaching materials is problematic. Because the internet sways from time to time. (T2)

T10 described that within a LMS there is no option to turn off spell-check which makes examinations difficult when working with language.

It is not possible to turn off the spelling there. Then I must check their knowledge of spelling in some other way. It is not possible to remove spelling as it's always activated., it's not good. (T10)

4.3　Theme: Collaboration and Competence Development

Some teachers mentioned that the LMS is used to share course material with other teachers. Their experience is that they save time by building upon already established material.

That's really good, because then not everyone needs to invent the wheel. If I have to have a sample about the Middle Ages, I take inspiration from someone else. (T4)

I collaborate with others and share material. If I have done a task, I share it so that the other class also gets the same thing. We share everything, it is fantastic that we do it. It is a strength. (T5)

It's good, then you do not have to invent new stuff every year. We have a template, so you can take inspiration based on it. On some theme days and so it's already done, and you come up with something new. You fill up in that bank. (T6)

When asked about how they learn about the LMS the majority referred to their colleagues as being the source of inspiration and support for adopting the LMS in their teaching.

We share ideas and thoughts between colleagues and help each other is my experience. (T9)

We have meetings like this where we teach each other different things. So, we have had it at school before, teach meets which are focused on teaching each other digital things. We run it with colleagues. We advise each other. It's great, there is a lot of information you get. (T8)

No one teaches us how to use Google Classroom because we only do it between coworkers. When a new coworker joins, I show how it works. (T4)

We show each other, we help each other. I started as a student assistant and then I saw how they did. When you use it a lot you know how to do it (**T3**).

Previously we were better at having teach meets. Then we ended up in a period where teachers felt that it was a bit prestigious and performance requirement, which I think is a bit of a shame. We should not sit on our ideas ourselves and it is important that we share with us. (T9)

I learned from my mistakes, and then by talking to my colleagues. (T5)

Some teachers expressed that the reason for using a LMS is because of the colleagues.

I started working with Google Classroom as I do because I saw other colleagues work so then I thought it looked good (...) you help each other. (T3)

Everyone at school uses Google Classroom as far as I know. (T4)

It is also about an expectation that together with colleagues when we plan teaching, we also plan the choice of digital tools in the form of software and where the didactic design also includes digital choices. (T1)

Some of the teachers expressed frustration with the amount of different LMS that they used in their teaching. One of those frustrations was that they are required to upload documents to more than one LMS due to using different systems.

*Some things get weird because we have two places like, where is this located? So, you start to think, from the beginning everything was on Tango. And then when we got Google. When we finished the protocol, we will now and then post it on Tango? *laughs* it's really weird. It's actually confusing to have two similar systems.* (T7)

I think it's good if most things are gathered in one place, so you do not have so many different LMS, and learn them. We have a little on Google, and a little on Tango. And then I get confused where to be. (T6)

All our meetings, plans are being made in two places right now. The collaboration is available both on Tango and on Google because we have not decided that we will work with either or. It is the choice that exists, we must add up it in two places as there are those who do not use vise-verse LMS. It is mostly for the colleagues that you post it in two places. (T8)

The teachers expressed that the LMS used in a flexible learning environment allows for teaching that changed the barriers that schools previously had. As students are allowed to move between rooms the LMS supports the teachers to perform their teaching across rooms and even to students who are not present at school that day.

The computer allows you to sit a little anywhere, and just as if the student is sitting at home, the student can connect from home. (T5)

The students can work in different places, and we get a little idea of what is happening. That they also know that we are with them, that I get a little overview. (T8)

Google gives me an insight into how they work. But Tango does not, except that I see a result. Google supports the process in the flexible learning environment. It allows me to be like an eye over the shoulder. But not in everything. (T10)

Another way the teachers use the LMS is by adding material to the LMS before the lectures start. This allows the lecture to move beyond the classroom and into the LMS.

Before the lecture you put in the material early so the students can check if they want and get to know what they are going to do. (...) And is a help for those who are on holiday or sick or so, to follow from home. (T2)

Before the lesson I usually write, today we will go through this. Partly for those who want to check 2-3 times and for those who are at home and sick. (T3)

The flexible learning environment was described as well thought out and enabled the teachers to use the environment in combination with digital resources.

We do not have the old classic school building, here it is well thought out from the first sod. (T9)

I usually have QR codes in the classroom so they can scan if they want an instruction or so. Like, this is how you do it. It's great because I can give instructions and then they forget, they can check afterwards. (T7)

It can be a QR code If I want to refer to a certain page. (T3)

4.4 Theme: Direct Feedback and Interactions

The teachers expressed that the direct feedback that some LMS offer are of great value for them in the flexible learning environments that they teach in. Google Classroom is said to be the main system that the teachers use when they want to have real-time-feedback on their students when they work in other rooms.

I keep track with the help of Google Classroom and see their documents how they work if they are in another room. (T5)

I can go in and give comments immediately when they write, control function but also interest function. (T8)

Sometimes they sit in the square and work, and some manage it well. The pedagogue has the documents up, and we can see if it is written or if it stands still. Then you can go and look at them and ask how it is going. (T6)

Say that the students should work with a text. I have access to it all the time. How far they have come and give direct feedback. (T9)

We use certain LMS like Google where you see exactly what they have done and who has done what. Then it is usually enough to say, you know I can check? Google docs are good in the way that I can follow exactly what they write in real time. So, in that way it is fantastically good. (T10)

T10 and T9 expressed their feelings when they did not use a LMS that had the real-time feedback function.

Before we used Google, I had to follow what they wrote so they had to send it to me all the time. Periodically you could get 30 emails and then you had to download all documents on your own, read, give feedback, and send back. Now it's smoother in the way that I can connect to them, in that way I can follow their development much easier. (T10)

If it is in the other LMS then they must upload it. It creates more steps that do not allow direct feedback. (T9)

Some teachers talked about the challenges with working in flexible learning environments. The teachers explained that trust is important to allow the students to work outside the teacher's supervision.

Flexible learning environments enable us to spread out. You do not have to be in the same room. We coined the term freedom under responsibility. Meaning that you can also take responsibility to be in other rooms and work. (T8)

It demands of me as a teacher that I have control over my group in these flexible environments so that you have peace of mind and an agreement with the students. A lot is about trust. (T10)

The room is like the third educator, say I'm the first, the screen is the other. The physical environment being the third. And that's how you get all these pieces together and connect with what we do. (T9)

4.5   Final Remarks on the Empirical Findings

A potential interpretation of the teachers' experiences with the LMS is that even if they are supporting in many areas in the daily teaching, there seems to be a lack of standardization. This creates additional workload for the teachers. As some of the LMS do not seem to fulfill all the needs of the teachers; additional LMS are used to support it. In the first theme "Lack of adaptation" there were comments about the design of the LMS not being inspiring and created for a broad target group. Furthermore, LMS seem to be created for a global market and were not built with the Swedish curriculum in mind. The second theme "Control within the system" highlights the areas where the teachers express that they do not have full control of the LMS itself. The students are given privileges that create additional workload for the teachers due to removal of assignments. Additionally, as one teacher mentioned there was no option to turn off spell check in the LMS creating problems with examinations within subjects of language that the LMS is supposed to support. The area where teachers expressed that control was present was in the collection of material and direct feedback, where the participants expressed that as they work in flexible learning environments it's of great value to be able to have control and oversee the students across the school. Teachers share their experiences with the LMS among their coworkers allowing for development of skills and understanding on how to use the LMS efficiently. Our interpretation is that within a flexible learning environment, teachers prefer LMS that allow for direct feedback, and interaction with the students.

5   Discussion

The analysis resulted in four themes of experiences that teachers have from using LMS in flexible learning environment (1) Lack of adoption, (2) Control within the system, (3) Collaboration and competence development, (4) Direct feedback and interactions (Table 5).

Table 5. Summary of themes

Theme	Description
Lack of adaption	Experiences with the LMS in the flexible learning environment are generally positive, but there are also disruptions that the LMS have that make the teachers choose to use several LMS to meet their needs in the flexible learning environment
Control within the system	LMS both give and take control of how to work in the flexible learning environment
Collaboration and competence development	Digital competence development is aquired when interacting with their coworkers and using the LMS in their own teaching
Direct feedback and interactions	Within a flexible learning environment, it is preferred that the LMS supports direct and real time feedback for the students

Lack of adaption can, as shown in this study, influence how teachers work in flexible learning environments. As argued by Godhe and Hashemi (2019) the implementation of LMS can have an influence on how the schools are digitized. Teachers for example adapted not to use certain features such as grading when the Swedish Curriculum and grading system were not available in the LMS. Instead, they tend to avoid the feature altogether or use another system that had the grading system that they wanted. Extra workload due to the design of systems can cause technostress (Ayyagari et al. 2011). As shown by Al-Fudail and Mellar (2008), stress may happen when there is a misfit between the integration of technology in the classroom and the skills and needs of the teachers. As shown in this study teachers avoided features that cause stress due to a mismatch of needs; furthermore, teachers use multiple LMS due to there being a lack of features and limitations within each of them. The teachers expressed the need to tailor the us for the flexible learning environment in lower and middle school education.

Control within the system represents the importance of teachers' control within the LMS. As previous research shows, teachers' confidence increases when they have successful experiences with technology (Ertmer and Ottenbreit-Leftwich, 2010). In this study there are several examples of teacher's frustration over not being in control, and not being able to control what the students can and cannot do in the LMS. There were also positive experiences, for example of being able to control access to material.

Collaboration and competence development regards the importance and expectations of digital competence development in flexible learning environments. According to Instefjord and Munthe (2017) there is a societal demand on teachers to be digitally competent and finding new ways of implementing technology within the classroom. As Engen (2019) shows digitalization changes the teacher's role within the classroom and brings expectations of digital competence. As this study shows the LMS add value when it comes to sharing material with colleagues. In fact, the colleagues showed to be the main source for competence development in this study. When the classroom structure is changed into flexible learning environments, it allows teachers to collaboratively work due the breakout from traditional structures (Niemi, 2021). In this study, the collaboration and fellowship between the teachers were expressed to be high and the teachers expressed an interest in learning from each other. However, some teachers expressed that too many LMS divide workflow forcing them to post protocols and resources in multiple places in order to reach all the coworkers. Wood (2018) showed that people are often forgotten of the equation in flexible environments. This adds up with the finding that the LMS still requires the teacher to upload material and use it in the teaching to fit in the flexible learning environment. Teachers often use the LMS before the lectures to upload material for students so they can prepare outside school hours. This adds up with Cleveland (2018) statement about the physical and digital resources overlap facilitates students' ability to learn from home. This study provides a picture of the LMS in the flexible learning environment as an enabler of collaboration and connection between the students and teachers; between rooms and overbridging the physical boundary when students are working from home.

The theme *Direct feedback and interactions* concerns the experiences of interacting with students in the flexible learning environment. In this study, the teachers regard direct feedback and interactions with the students to be of great value when working in a flexible learning environment. This is of importance to consider when choosing LMS for flexible learning environments. As Rasheed et al. (2020) argues, educational institutions sometimes have issues choosing the adequate technology to support its teachers. In this study the teachers seemed to identify the shortcomings of the LMS when interacting with students, and then choose to use external ones to fulfill their needs when following the student's progression and support students with feedback as well as interacting with students in real time.

6 Conclusion and Future Research

This study examined the question: *"How do teachers experience learning management systems within flexible learning environments?"* with the aim to provide insights of value when choosing LMS to be integrated flexible learning environments. If well designed and integrated the LMS can be a vital digital recourse in a flexible learning environment. However, if there is a misfit there are risks of workarounds, stress, and hindrance for teachers to work with the flexibility as intended. From this study we can conclude that teachers have experiences relating to how the LMS is adapted, to the control within the system, to collaboration and competence development, and to feedback and interaction with students. The insights gained from this study are of value when integrating LMS in flexible learning environments. These insights can inform the integration by taking the following implications into account when choosing and implementing an LMS into a flexible learning environment: Choose an LMS that.

- allows the flexibility for teachers to customize functions
- gives teachers the control and balance of what students can and cannot do
- allows for collaboration and knowledge exchange between teachers

• enables feedback and direct interaction with students

This study limited its scope to teachers working in lower and middle school education and therefore could future studies investigate how teachers in higher education experiences LMS in their teaching. The role of digital competence development towards LMS could be investigated when teachers are alone in their teaching subject to learn how they develop their digital competence towards LMS.

References

Al-Fudail, M., Mellar, H.: Investigating teacher stress when using technology. Comput. Educ. **51**(3), 1103–1110 (2008)

Ayyagari, R., Grover, V., Purvis, R.: Technostress: technological antecedents and implications. MIS Q. **35**(4), 831–858 (2011). https://doi.org/10.2307/41409963

Braun, V., Clarke, V.: Using thematic analysis in psychology. Qual. Res. Psychol. **3**(2), 77–101 (2006)

Cleveland, B.: Innovative learning environments as complex adaptive systems: enabling middle years' education. In: Benade, L., Jackson, M. (eds.) Transforming Education, pp. 55–78. Springer, Singapore (2018). https://doi.org/10.1007/978-981-10-5678-9_4

Engen, B.: Understanding social and cultural aspects of teachers' digital competencies. Comunicar **61**, 9–19 (2019). https://doi.org/10.3916/C61-2019-01

Ertmer, P.A., Ottenbreit-Leftwich, A.T.: Teacher technology change: how knowledge, confidence, beliefs, and culture intersect. J. Res. Technol. Educ. **42**(3), 255–284 (2010)

Fejes, A., Thornberg, R. (eds.): Handbok i kvalitativ analys, 3rd edn. Liber, Stockholm (2019)

Fernández-Cruz, F., Fernández-Díaz, M.: Generation Z's teachers and their digital skills. Comunicar **46**, 97–105 (2016)

Godhe, A., Hashemi, S.S. (eds.): Digital kompetens för lärare, 4th edn. Gleerups, Malmö (2019)

Gudmundsdottir, G.B., Hatlevik, O.E.: Newly qualified teachers' professional digital competence: implications for teacher education. Eur. J. Teach. Educ. **41**(2), 214–231 (2018)

Instefjord, E.J., Munthe, E.: Educating digitally competent teachers: a study of integration of professional digital competence in teacher education. Teach. Teach. Educ. **67**, 37–45 (2017)

Kariippanon, K.E., Cliff, D.P., Lancaster, S.L., Okely, A.D., Parrish, A.-M.: Perceived interplay between flexible learning spaces and teaching, learning and student wellbeing. Learn. Environ. Res. **21**(3), 301–320 (2018). https://doi.org/10.1007/s10984-017-9254-9

Krumsvik, R.J.: Situated learning and teachers' digital competence. Educ. Inf. Technol. **13**(4), 279–290 (2008). https://doi.org/10.1007/s10639-008-9069-5

Neill, S., Etheridge, R.: Flexible learning spaces: the integration of pedagogy, physical design, and instructional technology. Mark. Educ. Rev. **18**(1), 47–53 (2008)

Niemi, K.: 'The best guess for the future?' Teachers' adaptation to open and flexible learning environments in Finland. Educ. Inq. **12**(3), 282–300 (2021)

Player-Koro, C., Bergviken Rensfeldt, A., Selwyn, N.: Selling tech to teachers: education trade shows as policy events. J. Educ. Policy **33**(5), 682–703 (2018)

Rasheed, R.A., Kamsin, A., Abdullah, N.A.: Challenges in the online component of blended learning: a systematic review. Comput. Educ. **144**, 103701 (2020)

Rienecker, L., Stray Jørgensen, P.: Att skriva en bra uppsats, 4th edn. Liber, Stockholm (2018)

Skolverket: Adekvat digital kompetens – ett svårfångat begrepp, 11 December 2019. https://www.skolverket.se/skolutveckling/forskning-och-utvarderingar/artiklar-om-forskning/adekvat-digital-kompetens---ett-svarfangat-begrepp

Skolverket: Leda digitaliseringen på skolor och förskolor, 13 January 2022. https://www.skolve rket.se/skolutveckling/leda-och-organisera-skolan/leda-digitaliseringen-i-skola-och-forskola

Spante, M., Hashemi, S.S., Lundin, M., Algers, A.: Digital competence and digital literacy in higher education research: systematic review of concept use. Cogent Educ. **5**(1), 1519143 (2018)

Strayer, J.F.: How learning in an inverted classroom influences cooperation, innovation and task orientation. Learn. Environ. Res. **15**(2), 171–193 (2012). https://doi.org/10.1007/s10984-012-9108-4

Swedish Research Council: Forskningsetiska principer inom humanistisk-samhällsvetenskaplig forskning. Vetenskapsrådet, Stockholm (2002)

Walsham, G.: Doing interpretive research. Eur. J. Inf. Syst. **15**(3), 320–330 (2006)

Webster, J., Watson, R.T.: Analyzing the past to prepare for the future: writing a literature review. MIS Q. **26**(2), xiii–xxiii (2002)

Wells, A., Jackson, M., Benade, L.: Modern learning environments: embodiment of a disjunctive encounter. In: Benade, L., Jackson, M. (eds.) Transforming Education, pp. 3–17. Springer, Singapore (2018). https://doi.org/10.1007/978-981-10-5678-9_1

Wood, A.: Selling new learning spaces: flexibly anything for the twenty-first century. In: Benade, L., Jackson, M. (eds.) Transforming education, pp. 95–106. Springer, Singapore (2018). https://doi.org/10.1007/978-981-10-5678-9_6

Concept-Based Modeling as a Method Combining Digital and Analogue Means for Problem-Solving

Björn Sjödén[✉] [iD], Patrik Lilja Skånberg[iD], and Hans B. Löfgren[iD]

Halmstad University, Box 823, 301 18 Halmstad, Sweden
bjorn.sjoden@hh.se

Abstract. In this paper we present Concept-Based Modeling (CBM), an innovative pedagogical method for problem-solving in engineering education, which combines analogue and digital tools. We outline the scientific rationale for CBM and discuss how it compares to traditional teaching with respect to optimizing the pedagogical value of both analogue and digital means. CBM is based on conceptual modeling of quantities derived directly from first principles and streamlined for the use of computer algebra systems (CAS). The method was evaluated in a pilot survey in a statics course for engineering students in their freshman year at Halmstad University. We conclude that CBM improves students' problem-solving skills by the reciprocal action between conceptual understanding and modeling of a problem. Student evaluations suggest that CBM enables students to handle more realistic problems and that CAS as a professional tool prepares them for their future working life. Future studies will address CBM for more advanced courses, as the students' knowledge develops over time.

Keywords: Concept-Based Modeling · Digital · Analogue · Problem-Solving · Computer Algebra System

1 Introduction

Problem-solving is a complex skill that requires both domain knowledge and knowing what strategies to apply in which problem situations. Teaching problem-solving skills carries the additional challenge of arranging teaching tools and materials that support the student's process of identifying relevant knowledge and rules, while allowing sufficient degrees of freedom for students' own creativity, exploration and independence. In this paper, we propose one pedagogical method that combines analogue and digital tools, where traditional, "pen-and-paper" methods precede the use of a computer algebra system for processing calculations, in the engineering and physics domains. Together, these two approaches have shown to increase the problem-solving capabilities of students.

Our aim is to highlight how conceptual thinking and creative exploration can work together with a computer algebra system (CAS) in a way that takes optimal advantage of both human and machine capacities. At the centre of this enterprise is a technique

© ICST Institute for Computer Sciences, Social Informatics and Telecommunications Engineering 2023
Published by Springer Nature Switzerland AG 2023. All Rights Reserved
E. Brooks et al. (Eds.): DLI 2022, LNICST 493, pp. 22–37, 2023.
https://doi.org/10.1007/978-3-031-31392-9_2

referred to as *Concept-Based Modeling* (CBM), which has been developed and assessed over five years of teaching in mechanical engineering at the university by the project leader and author (HL). In addition, we suggest how the CBM technique can be further empirically evaluated and developed as a pedagogical method, drawing from the input and course evaluations by students.

Hence, our guiding questions for the present paper can be formulated as follows:

- What is the scientific rationale for combining analogue and digital means in a common instructional design, in the form of CBM?
- How does teaching using CBM add pedagogical value to other, traditional methods of teaching for students in the engineering domains?
- What are the implications of CBM for educational interventions that optimize the combination of analogue and digital teaching tools?

The outline of this paper is as follows. First, we provide a background as to the relevance and rationale of our approach to teaching and learning problem-solving skills in the engineering domain. We specifically address the added value of combining digital and analogue means in a common pedagogical design, using CBM. Then, in the main part of this paper, we describe how CBM works in practice, including the results of a pilot survey among university students who used CBM in a course on statics. Finally, we make some concluding remarks and suggest some areas for follow-up work.

2 Background

2.1 Learning and Teaching How to Solve an Engineering Problem

Decades of research have failed to demonstrate any general problem-solving strategies independent on substantial subject knowledge; this is the case also for ostensibly less fact-based subjects like mathematics (Sweller, Clark & Kirshner, 2010). In order to become an expertise problem solver, such as an engineer who uses mathematics, one must learn how and when to apply one's general knowledge of mathematical laws and methods to quite specific contexts and situations – whether this concerns calculating an orbit to the moon, the construction of a bridge or figuring out when a stool remains at rest (an example which we will return to).

The vast range of possible, including hypothetical and yet unknown, problems to be solved leaves great room for creativity and motivational factors in the process. This concerns not only what is the most effective solution but also which is the more interesting, desirable and even aesthetically pleasing way to go about it. In short, if anything general can be said about actual problem-solving as carried out by human beings, we hold that it is driven by three main factors: will, creativity and knowledge.

Whilst education traditionally focuses on the latter (different forms of knowledge), teaching problem-solving must not become a task of simply having the student to recognize facts and mechanically perform calculations to reach a particular, by the teacher intended, solution. If good learning assumes willingness to solve a problem and creative insight, then good teaching should provide situations designed to offer such opportunities as part of the problem-solving process.

As a case in point, consider traditional engineering education, which leans heavily on mathematics. A main ingredient in traditional mathematics teaching consists of the teacher demonstrating procedures on blackboards/whiteboards, a form of pedagogical practice analysed in detail by Greiffenhagen (2014). Interestingly, traditional teaching of computer programming consists of similar practices (Tenenberg et al., 2018). Code is being written on whiteboards by the teacher who comments on each step.

In these contexts, examples and illustrations are often math heavy. To make sure the mathematical aspects are covered in all steps of the solution to the engineering problems, they are presented from the outset. This imposes great demands on well-developed mathematical abilities of the students – requirements that are becoming more difficult to defend given today's powerful computer algebra systems and the growing complexity of the problems that engineers must be able to deal with.

Hence, we see several issues that call for innovative teaching practices in engineering. First, creative and conceptual thinking are vulnerable mental processes that are easily disrupted. As soon as algorithms, programming or mathematical methods become in focus, the big picture is often backgrounded or lost. Second, students' problem-solving process is often hidden, in that the steps taken to reach a solution is not made visible and open to scrutiny for both the teacher and the students themselves. Learning implies making errors, revising and understanding where the errors come from, such that conceptual errors are not confused with syntax errors in a line of code. Third, the availability of digital educational resources today offers complements to traditional teaching materials which may effectively address these previous limitations. This calls for a closer examination into the role of traditional, "analogue", and innovative, "digital", means for problem-solving and, most importantly, how they should be combined for improving problem-solving practices in engineering education and related domains.

2.2 Adding Pedagogical Value by Combining Digital and Analogue Means

Thinking requires hard effort and although people seem naturally inclined to solve problems, we are not naturally good at it. As Willingham (2009, p. 3) puts it, "People are naturally curious, but we are not naturally good thinkers; unless the cognitive conditions are right, we will avoid thinking". The argument goes, that hard thinking is so demanding, that our brain works to save us from the effort whenever possible, resulting in what Kahneman (2011) referred to as the fast, automatic "System 1" thinking (in contrast to the slow, effortful "System 2" thinking). At the same time (and cogently), successfully solving a problem is rewarding and pleasurable, to make the effort worth it. The implication for education is that teachers carefully need to consider how they make students engage in purposeful cognitive processes. Any external support or tools should serve to encourage students' own, and *the right kind of,* efforts.

What then are "the right kind"? First, we must acknowledge that students need tools to help their thinking; some tools target specific cognitive processes (e.g. a calculator) whereas others serve to generally off-load information onto the environment (e.g. a keyboard, or a pen). Second, as noted above, students need knowledge. In education, we cannot assume that students (or anyone else) are cognitively well-equipped enough to learn new concepts or skills simply from exposure to a problem, which then triggers thinking in the direction of an intended learning outcome. However, provided with the right tools, and the right knowledge, which trigger efforts in the right direction for solving a problem, human beings are exceptionally good learners. In learning, we form ideas and hypotheses, using different tools to off-load our "thinking" onto the environment, and repeatedly compare outcomes of internal states to events in the outside world. In doing so, people can develop professional skills and produce outstanding results, as exemplified by the engineering ingenuity of modern society.

Computers, on the other hand, are not equipped to generate ideas, to formulate hypotheses or conceive of models in line with human thought and creativity. Computers are good at executing problem-solving steps, as programmed by humans, following algorithms and processing vast amounts of information in terms of predefined data – that is, computation. Although computers have been shown to surpass human performance in delimited domains such as playing chess, Go and trivia quizzes (Silver et al., 2017), present discourse emphasizes that the *collaboration* between human beings and computers is even more efficient in achieving specific outcomes, than either part alone (Tegmark, 2017; Polson & Scott, 2018).

For example, a study by Wang et al. (2019), which involved 20 professional data scientists, revealed that computers using artificial intelligence (AI) are not necessarily perceived as a threat or competition to human performance, even when it concerns the development of techniques which serve to automate the work practices of data scientists themselves. The authors concluded that the interviewees maintained a general view that "…the future of data science work will be a collaboration between humans and AI systems, in which both automation and human expertise are indispensable". If this is true from the extensive experience of professionals in the field, who work with actual problems, it would make sense to foster a similar view in education for students who anticipate this future. In other words, students would benefit from learning to assess and use their own expertise in relation to the functions of computer systems.

Importantly, from our perspective, digital tools such as computers and computer software, make people better equipped to solve problems by the innovative means they offer for complementing human functioning. Considering technological development over time, the distinction between digital and analogue technologies has become increasingly blurry. For the objectives of this paper, we intend technologies that allow capturing human bodily movements in a way that is analogous to the movement and traces on a medium. Pens or brushes used on paper is a prime example. However, todays' digital technologies, like tablets, can emulate the use of pens or brushes on paper in ways which allow for very similar or identical actions by the drawing hand. When we refer to use of "analogue means" we therefore include drawing tablets, when used to emulate analogue technologies, because they allow for more or less identical bodily actions to creative drawing using a hand-held pen or brush.

Our suggestion here is, that analogue and digital means, in this sense, respectively might serve different pedagogical functions. More precisely, the analogue means of drawing and writing on paper seem more apt at aiding our slow, conceptual thinking and generation of ideas, whereas the digital means of computation and automation seem more apt at performing the actual calculations which, once conceived of, produce the outcome that informs us of the next step in the problem-solving process.

CBM takes into account both students' need for analogue "thinking" (conceptualization) and the computer's capacity of digital "automation" (through algorithms and calculation). In learning with CBM, the student typically has to reconceive and revise her model from the results it generates from a Computer Algebra System (CAS). A central aspect of CBM is that the CAS is used to free the analogue means (the modeling using pen and paper) from the demand to represent all mathematical aspects. The presence of digital means thus opens new possibilities for using analogue means.

In CBM, analogue means are used to model the concepts of "first principles" (see below), letting the computer algebra system take care of all the algebra, arithmetic or more advanced mathematics. The reduction of the mathematical content is intended to help the students to get an aerial view of the engineering problem, which allows them to use cognitive resources to address the fundamental levels of the problem. More specifically, the analogue means are introduced to help the students clarify how the relevant first principle applies to the problem.

The primary concern of CBM is not whether the outcome at first constitutes a "correct" solution (although this would be the ultimate goal of any problem-solving) but that the student makes the critical parts of her own problem-solving process more precise, identifiable and visible, in order to guide her learning further. In the following paragraphs we detail how CBM meets these criteria and is carried out in practice, starting with its theoretical foundation and then exemplifying its use with a sample problem.

3 How Concept-Based Modeling Works

3.1 The Foundation of CBM in Scientific Theory and Knowledge

Scientific knowledge can be described in terms of theory, principles, and concepts. At the core of our scientific knowledge, we find what we call theories. These are separate and non-overlapping descriptions of the world. For example, the theory of Newtonian mechanics and the theory of thermodynamics deals with two different aspects of the world. While Newtonian mechanics efficiently describes the detailed motion of particles, thermodynamics tells us how energy may be transported and what forms it can take.

Each theory is furthermore founded on a complete set of laws or first principles. In Newtonian mechanics we find Newton's three laws of motions and Newton's universal law of gravity, and in thermodynamics we have the zeroth to the third law of thermodynamics. Every law contains fact-based universal pieces of information about nature that we call concepts. These concepts are fundamental to our understanding of the world. Some concepts are non-divisible "atomic facts" (Wittgenstein, 1962) like the mass, or the speed of a body. Others are combinations of atomic facts like the concept of momentum. To simplify this hierarchy of facts, we will call every piece of fact a concept.

3.2 The Three-Step Process of CBM

CBM divides the problem-solving process into two distinct tasks: modeling, and computation. Following the computation, the final result is assessed, a "reality check". This three-step process is depicted in Fig. 1.

The modeling task is to identify the first principles of the problem, for example Newton's second law of motion or the first law of thermodynamics, and to model each of the involved physical concepts, part by part, all the way down to the most basic of mathematical concepts. In the computation task, the analyst merely transfers the conceptually modelled first principles into a computer algebra system of choice for the succeeding mathematical treatment. These two tasks require completely different mindsets and are advantageously separated. In the CBM process, it is crucial that the initial modeling activity precedes the coding and execution of digital programs in the CAS. Modeling and computation are thus clearly separated. This serves to create a space in which pen and paper are used to create visual images to support the conceptual exploration of the engineering problem, before the mathematical processing commences.

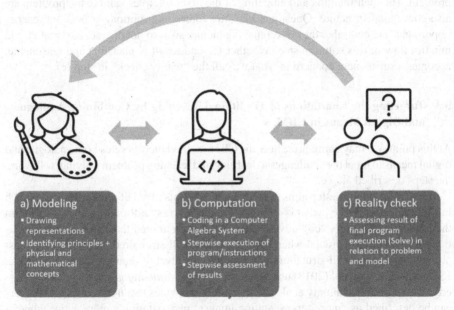

Fig. 1. The three-step process of CBM.

In the modeling step (a), the students creatively draw and write models, equipped with colored pens and paper or drawing tablets. The computation step (b) can be described as a stepwise process involving several iterations of coding, execution, and assessment. The final step in the process, the reality check step (c), begins when the entire code is run and a final result in the system is presented. It differs from the stepwise assessments in step (b) in that the students need to assess the plausibility of the final result (for example, that it is not a negative number if it needs to be positive). Errors that cannot be detected in step (b) can potentially show up in step (c).

If a step does not function as intended, something is wrong in the code and/or the mathematical conceptualization, and that needs to be addressed. The computer is the indispensable dialogue partner in this process, but it is the students who build the structure in which the computation flows. This way of structuring solutions in a transparent and logical way is a crucial part of the students' learning process.

When the engineering problem has been presented by the teacher/textbook (or defined by the students), but before the proper modeling (step a) has begun, initial cognitive activity which has been referred to as *problem conceptualization* (Delahunty et al., 2020) takes place[1]. This relates to our points above (Sects. 2.1–2.2) and is important for the subsequent activities in CBM, since the students' previous knowledge will be of consequence for how the problem-solving task is approached.

When the students move on to modeling, their internal conceptualizations of the problem begin to be externalized through the drawing of visual representations in a way which resonates with the students´ understanding. They are encouraged to be artistic and creatively draw nice colourful pictures, so that their minds really get a feel for the problem. The identification and modeling of the first principles valid to the problem are also conceptual in nature. Questions like "are forces and motion, or heat and energy important?" are central to the conceptual big picture so as to not distract the creative and mindful flow of this solution step. Whether the end result is plausible and reasonable, becomes a subsequent concern in what we call the "reality check" in step (c).

3.3 Targeting the Limitations of Traditional Teaching by Combining Analogue and Digital Means in CBM

At this point, we may summarize how the CBM method incorporates both analogue and digital means to meet the challenges to learning and teaching problem-solving, following the steps described above.

First, the modelling step aims to off-load the students' need of representing too much information at once (i.e., what is commonly referred to as "information overload" or, in the academic literature, "cognitive load"). It has been argued that external representations are particularly crucial when people are facing ill-structured problems, or at least problems that appear ill-structured in relation to the level of their previous knowledge. Kiverstein and Rietveld (2018) uses the term *representation hunger* to denote this property of cognition. Delahunty et al. (2020, p. 399) concludes that novice problem solvers can be described as "more'representation-hungry' necessitating a more active engagement with discrete cognitive schema and mental models as well as active combination and modification mechanisms".

Based on this literature, we conclude that the initial problem conceptualization and the following creative drawing in CBM are often highly cognitively demanding. The students need to form a representation of the engineering problem, using the relevant first principles with corresponding physical and mathematical concepts. Drawing can be extremely helpful in this phase and since the students are generally more or less novice in the domain and can creatively interact with the external representations that is being produced during the drawing.

---

[1] Delahunty et al. (2020, p. 399) define problem conceptualization as "the period of cognitive processing occurring before the externalization of any representation (e.g. a sketch, mathematical expression, verbal communication etc.)".

Furthermore, premature involvement of mathematical operations and calculations will activate different knowledge networks, potentially competing for resources in the working memory that is needed to identify and model the relevant first principles and concepts. Less formally expressed from the practical teaching viewpoint informing CBM, conceptual thinking and creative problem conceptualization and representation are vulnerable processes that can easily be disrupted by the details of analysis. Finally, drawing also makes aspects of the student´s reasoning available to both teachers and peers for comments and feedback which are important aspects of the learning setting.

Second, in contrast to modeling in the CBM process, the computation step is supported by digital means. The student turns to the functions of the digital tools. The creative mindset is temporarily left to focus on the details and get every number, variable and equation correctly declared. Here, the big picture disappears in favour of the details. The student starts to create a simple program, which is solved in small steps by trial and error until the final result or answer appears on the screen.

Step (b) can be described as a dialogue with the computer, in which inputs are made and temporary results are reviewed. The dialogue with the computer also affords a trial-and-error approach where different coding options can be tried out to assess which one seems to work. However, in order to successfully complete the computation step, the student needs to build a structure for the code that relates the appropriate concepts to the relevant first principles (see the sample problem in the Appendix, in which Positions, Forces, Moments are stepwise modeled and finally put into the equation for equilibrium - the relevant first principles). While part of this process can consist of trial-and-error solutions, the students also need to organize the code in an appropriate way (see Appendix).

The digital tools (here, the CAS) ideally contain as many pre-defined high-level functions and algorithms allowing automated operation as possible. This means that as much as possible of the mathematical and computational processing will be black boxed and not directly accessed by the students. This is to allow them to focus on the most conceptual part of the work with mathematics and to avoid introducing cognitively demanding coding.

The CAS is utilized to off-load the highly knowledge intense mathematical processing to the computational system, thereby minimizing the need for attention and previous knowledge. This does not mean that the CAS approach is simply made easier than traditional methods. Rather, we suggest that the combination of low-stakes trial and error approach in combination with the need to structure the whole problem-solving process, from step (a) to step (c), are very important for deep learning, or what Ohlsson (2011) refers to as non-monotonic change. There are many potential instances of positive or negative feedback (from the computer as well as from teachers and peers) which can gradually and qualitatively alter the cognitive networks activated in the students. Next, we show how these steps manifest in practice by illustrating how a sample problem is solved by using CBM.

3.4 Sample Problem

For a concretisation of the CBM problem-solving process, we refer to the Appendix. There we work through a typical statics problem, which combines text and a picture, detailing the modeling and computation steps from Fig. 1. Importantly, all the problem-solver does is to model the concepts of the first principles that governs the problem. All arithmetic, algebra and more advanced mathematics are handed over to the CAS.

3.5 Evaluation with Students

To study the student experience of CBM as a problem-solving method, we conducted a pilot survey at the end of the CBM course in statics for engineering students in their freshman year, 2019 and 2021. During the pandemic year 2021 all teaching was online, but there were no indications that this affected the overall student experience and learning with CBM, probably because CBM made use of digital drawing tablets and computers that connected well with web seminars. In total, 33 students responded.

The survey was divided into two parts: CBM in teaching and CAS as a tool. The full survey comprised twelve items, including items relating to the student experience which are beyond the scope of the present paper (e.g., if CAS had increased one's curiosity for mathematics and physics). Here, we focus on three stand-alone, free-response items of the first part (CBM in teaching) and three rating items of the second part (CAS as a tool), which all targeted engineering-relevant problem-solving skills. In the first part, the students were asked to describe their overall experience of CBM in relation traditional teaching (where problem-solving is made purely by hand) as well as with respect to special skills required by the teacher, and for meeting the needs of the labour market. In the second part, the students rated their agreement with different statements about using a CAS (e.g. *"CAS facilitates the use of mathematics"*) on a 5-point likert scale, where 1 meant "Disagree" and 5 meant "Totally agree". The results of the second part are summarized in Table 1. The averaged total can be seen as a measure of students' general attitude to the utility of using CAS in the context of CBM.

Table 1. Student ratings of agreement with statements about CAS (1 to 5; 1 = Disagree, 5 = Totally agree).

Statement	Student average rating ($N = 33$) M (SD)
CAS facilitates the use of mathematics	4,0 (1,2)
CAS works well as a tool for problem-solving	4,1 (1,0)
CAS has helped to develop my programming skills	3,4 (1,1)
Total	**3,8 (1,1)**

The main result from Table 1 is that students experienced CAS as an effective tool, particularly with respect to facilitating the use of mathematics and problem-solving, and to somewhat less degree for developing programming skills.

The students' free responses were reviewed by two of the authors (HL and BS) for common themes. As a pilot survey, we were primarily interested in finding out how the items in the survey would capture relevant student experiences of CBM, as a basis for constructing a more precise questionnaire for future studies. We took special interest in student free-response reflections on the relevance and effectiveness of the method, relating to the items in Table 1. In addition, we were interested in what special qualities or skills that students considered the teacher to need when using CBM (e.g., whether they would point to the teacher's digital competence as to skills in combining analogue and digital means, or more general pedagogical qualities such as communication skills).

Overall, students did not express any major differences between CBM and traditional teaching (e.g. "It is basically the same, it all starts on paper, the difference is that you type in everything on a computer.") but several pointed out that the use of computers seemed to make CBM more relevant, and that problem-solving became "easier" and "more efficient". Students also stressed the importance of combining approaches, e.g. "A combination is important. The computer helps a lot, but knowledge also decreases. You learn more by hand, but the computer makes the work much more efficient.". Only one response expressed a preference for traditional teaching, but did not specify why.

As to special skills needed by the teacher of CBM, students pointed particularly to the importance of good conceptual thinking and programming skills. Both analogue and digital skills were mentioned in this context (e.g. "both be able to explain on paper and be able to program", "Knowledge of the software and to be able to explain how the code is interpreted"). As to the role of CAS for courses that meet the needs of the labour market, the main themes related to introducing professional tools (e.g. "My experience is that CAS is used more and more in the labor market in general and in an increasingly digitalized world it feels like this will be the future.") and solving more realistic problems (e.g. "CAS allows us to solve more advanced problems that reflect reality and are not as dumb down as the typical school problems.").

4 Discussion

In this paper, we aimed at presenting how and why analogue and digital means can be combined in a common instructional design, in the form of CBM. We specifically targeted how teaching using CBM adds pedagogical value to other, traditional methods of teaching in engineering. In this section, we further address the implications of CBM for educational interventions that optimize the combination of analogue and digital teaching tools.

In short, our two-fold, analogue and digital, approach was motivated by considering basic qualities of human cognition in relation to the functionality of computerized systems. CBM exemplifies how learning can be made more appealing and efficient, through directing students' efforts towards practices that better meet the demands of complex problem-solving, such as that reflected in engineering education. The educational aspect is important, since learning involves iterative cycles of modeling and computation in relation to the outcome (Fig. 1) – in other words, practice and feedback – before students' have developed the professional skills needed in their actual work. Considering how human-computer interactions are likely to develop along these lines, the experience of using a multi-faceted approach like CBM makes an important preparation for students' future work practices.

As to how CBM is carried out in practice and what it means for optimizing the combination of analogue and digital teaching tools, we find a few points particularly worth highlighting. For example, the students associated CBM with solving more realistic problems and that problem-solving became more time efficient. Many students stated that the skills and methods trained in the classroom were the same as the ones they will use in their future working life. This makes CBM stimulating for the student, as well as for the teacher. Interestingly, students made less pronounced associations between programming skills and using CAS. One reason might be the high level of automation built into the systems in today's mathematical software. This often makes the creation of the solution so simple and straightforward that the student becomes unaware of the programming process.

Traditional teaching in the engineering sciences is mainly knowledge-based and emphasizes on breadth rather than understanding and depth. Facts can only be memorized and known, not (normally) understood. On the other hand, principles and concepts are the very foundation of our understanding. Hence, a concept-based teaching approach is focused on understanding and opens for deeper knowledge, also stated by Stern et al. (2017) and Alhumaid (2020). It is in this context we conclude that CBM is beneficial to teaching engineering science and problem-solving. Both are strengthened by the power of conceptual thinking (and CAS). The combination of the analogue and the digital further helps the student to structure his or her own thinking, and to separate the creative from the analytic processes of problem-solving. The analytic processes connected with mathematics are significantly simplified using CAS. Given the complexity of todays' engineering problems, it seems no longer defendable to do most of the calculations by hand. In fact, CBM proposes the contrary; the computer performs all computations and lets students focus on the problem formulation, modeling and reflection.

The main technical difference between what we call traditional teaching and teaching by means of CBM lies in the all-out use of a CAS. Ultimately, without the need of teaching mathematical tricks and clever simplifications a lot of time is freed to deepening the students conceptual understanding. However, trading the mathematical solution techniques of traditional teaching with the manipulation of a CAS is not only time saving, but it also makes a massive impact on how theory is being presented. In CBM, every concept and physical law are derived and applied in its most general form. This makes a contrast to the traditional teaching that typically derives partial facts and approximations and through lengthy explanations finally come up to (but seldomly reaching) the general form. Simply adding a CAS to an otherwise traditional teaching philosophy does not make it CBM. CBM is above all a problem-solving process which makes full use of the CAS.

Notably, some students remarked that the use of computers makes the learning more difficult due to the programming part. If you are new to a math-software, there is a learning curve that initially takes focus away from the course and the problem-solving process. Some students also expressed fears that knowledge was being lost when using computers, and there is a belief that you learn more by hand. This fear is widespread, also among teachers, but is historically unjustified (Schramm, 1998). This fear or anxiety of using CAS can, however, be overcome if it is blended into their everyday class work and systematically introduced (D'Souza et al., 2005). A good way of letting the students familiarize themselves with the software is to combine programming and CAS in the creation of new functions (Galán García et al., 2005). Such projects may help to transform the feared Black Box experience into a White Box experience.

5   Conclusions and Future Studies

Our work with CBM has demonstrated how analogue and digital means can be fruitfully combined for the teaching and learning of problem-solving in engineering, on a scientific basis. By using CAS, the students' mathematical abilities no longer set a definitive limit to what kind of problems that can be studied. Instead, the limit is set based on the conceptual understanding and the modeling capability of the student, in reciprocal action. An important educational implication of CBM, substantiated by evaluation with students, is that more realistic problems can be studied and that CAS as a professional tool prepares the student for their future working life. Finally, we conclude that CBM is important to the curriculum in engineering education due to its potential to match the future demands of a growingly complex technological development. Future work will extend our work with CBM to other and later topics, like Dynamics and Thermodynamics. This will show how conceptual modeling and computation using CAS can be further effectively combined for more advanced courses, as students' knowledge develops over time.

Acknowledgements. The authors wish to thank all the students that responded to the survey, Per Högström and Pernilla Nilsson at Halmstad University for contributing to the ideas behind this paper, and Anders Gåård at Karlstad University, as well as the anonymous reviewers, for their valuable comments and contributions to the construction of the survey.

Appendix

Sample Statics Problem Resolved Using CBM
Here, we work through a typical statics problem using CBM (see Fig. A1).

a) **Modeling**
   Given the question, we embark on the first task of the solution process, the conceptual modeling of the problem. We need to decide the first principles that governs the problem. This is a static problem for which it is know that the stool needs to be in equilibrium with its surroundings, that is, the resulting forces and force-couples are zero ($\sum \mathbb{F} = 0$ and $\sum \mathbb{M}_C = 0$). This means that a free-body diagram must be drawn, and all the forces and force-couples must be modeled.
   A free-body diagram is a careful drawing of the specific part (the body) that is to be studied (see Fig. A2). Here, we introduce the known lengths and angles along with an appropriate coordinate system (x, y, z). This is the part of the solution process where we really see the problem. Remember that we cannot draw what we have not seen.
   Once the stool is drawn, we start to model the forces conceptually by adding vectors (arrows) in the direction of their application onto the stool. Generally, assuming

Sample problem

A three-legged stool is subjected to an oblique force P applied at center of the seating area. Based on the dimensions of the stool, calculate the minimum static coefficient of friction that makes the stool remain at rest.

Neglect the mass of the stool.

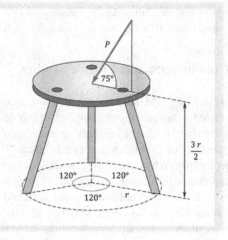

Fig. A1. A typical problem in a university level course in statics.

that each of the three legs are in contact with the floor, their reaction forces must be a combination of normal and friction forces. In finding the minimum static coefficient of friction we must assume that the friction forces are fully developed and equal to the coefficient of friction times the normal force. The load P is already given in the problem.

b) **Computation**

The next step of the solution process is to transform the conceptual models into a code that can be processed by a computer. In this example we make use of the CAS *Mathematica* ®. The coding always starts with defining the most basic of all concepts, the base vectors. Once we have these base vectors, we can define our rotation matrix and so on.

Base vectors

```
i = {1, 0, 0};
j = {0, 1, 0};
k = {0, 0, 1};
```

Rotation matrix

```
R = RotationMatrix[(i - 1) 120 °, k];
```

After the mathematical concepts are defined, we are ready to go on and model all our physical concepts. Note that the concepts always appear on the left-hand side of the equal signs and their definition and models on the right:

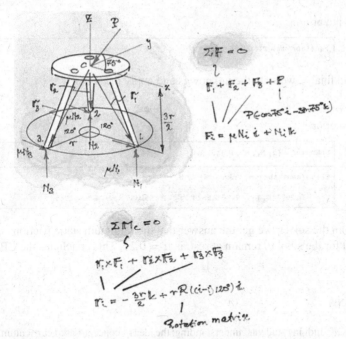

Fig. A2. The conceptual modeling of the loaded stool. The shaded equations represent the first principles valid for equilibrium. Each of the physical concepts are here modelled in steps all the way down to the most basic, the base vectors of the coordinate system.

Positions

$$r_i = -\frac{3}{2} r \, \mathbb{k} + r \, \mathcal{R} . i ;$$

Forces

$$F_i = \mu \, N_i \, i + N_i \, \mathbb{k} ;$$
$$P = P \, (-\text{Cos}[75°] \, i - \text{Sin}[75°] \, \mathbb{k}) ;$$

Resultant

$$\Sigma F = P + \sum_{i=1}^{3} F_i ;$$

Moments about C

$$\Sigma MC = \sum_{i=1}^{3} r_i \times F_i ;$$

Now we are ready to state the 1st principles, the equations for equilibrium:

Equilibrium

```
equilibrium = ΣF = 0 && ΣMC = 0;
```

And finally, we state the unknowns and apply the solver:

Solution

```
unknowns = {μ, N₁, N₂, N₃};

Solve[equilibrium, unknowns] // N

{{μ → 0.267949, N₁ → 0.0631562 P, N₂ → 0.451385 P, N₃ → 0.451385 P}}
```

From the solver, we get the answer that the minimum static friction coefficient, needed for the stool to remain at rest, is $\mu = 0.27$. This concludes the CBM study.

References

Alhumaid, K.F.: Judging students' understanding: the idea of concept-based curriculum. Humanit. Soc. Sci. Rev. **8**(5), 319–325 (2020)

Delahunty, T., Seery, N., Lynch, R.: Exploring problem conceptualization and performance in STEM problem solving contexts. Instr. Sci. **48**(4), 395–425 (2020). https://doi.org/10.1007/s11251-020-09515-4

D'Souza, S., Leigh Wood, L., Petocz, P.: Proceedings of Blended Learning in Science, Teaching and Learning Symposium, pp. 37–42. UniServe Science, Sydney (2005)

Galán García, J.L., Galán García, M.A., Gálvez Galiano, A., Jiménez Prieto, A.J., Padilla Domínguez, Y., Rodríguez Cielos, P.: Computer algebra systems: a basic tool for teaching mathematics in engineering. In: 3rd International Conference on Multimedia and Information and Communication Technologies in Education (m-ICTE2005). Formatex, Spain (2005)

Greiffenhagen, C.: The materiality of mathematics: presenting mathematics at the blackboard. Br. J. Sociol. **65**(3), 502–528 (2014)

Kahneman, D.: Thinking, Fast and Slow. Farrar, Straus and Giroux, New York (2011)

Kiverstein, J.D., Rietveld, E.: Reconceiving representation-hungry cognition: an ecological-enactive proposal. Adapt. Behav. **26**(4), 147–263 (2018)

Ohlsson, S.: Deep Learning. How the Mind Overrides Experience. Cambridge University Press, Cambridge (2011)

Polson, N., Scott, J.: AIQ: How Artificial Intelligence Works and How We Can Harness Its Power for a Better World. Bantam Press, London (2018)

Schramm, T.: Computer algebra systems in engineering education. Glob. J. Eng. Educ. **2**(2), 187–194 (1998)

Silver, D., Schrittwieser, J., Simonyan, K., Antonoglou, I., Huang, A., Guez, A., et al.: Mastering the game of go without human knowledge. Nature **550**, 354–359 (2017)

Stern, J., Ferraro, K., Mohnkern, J.: Tools for Conceptual Understanding. SAGE Books (2017)

Sweller, J., Clark, R., Kirschner, P.: Teaching general problem-solving skills is not a substitute for, or a viable addition to, teaching mathematics. Not. Am. Math. Soc. **57**(10), 1303–1304 (2010)

Tegmark, M.: Life 3.0: Being Human in the Age of Artificial Intelligence. Random House–Knopf, New York (2017)

Tenenberg, J., Roth, W.-M., Chinn, D., Jornet, A., Socha, D., Skip Walter, S.: More than the code: learning rules of rejection in writing programs. Commun. ACM **61**(5), 66–71 (2018)

Wang, D., et al.: Human-AI collaboration in data science: exploring data scientists' perceptions of automated AI. In: Proceedings of the ACM on Human-Computer Interaction, vol. 3, no. CSCW, pp. 1–24 (2019)

Willingham, D.:Why Don't Students Like School? Wiley (2009)

Wittgenstein, L.: Tractatus Logico Philosophicus. Routledge & Kegan Paul Ltd., London (1962)

Promoting Life-Long Learning Through Flexible Educational Format for Professionals Within AI, Design and Innovation Management

Jeanette Sjöberg$^{(\boxtimes)}$ [iD], Stefan Byttner [iD], Pontus Wärnestål [iD], Jonathan Burgos [iD], and Magnus Holmén [iD]

Halmstad University, Kristian IV:s väg 3, 301 18 Halmstad, Sweden
{jeanette.sjoberg,stefan.byttner,pontus.warnestal,
jonathan.burgos,magnus.holmen}@hh.se

Abstract. In recent years, the concept of lifelong learning has been emphasized in relation to higher education, with a bearing idea of the possibility for the individual for a continuous, self-motivated pursuit of gaining knowledge for both personal and professional reasons, provided by higher education institutions (HEI:s). But how can this actually be done in practice? In this paper we present an ongoing project called MAISTR, which is a collaboration between Swedish HEI:s and industry with the aim of providing a number of flexible courses within the subjects of Artificial intelligence (AI), Design, and Innovation management, for professionals. Our aim is to describe how the project is setup to create new learning opportunities, including the development process and co-creation with industry, the core structure and the pedagogical design. Furthermore, we would like to discuss both challenges and opportunities that come with this kind of project, as well as reflecting on early stage outcomes.

Keywords: Flexible education · Lifelong learning · Pedagogical design · Learning for professionals · AI education

1 Introduction

Contemporary higher education institutions (HEI:s) are undergoing change; some changes are incremental in nature, while others are a result of world events, most notably the covid-19 pandemic that swept over the world recently and forced universities globally to switch to digital and/or remote teaching almost overnight. In the public debate, much of the changes are due to the ongoing digitalization of society [e.g., 1–3]. Another change for HEI:s has to do with challenging the idea that students in higher education today are persons who come to higher education straight out of high school, complete an education program after a few years and then disappear into working life never to return. Rather, this change can be linked to the idea that HEI:s should offer continuous access to learning through all phases of life. One such phase is education aimed at people who have been professionally active for a longer period of time. In this paper, we present

E. Brooks et al. (Eds.): DLI 2022, LNICST 493, pp. 38–47, 2023.
https://doi.org/10.1007/978-3-031-31392-9_3

a substantial collaborative project between HEI:s and industry called MAISTR (Data Analytics and Service Innovation based on Artificial Intelligence) which aims to develop an educational concept consisting of a number of different courses with flexible format within limited fields of content aimed at professionals.

The involved HEI:s are Halmstad University, Skövde University, Blekinge Institute of Technology and RISE which are known for performing high quality AI research in collaboration with industry, as well as delivering campus-based education in the fields of AI, Design and Innovation management. These universities decided to develop content for lifelong learning directed towards professionals through the support from KK-foundations "Expertkompetens" program. The content that was proposed was a program consisting of 26 courses on advanced level in the fields of AI, Design and Innovation management with a flexible format that is suited for professionals. Developing the education in collaboration with industry is an expectation from the KK-foundation and the initiative is supported by about a dozen Swedish industrial partners from both the Swedish production industry as well as from the Swedish service industry.

In this paper we would like to address issues concerning the development of flexible formatted courses aimed at professionals and highlight the importance of these in relation to the concept of lifelong learning. Examples of issues we face in the project are about acquiring insight about competence needs from the companies, design of courses that achieve sufficient flexibility, and scalable examination. The MAISTR project provides a competence development framework for non-traditional students (i.e., working professionals) who would otherwise not be able to participate in higher education.

1.1 Learning Perspective

To be able to start talking about the framework of the courses included in the MAISTR project and the learning that is supposed to take place there, we need to start off by saying something about learning itself. Generally speaking, one pedagogical principle is that as a learning individual you have your own responsibility for your learning through your actions. This can be expressed in different ways; partly through the approach the individual has towards his or her own learning and whether there is an expectation of gaining knowledge or to generate knowledge, partly through the individual's participation in the learning situation and if this participation appears to be active or passive. A starting point that derives from this and is based on pedagogical research [e.g. 4], stems from the belief that learning is promoted by one's own activity rather than by passively listening to a lecturer. Researchers Lave and Wenger [5] discuss different kinds of participation; from peripheral to central participation, and that a person can be part of a context, that is to say participate, without he or she actually participating. It may be about being denied participation, but it can also be about choosing not to participate [5].

In addition, Lave and Wenger claim that learning is situated, i.e., takes place within the framework of a specific context and for a specific situation [5]. Based on this, most course elements in higher education should be about the students themselves 'deciding' or regulating their own learning based on their participation. Another angle of participatory learning is connected to an interactionist approach [e.g. 6] and has to do with learning taking place in interaction with others; it's in the interpersonal meeting in which development mainly takes place. From a sociocultural perspective on learning [e.g. 7, 8], then you primarily focus on communication and language – which is absolutely the most important symbol within even symbolic interactionism [6] - and its social character [e.g. 8–10] as everyday action. This focus on dialogue and the importance of conversation in relation to learning - that we learn in interaction with others - can therefore not be emphasized enough [6]. The approach may seem obvious, but many institutionalized teaching contexts have traditionally focused rather on the individual's learning in relation to their own studies of literature (see for example [11]).

In the case of the current courses included in the project, they are primarily aimed at professionals in a few limited areas. This means that the students who are part of the project differ significantly from what could be called traditional students, in that they come from practical experience within professional practices. It is therefore of essence that they choose to actively participate in any educational endeavor, and in order to make it easier for them the format of courses offered in the MAISTR project are flexible. Coming from the experience of the working field, professionals develop so called "silent knowledge" within their practice [12]. This knowledge can be described vaguely as in "one's spine" and is usually brought to the fore in relation to professions such as nurses and craftsmanship, but professionals in all occupations more or less develop some sort of silent knowledge in their field. This knowledge, alongside the work experience, are crucial elements that professionals bring with them into an educational context. The idea, thus, is that the experience of the practice adds value for the student in the learning situation, which leads to a greater enhancement for the professional skills acquired.

2 Related Work

2.1 Flexible Education and Flexible Learning

Flexible education usually means that the education is available to students in for example adaptations in both time and space, but also in terms of the teaching mode or format. Closely connected to flexible education is the concept of flexible learning. Flexible learning is usually defined as concerning approaches to teaching and learning that are learner centered as well as the use of appropriate technologies in a networked environment [e.g., 13, 14]. Furthermore, flexible learning is more or less "free" regarding time, place and methods of learning and teaching. Flexible learning has been used within diverse areas such as learning environment [e.g., 15, 16], emergent frameworks for new learning opportunities [e.g., 17, 18], as well as teachers' adaptations to digital teaching [e.g., 19]. The term is commonly used as a means to describe changed classroom conditions [e.g., 20, 21] moving from physical to digital classroom with different options for students in terms of pace of studies. Basically, the term flexible learning describes a learning design perspective deeply rooted in the perceived needs of students, with the main objective being to provide them with the most flexibility about the learning content, schedules, access, and learning styles as possible. A flexible learning design customizes learning environments to meet the needs of learners, using both technological and non-technological tools and it includes an approach to learning in which the time, place, and pace of learning may be determined by learners [22]. The term most often includes varieties of learning such as blended learning, flipped learning, m-Learning (mobile), networked learning and digital learning [e.g., 23]. It is often incorrectly used in an interchangeable manner with other terms such as open learning, distance learning, work-based learning, as well as e-learning, which are all instances or forms of flexible learning in that they provide flexibility to the student in terms of time/pace, place, access, content, and/or delivery mode [24]. The term is broadly used in descriptions of programs and courses delivery and design, in such a way as to cater for student demands for variety, access, recognition of diverse learning styles, and student control over the learning experience [24].

In addition, flexible learning is also a teaching strategy designed to empower students to learn in various ways. While working with and preparing for flexible learning and flexible education, there are many aspects to consider: content, time, space, learning styles, methods, requirements, organization and infrastructure. All these aspects are vital for the success of education [22]. The benefits for the students involved in flexible learning can be multiple: improved learning outcomes resulting from evidence-based and technology-enabled teaching methods [e.g., 25]; more choice in different kinds of learning (online, face-to-face, blended, MOOC:s, etc.); flexible learning delivers more scheduling options (e.g., day/night, on-/off-campus); enhanced personalization of degree programs; more just-in time learning options for career learners; improved learning experiences including more experiential and community-based learning options; more global learning options; more open content - learning materials are often free and not restricted to students registered in a degree program [26].

In the case of the MAISTR program flexibility looks as follows. At a program level, while there are recommendations for the order courses are taken (Fig. 1), the students may freely choose which courses to take and in the order they prefer. This freedom of choice is in line with the view that learning is situated and that the experience, motivation and wants of the students should inform learning objectives and activities. By allowing professionals to actively choose the courses in any order and from any track they deem relevant, MAISTR's flexibility provides a low-risk opportunity for them to expand their knowledge and comfort zones. To nudge such cross-coupling, mixing between courses in different tracks is not only feasible but encouraged.

2.2 Life-Long Learning

A concept that works well together with a flexible approach to education is life-long learning. There is no formal or final definition of the term life-long learning rather many co-existing definitions [e.g., 27], but generally the meaning concerns learning that is taking place outside a formal institution (such as a school). UNESCO has a broader definition of the term and describes life-long learning as follows: "All learning activities undertaken throughout life, with the aim of improving knowledge, skills and/or qualifications for personal, social and/or professional reasons" [28]. This definition implies that life-long learning also includes the opportunity to learn throughout the different stages in life, in both formal and informal contexts. Moreover, it implies that life-long learning is self-initiated in such a way that it is the individual's own choice and personal drive for personal development that is the basis for learning. In 2015, UNESCO released the book *The Role of Higher Education in Promoting Lifelong Learning*, in which the authors are advocating for the practical implementation of lifelong learning in higher education, both within their own regional context and globally, and they are pointing out that life-long learning has been emphasized in relation to higher education more frequently in recent years [29]. Lessons learned from a Swedish national perspective on life-long learning in AI-education have been summarized in [30], which includes the importance of adapted learning formats and the specific challenges associated with adult learning in the AI field (e.g., the need to be able to do simple programming). The MAISTR programme is part of the Swedish national initiatives in life-long learning and aims to evaluate how different approaches to teaching in this context can be done in an efficient way, for both the professionals and for the university. Evaluation will be carried out by using different methods, such as standardized questionnaires for course evaluation as well as follow-up interviews with participants, industry partners and instructors.

3   The MAISTR Program Setup

3.1   Background

The program has three tracks: Machine learning (ML), Human-centered design (HCD) and Innovation management (IM). The courses are defined as free-standing so students do not apply to a program. Instead, there is a specific website (link) developed in the project where the courses are presented along with a link for each course to the national admission system. This allows the students to pick any combination and order of courses they like, as long as they fulfill the prerequisites of a specific course. The three tracks are balanced in terms of number of courses, ten in the ML track, nine in the HCD track, and seven in the IM track, see Fig. 1.

The course offerings in the MAISTR program vary in terms of instruction modality, length of study, instruction frequency, and examination styles. All of the courses are given online at a pace of approximately 20% full-time studies, with real-time instruction ranging from weekly to monthly. Some courses are completely self-paced with a reading guide that students can follow at their leisure during the course term, while others offer students the possibility to meet in person and participate in physical-digital hybrid discussions. Technical courses can run over a longer period than others to give students the opportunity to complete practical coding exercises and project work. Examination types vary from rating assignment completion to final projects and oral examinations. This variability of course characteristics ensures that the instruction method is accommodating to the subject area as well as the prospective student groups.

3.2   Courses and Tracks

Machine Learning Track: Machine Learning (ML) is a subfield of artificial intelligence that gives machines the ability to learn and improve automatically through experience and by the use of data. It has become a significant competitive differentiator for many companies, and we all probably use it several times throughout our day without knowing it. The machine learning track consists of courses related to topics such as learning algorithms, data mining and statistics with applications to domains like healthcare and predictive maintenance of vehicles. The courses assume some prerequisite knowledge of python programming and equip the student with both theoretical knowledge and practical skills to apply the latest state-of-art techniques in machine learning.

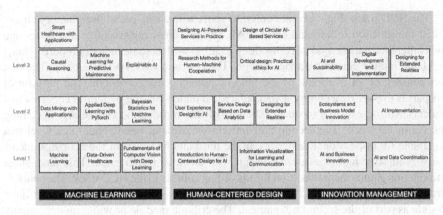

Fig. 1. Track and course disposition in the MAISTR program.

Human-Centered Design Track: As AI-powered functionality in digital services increases in availability, the need for thoughtful interaction and service design increases as well. However, in order to create valuable and usable AI-powered services, designers have to make sure that they understand who the service is for, how it creates value, and how it affects existing workflows and business offerings. Translating AI technology into real-world socio-technical systems is the domain of human-centered design [31]. The Human-Centered Design track consists of courses related to design thinking, service innovation, UX design, research methods and information visualization. All courses are built from an AI-first perspective, which means that various kinds of AI are seen as a new "design material" for designers, and that methods and approaches are taking AI-specific features into consideration.

IM Track: Data is intermittently seen by practitioners, business and other organizations as 'the new oil', with AI–and particularly ML–acting as "refineries" that produce rapid and cheap prediction machines; the capacity to destroy and create new jobs, business opportunities and professions; but also as being terribly overhyped. The IM track addresses all of these aspects by focusing on the management of AI-oriented innovation processes, structures, and resources by explaining and reflecting upon what is new with AI. Participants have heterogeneous backgrounds, ranging from data science, nursing, engineering, and business studies, and covering any type of industry or public sector. All courses are based on blended learning, with a combination of pre-recorded lectures, online group discussions, and situated learning-oriented assignments.

3.3 Example Pedagogical Design and Learning Approaches

As previously stated, MAISTR consists of over two dozen courses given at the master's level. For the purposes of this paper, we use the case of human-centered design as an example of how MAISTR courses combine flexibility and life-long learning into the program.

The HCD track (Fig. 1, center column) starts with a self-paced introductory course called Introduction to human-centered AI. The resources consist of academic journal and conference papers, podcast episodes [cf. 32] as well as some industry reports related to AI and human-centered service design. The course consists of three parts: The first part consists of an overview of the field of human-centered design. The purpose of this part is to provide a common vocabulary and understanding of central concepts that students will be exposed to during the rest of the introduction course and upcoming courses in the track. The second part introduces artificial intelligence on a level that is suitable for professional designers. In the third and final part of the course, students try to synthesize human-centered design with artificial intelligence. This three-stage introduction equips them to take on the upcoming courses in the HCD track. The course's three parts are examined by three written assignments. There is also one peer critique module as part of the second assignment. The critique module provides an opportunity for social interaction and consists of reading another student's submitted assignment and writing a rebuttal.

Later in the HCD track, students can take the Service Design based on Data Analytics course. It is a three-credit course where the focus lies on using data analytics and machine learning for service design. The course allows the students to expand from user experience and interaction design to strategic and holistic service experiences. The course consists of a series of invited lectures from industry. All video lectures are recorded so that students can consume the content at different times. Since the course has been given several times, there are several video recorded case studies that can be reused in future courses. There are also traditional video lectures that are given live digitally and recorded for students that do not have the possibility to attend the live sessions. Apart from traditional readings, the course makes use of selected episodes from a podcast-based course called Human-Centered Machine Learning [32]. Podcast episodes are also examples of readily available resources that can be reused and accessed "life-long" and in a flexible manner.

4 Current and Expected Outcomes

The MAISTR project has defined a number of different kinds of impact that should be achieved by the program for both students, companies and universities. This is related to aspects such as increased ability and skills in AI, increased opportunities for flexible learning, strengthened relations between companies and universities, increased employer branding, etc. We are considering several ways to measure the level of impact, including the formulation of additional questions in the final course evaluation, as well as having interviews with company staff and managers to get testimonials.

4.1 The Student Perspective

As of September 2022, eight courses have been given in the program (three in ML, three in HCD and two in IM) and course evaluations indicate a general success and high appreciation of both content and format. Standard course evaluations from the students have been carried out at the end of each course. In particular, self-paced reading-based courses–such as those described in Sect. 3.3–have been favored by the course participants.

Participants in the course evaluations voice the importance of flexibility, and the advantage of being able to access resources in flexible formats, such as reading PDF files on any kind of device, listen to podcasts via existing platforms, or being able to run the written content through a text-to-speech service to consume the content via audio. Through course evaluation responses and dialogues with instructors, some MAISTR students have indicated that they would not have otherwise been able to participate in such continued education programs.

4.2 The Industry Partner Perspective

The MAISTR leadership group meets regularly with industry partners to present the status of the program, course evaluations, and strategic plans. Industry partners provide feedback on how the content of the courses are aligned with general competence development needs that exist in the labor market. Similar to students themselves, project leaders and supervisors may also notice improvements in performance indicators that after a colleague took a MAISTR course. Long-term follow-ups with industry partners are necessary to evaluate any effects on workplace impact.

Time is a big challenge for professionals taking courses while working. Professionals may not be able to take time off from work to pursue higher education, and employers do not want to lose productive hours on their skilled staff. Self-paced content and long course duration are two qualities that are appreciated by the students and employers alike, based on the initial course evaluations.

4.3 The HEI Perspective

Course evaluations have identified a risk for lack of interaction (both student-student and student-teacher) due to the high degree of self-paced content. As a whole, the program is a mix of approaches, where flexibility differs between courses. This makes the program different from completely self-paced online courses where there is no teacher interaction at all and teaching is limited to pre-recorded videos.

HEIs need not develop full education programs and compete with other institutions. The MAISTR project gives partnering HEIs the ability to develop stand-alone courses in line with their respective profiled areas, potentially easing in staffing and other resource management concerns. Students benefit from being able to take a cohesive set of stand-alone courses across multiple HEIs in ML, HCD and IM, without needing to compromise for a generalized program given by one university.

4.4 Future Plans

At present, the MAISTR project has not yet run its full 26-course curriculum. As more information is gathered from course evaluations, follow-up interviews and workshops with industry partners, we will be able to formally evaluate whether the design (and subsequent adjustments) of the MAISTR project and its courses are meeting the expected outcomes from each stakeholder's perspective.

Participants have expressed some worry that they are "alone" in their new competency development after having completed a course. A significant challenge consists of actually changing work practice in the home organization after finishing the course. A critical mass of team members needs the new knowledge, as one person cannot change work practices on his or her own. This implies that we should encourage several team members from the same division or organization to participate. One way to approach this is to modify some courses to be (a) domain-specific, and/or (b) be designed for team participation. To this end, we are planning to deliver at least one course in conjunction with a real industrial project (more specifically, the course "Designing AI-powered services in practice") where we aim to test a project course concept where practical training and mentorship from the teachers are combined with work at a company to support the professionals' learning and future dissemination in the home organization.

References

1. Sjöberg, J., Lilja, P.: University teachers' ambivalence about the digital transformation of higher education. Int. J. Learn. Teach. Educ. Res. **18**(13), 133–149 (2019)
2. Erstad, O., Kjällander, S., Järvelä, S.: Facing the challenges of 'digital competence'. A Nordic agenda for curriculum development for the 21st century. Nord. J. Digit. Literacy **16**(2), 77–87 (2021)
3. Rapanta, C., Botturi, L., Goodyear, P., Guárdia, L., Koole, M.: Balancing Technology, Pedagogy and the New Normal: Post pandemic Challenges for Higher Education. Postdigital Sci. Educ. **3**, 715–742 (2021). https://doi.org/10.1007/s42438-021-00249-1
4. Ramsden, P.: Learning to Teach in Higher Education. Routledge, New York (2003)
5. Lave, J., Wenger, E.: Situated Learning. Legitimate Peripheral Participation. Cambridge University Press, Cambridge (1991)
6. Bron, A., Wilhelmsson, L.: Lärprocesser i högre utbildning. Liber, Malmö (2005)
7. Vygotsky, L.: Thought and Language. Harvard University Press, Cambridge (1934/1986)
8. Wertsch, J.: Mind as Action. Oxford University Press, New York (1998)
9. Billig, M.: Arguing and Thinking: A Rhetorical Approach to Social Psychology, Revised Version. Cambridge University Press, Cambridge (1996)
10. Säljö, R.: Learning & Cultural Tools. About Learning Processes and Collective Memories. Norstedts Akademiska Förlag, Stockholm (2005)
11. Biggs, J., Tang, C.: Teaching for Quality Learning at University. Open University Press, Maidenhead (2011)
12. Molander, B.: The Practice of Knowing and Knowing in Practices.Peter Lang GmbH, Internationaler Verlag der Wissenschaften (2015)
13. Goodyear, P.: Flexible Learning and the Architecture of Learning Places. Routledge, London (2008)
14. Collis, B.A., Moonen, J.: Flexible Learning in a Digital World: Experiences and Expectations. Open & Distance Learning Series (2001)
15. Frelin, A., Grannäs, J.: Teachers' pre-occupancy evaluation of affordances in a multi-zone flexible learning environment–introducing an analytical model. Pedagog. Cult. Soc. **30**(2), 243–259 (2022)
16. Vercelotti, M.L.: Do interactive learning spaces increase student achievement? A comparison of classroom context. Act. Learn. High. Educ. **19**(3), 197–210 (2017). https://doi.org/10.1177/1469787417735606

17. Andrade, M.S., Alden-Rivers, B.: Developing a framework for sustainable growth of flexible learning opportunities. High. Educ. Pedagogies **4**(1), 1–16 (2019). https://doi.org/10.1080/23752696.2018.1564879

18. Barnett, R.: Conditions of flexibility: securing a more responsive higher education system. Higher Education Academy, York (2014)

19. Deed, C., et al.: Teacher adaptation to flexible learning environments. Learn. Environ. Res. **23**(2), 153–165 (2019). https://doi.org/10.1007/s10984-019-09302-0

20. Müller, C., Mildenberger, T.: Facilitating flexible learning by replacing classroom time with an online learning environment: a systematic review of blended learning in higher education. Educ. Res. Rev. **34**, 100394 (2021)

21. Byers, T., Imms, W., Hartnell-Young, E.: Evaluating teacher and student spatial transition from a traditional classroom to an innovative learning environment. Stud. Educ. Eval. **58**, 156–166 (2018). https://doi.org/10.1016/j.stueduc.2018.07.004

22. Sturm, M., Kennell, T., McBride, R., Kelly, M.: Handbook of Research on Web 2.0 and Second Language Learning (2009)

23. Whyte, B.: Collaborative teaching in flexible learning spaces: capabilities of beginning teachers. J. Educ. Leadersh. Policy Pract. **32**, 84–96 (2017)

24. Lee, M., McLoughlin, C.E.: Applying Web 2.0 tools in hybrid learning designs, pp. 371–392. IGI Global (2010)

25. Nortvig, A.M., Petersen, A.K., Balle, S.H.: A literature review of the factors influencing e-learning and blended learning in relation to learning outcome, student satisfaction and engagement. Electron. J. e-Learn. **16**(1), 46–55 (2018)

26. Joan, R.: Flexible learning as new learning design in classroom process to promote quality education. J. Sch. Educ. Technol. **9**(1), 37–42 (2013)

27. Laal, M.: Lifelong learning: what does it mean? Soc. Behav. Sci. **28**, 470–474 (2011)

28. United Nations Educational, Scientific and Cultural Organization (UNESCO): Terminology of Technical and Vocational Education (1984)

29. Yng, J., Schneller, C., Roche, S. (eds.): The Role of Higher Education in Promoting Lifelong Learning. UIL Publication Series on Lifelong Learning Policies and Strategies: No., UNESCO (2015)

30. Heintz, F., et al.: AI competence for Sweden - A National Life-Long Learning Initiative. In: EDULEARN 2021 Proceedings, pp. 2560–2567 (2021)

31. Wärnestål, P.: Designing AI-Powered Services. Studentlitteratur, Lund (2022)

32. Wärnestål, P., Sjöberg, J.: Rethinking continuous university education for professionals – a podcast-based course on service design and AI. In: Stephanidis, C., Antona, M., Ntoa, S. (eds.) HCII 2020. CCIS, vol. 1294, pp. 324–332. Springer, Cham (2020). https://doi.org/10.1007/978-3-030-60703-6_42

AI-Supported Acquisition of Argumentation Skills: Use Case 'The Argueniser'

Veronika Hackl[(✉)] [iD] and Christian Müller[iD]

Universität Passau, Innstraße 41, 94032 Passau, Germany
veronika.hackl@uni-passau.de

Abstract. A growing number of students enrolls at universities, while capacities – above all in terms of teachers – to support their learnings stay limited. In particular, individualised feedback for students is not feasible in many courses. How can universities close this gap with the help of Artificial Intelligence (AI)?

This paper presents a use case for an AI-aided learning scenario that is expected to achieve high learning effectiveness: the acquisition of argumentation competence in the disciplines of law and economics. Emphasis is placed on good comprehensibility for the target group of students, despite the complexity of the setting. Also for this reason, the use case has been given a descriptive name, The Argueniser - Organise Your Arguments.

The focus of this paper is placed on the use case. Flanking topics are also highlighted: the concept of argumentation competence within the project, the role of feedback, and mutual learning between learners, teachers and AI. A preliminary study design illustrates the approach to measure learning effectiveness of the AI-aided learning situation. A notable aspect of the project is the involvement of the instructional design perspective already in the training phase of the AI.

DEEP WRITE is a project funded by the German Federal Ministry of Education and Research (BMBF) that aims to improve university teaching using AI. This paper is developed in the context of this project and it is based on thoughts developed within the team.

Keywords: Educational Design Research · Design-Based Research · AI-Aided Competence Development · Argumentation Competence · Toulmin Scheme · legal opinion style · ARS

1 Introduction

The work-in-progress paper contributes to a higher teaching quality in Higher Education. An innovative educational intervention will be developed to reach better learning outcomes. An overall view will be given about the ongoing pedagogical considerations and the implications for the development of a first prototype as well as about a following evaluation. The work follows a design-based research approach with the phases analysis, design, evaluation (McKenney 2012, p. 135).

Teaching quality consists of three basic dimensions: classroom management, cognitive activation and student support (Praetorius et al. 2018). A typical classroom management teaching scenario in lecture halls with a great many of students and only one

E. Brooks et al. (Eds.): DLI 2022, LNICST 493, pp. 48–54, 2023.
https://doi.org/10.1007/978-3-031-31392-9_4

person as mentor has the weakness of individual support for each student. Large sessions in the disciplines of law and economics at the University of Passau with more than 400 participants, especially in the basic courses, form the field for testing the use case for cognitive activation presented in the paper.

AI-technologies seem to promise a better learning experience for each student even in this type of university lectures. The AI in the project will be able to automatically evaluate texts of students as well as to give instant and effective feedback. It takes on the role of a computer-simulated personal mentor (EDUCAUSE 2017, p. 2) in this process. Students in mass study programs will be able to receive individual feedback on their performance in order to significantly improve their practical skills.

The presented use case 'Argueniser' is implemented into ClassEx, an advanced ARS that allows to configure complex intervention settings in stages. It integrates Mazur's effective Peer Interaction active learning strategy (Crouch and Mazur 2001, p. 975), while at the same time is capable to display AI-generated feedback. The Argueniser does not replace academic teaching with 'edutainment', but acknowledges the fact that 'Although enjoyment and interactivity do not determine learning, they are necessary conditions which predicate learning.' (Wood 2020, p. 24). In the use case, it is tried to keep up learners' intrinsic motivation through increasing interest, managing expectations, and clear goalsetting (Reinders 2015, p. 57).

As indicated by the design based research and the three basic dimensions of teaching quality, the approach taken in the project is marked by a high learner centricity. The individual learner, the learning experience and the target competencies set the frame for the intervention. The disciplines involved are brought together in a Learning Experience Design setting, usually consisting of pedagogical and psychological aspects, the subject domains as source of knowledge, and software development (Ebner 2021, p. 3). There is an interplay of the different disciplines designing the effective teaching-learning process.

In DEEP WRITE it is the following disciplines who contribute to the overall project: Data Science with a focus on Natural Language Processing (NLP), the knowledge domains of economics and law, ClassEx, the ARS system used in the project, and educational sciences. The different disciplines jointly plan, accompany and evaluate the use of AI in practical teaching, facilitate the formulation of learning objectives and develop feedback strategies and assessments.

2 Analysis

What makes a good written argumentation? The definition presented below takes into account different perspectives, ranging from existing writing and argumentation competency models, literary practices, taxonomy models, to study and examination regulations of the subject domains in the project (cf. Anderson 2001; Becker-Mrotzek 2022; Feilke 2016; Fix 2008; Sieber 2005; Toulmin 2003).

In the DEEP WRITE project, the term argumentation competence means the written argumentative discussion of an issue or a question within the disciplines of law and economic sciences. The argumentation formally follows a set pattern, legal opinion style ('Gutachtenstil') in the legal context, and the Toulmin scheme in the context of economics. In the DEEP WRITE project, argumentation competence includes not only the application of argumentation models, but also the convincing presentation of positions, for which content and arguments must be selected, weighted and arranged according to their relevance, correctness and completeness. Knowledge of norms and values, subject knowledge, world knowledge and language knowledge are also required.

The German Gutachtenstil and the use of language in law in general follows strict rules 'and the recourse to fixed formulas and locutions, which give little room for any individual variation.' (Bourdieu 1987, p. 819): The German Gutachtenstil, a specific legal opinion argumentation scheme as presented in Fig. 1, clearly regulates how a legal argumentation must look like in order to meet the quality criteria of the discipline of law. The Gutachtenstil is mainly used in law studies up to the First State Examination in Germany. In the practice of jurisprudence and administration, the verdict style dominates. Here, the result is put first (not the problem) and then systematically justified. This specific legal opinion argumentation scheme differs from the Anglo-American style of written argumentation.

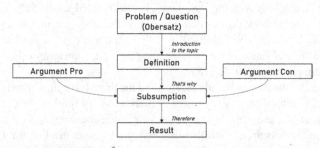

Fig. 1. The German legal opinion argumentation scheme (own visualization)

Based on the definition of argumentation competence provided above a preliminary criteria catalogue to rate student argumentative texts is being produced. The criteria are being located in the learning objectives taxonomy (LOT) (Anderson 2001, p. 28) (Table 1).

Table 1. Proposed evaluation criteria (own compilation)

Priority	Criteria catalogue	Expectation horizon	LOT
1	Argumentation structure (textualisation)	Student knows the domain specific argumentation model and applies it	C3 (procedural)
2	Correctness of content (referentialisation)	Student chooses correct content for argumentation and applies it	A3 (factual)
2	Relevance of content (alterisation)	Student evaluates and weighs the content of his/her argumentation	A5 (factual)
2	Completeness of content	Student must select and apply all appropriate content	A3 (factual)
3	Knowledge of norms and values	Student applies knowledge of general principles and models	B3 (conceptual)

3   Design

The Argueniser – Organise Your Arguments is a scaffolding exercise that provides the students with knowledge about the structure of an argumentation (Fig. 2). It transfers the theoretical framework of the respective argumentation schemes into a learning exercise within an ARS. The argumentation elements are labelled and explained. The exercise as cognitive activation is considered to be most effective when the following four phases are planned: declarative knowledge acquisition, reference to examples, forming rules, and lastly automation and flexibility allowing learners to transfer their knowledge to new tasks (Philipp 2021, p. 102–103, cf. Renkl 2014).

For economics, the Toulmin scheme is applied, offering Claim, Evidence, and Warrant as open text fields. For the German Gutachtenstil, open text fields are offered for the General Question, the Factual Requirements, the question whether the condition is fulfilled (Obersatz), the Definition of a factual requirement, the Subsumption, and the Result.

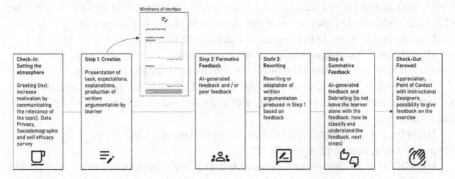

Fig. 2. Argumentation Style Scaffolding Use Case The Argueniser (own visualization)

The aim of any feedback in the use case is to close the gap between a learning objective and the current level of competence. It is intended to generate feedback for the students following the three-perspectives of effective feedback (Hattie 2007, p. 87): Feed-Back, Feed-Up, Feed-Forward. The learning analytics dashboard for the learner might include at a later stage "learning opportunities, self-assessments, recommendations, comparison to peers, social interactions, or additional links (Sahin and Ifenthaler 2021, p. 3). The AI-generated feedback will mainly focus on the Feed-Back perspective through analysis of the content produced by the student. AI evaluation options include, but are not limited to similarity checks in the first stages of the project. One decisive advantage of AI-generated feedback is immediateness: 'Prompt feedback allows students to confirm whether they have understood a topic or not and helps them to become aware of their learning needs. Instant feedback is not only useful for students but also enables teachers to make necessary pedagogical changes in order to address identified gaps in students' understanding.' (Wood 2020, p. 24). Putting this in context with the three basic dimensions of teaching quality, it pays directly into the improvement of student support.

4 Evaluation

The aim is to demonstrate students' competence development in written argumentation through AI-supported learning environments. Consequently, the Hypothesis 1 is: AI-supported ARS learning scenarios with the goal to acquire argumentation skills are more effective than ARS learning scenarios that integrate peer feedback or feedback by lecturer.

Figure 3 illustrates the schematic sequence of the preliminary field study design including repeated measurements. The number of participants per group will be n > 100. The study is expected to be conducted in October 2023. Three different treatments are being given, differing in the kind of feedback provided to the student: AI-generated feedback, peer feedback, feedback by lecturer. These three different treatments are being chosen in the current preliminary design as it is assumed that the AI-generated feedback and the feedback given by the lecturer will equalize in quality in the course of the project, while the peer feedback is used as a contrast. The result is demonstrated through the number of those who achieve the required competence. The required competence will be represented numerically. The measuring instrument is the trained correctors. A catalogue of criteria with detailed anchor examples is made available to the correctors.

More hypotheses are being discussed, such as the following:

Hypothesis 2: Sub-aspects of argumentation competence on which the AI can give feedback will develop better than those for which no AI feedback is given.

Hypothesis 3: Those who already show a good result in the baseline measurement achieve a smaller increase in proficiency than those who are rated poor in the baseline measurement.

Hypothesis 4: Students that receive AI-generated feedback in both treatments achieve the greatest increases in proficiency.

Hypothesis 5: Students with a positive self-efficacy expectation will achieve greater increases in proficiency regardless of the scenario.

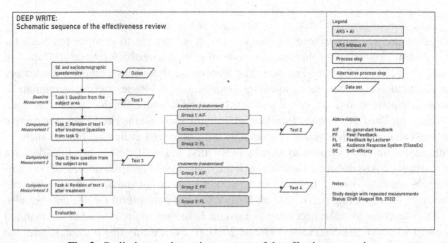

Fig. 3. Preliminary schematic sequence of the effectiveness review

5 Conclusion

As Akata puts it the central question is 'how to build adaptive intelligent systems that augment rather than replace human intelligence' (Akata 2020, p. 20). The use case presented in this paper is an attempt to bring together different perspectives to allow students to develop argumentation skills in a presumably effective AI-supported learning scenario. The study to be conducted in the course of the project will hint at strengths and weaknesses of the concept, giving the chance to improve it further and contributing to augmenting human intelligence.

'Human-centered AI needs [an] integrated approach where technical, social, legal and ethics approaches are used together for supporting the Human-in-the-loop principle.' (Rodríguez-Doncel 2021, p. 2). It is an irrevocable principle in educational sciences to put the learner in the center of the developmental process, rather than in the loop. There has been a discussion within the project whether there should actually be three actors in the center: the learner, the teacher, and the AI, mutually benefitting from each other and evolving together. From the point of view of the authors this question forms a very provocative perspective, nonetheless it might add to the general discourse of AI-development in educational sciences.

References

Akata, Z., et al.: A research agenda for hybrid intelligence: augmenting human intellect with collaborative, adaptive, responsible, and explainable artificial intelligence. Computer **53**(8), 18–28 (2020)

Anderson, L.W. (ed.): Longman, New York (2001)

Becker-Mrotzek, M., Roth, H.-J., Grießbach, J., von Dewitz, N., Schöneberger, C. (eds.): 1st edn. Kohlhammer Verlag, Stuttgart (2022)

Bourdieu, P.: The force of law: toward a sociology of the juridical field. Hastings Law J. **38**(5), 814–853 (1987)

Crouch, C.H., Mazur, E.: Peer instruction: ten years of experience and results. Am. J. Phys. **69**(9), 970–977 (2001)

Ebner, M., et al.: Learning experience design – zur gestaltung von technologiegestützten lern-erfahrungen mit methoden der design-entwicklung. In: Wilbers, K., Hohenstein, A. (eds.) Handbuch E-Learning. Expertenwissen aus Wissenschaft und Praxis – Strategien, Instrumente, Fallstudien. Fachverlag Deutscher Wirtschaftsdienst, Köln (2021)

EDUCAUSE: Artificial intelligence in teaching and learning. 7 things you should know about artificial intelligence in teaching and learning (2017). https://library.educause.edu/-/media/files/library/2017/4/eli7143.pdf. Accessed 13 Aug 2022

Feilke, H.: Literale Praktiken und literale Kompetenz. In: Deppermann, A., Feilke, H., Linke, A. (eds.) Sprachliche und kommunikative Praktiken. De Gruyter, Berlin (2016)

Fix, M.: Texte schreiben. utb GmbH, Stuttgart (2008)

Hattie, J., Timperley, H.: The power of feedback. Rev. Educ. Res. **77**(1), 81–112 (2007). https://doi.org/10.1007/BF03078234

McKenney, S.E., Reeves, T.C.: Conducting Educational Design Research. Routledge, London (2012)

Philipp, M.: Schreiben lernen, schreibend lernen: Prinzipien des Aufbaus und der Nutzung von Schreibkompetenz. Springer eBook Collection. Springer VS, Wiesbaden (2021). https://doi.org/10.1007/978-3-658-33253-2

Praetorius, A.K., Klieme, E., Herbert, B., et al.: Generic dimensions of teaching quality: the German framework of three basic dimensions. ZDM Math. Educ. **50**, 407–426 (2018)

Reinders, H., Ditton, H., Gräsel, C., Gniewosz, B.: Empirische Bildungsforschung. VS Verlag für Sozialwissenschaften, Wiesbaden (2015)

Renkl, A.: Toward an instructionally oriented theory of example-based learning. Cogn. Sci. **38**(1), 1–37 (2014)

Rodríguez-Doncel, V., Palmirani, M., Araszkiewicz, M., Casanovas, P., Pagallo, U., Sartor, G. (eds.): AI Approaches to the Complexity of Legal Systems XI-XII: AICOL International Workshops 2018 and 2020: AICOL-XI@JURIX 2018, AICOL-XII@JURIX 2020, XAILA@JURIX 2020, revised selected papers. Lecture Notes in Artificial Intelligence, vol. 13048. Springer, Cham (2021)

Pagallo, U., Palmirani, M., Casanovas, P., Sartor, G., Villata, S. (eds.): LNCS (LNAI), vol. 10791. Springer, Cham (2018). https://doi.org/10.1007/978-3-030-00178-0

Sahin, M., Ifenthaler, D. (eds.): Visualizations and dashboards for learning analytics. In: Advances in Analytics for Learning and Teaching. Springer, Cham (2021). https://doi.org/10.1007/978-3-030-81222-5

Sieber, P.: Didaktik des Schreibens – vom Produkt zum Prozess und weiter zur Textkompetenz (2005)

Spector, J.M., Merrill, M.D., Elen, J., Bishop, M.J. (eds.): Springer, New York (2014). https://doi.org/10.1007/978-1-4614-3185-5

Wood, R.: A systematic review of audience response systems for teaching and learning in higher education: the student experience. Comput. Educ. **153**, 103896 (2020)

Toulmin, S.E.: The Uses of Argument, 2nd edn. Cambridge University Press, Cambridge (2003)

Collaboration Between Parents and Children Using Robots

Anders Kalsgaard Møller[1]([⊠]) and Camilla Finsterbach Kaup[1,2]

[1] Aalborg University, 9220 Aalborg, Denmark
ankm@ikl.aau.dk
[2] University College of Northern Denmark, Hjørring, Denmark
cmf@ucn.dk

Abstract. In this paper we report from a study where families (children aged 10–15 and parents) work together in their own homes on programming tasks with an educational robot Robomaster S1. The purpose of the study is to improve the science, technology, engineering, mathematics (STEM) and computational thinking (CT) competencies for both parents and children. The data collection involves self-recording and self-assessment done by the families after each completed task. In this paper we present and evaluate the method along with preliminary results from the data collection. The preliminary results provided insights about the collaboration and interaction with the robot and initial feedback about the method and tasks. The preliminary results indicated that the family improved their understanding of technology and programming. Furthermore, the children in the study supported the parent with explaining the mathematics concepts. We hope that the future results and studies can contribute to understanding the children-parent collaboration and how children use STEM and CT to solve problems while working with robotics.

Keywords: Mathematics · Robotics · STEM · Out-off-school activities · learning Computational Thinking

1 Introduction

There are currently many experiments aiming at introducing programming and computational thinking (CT) to children in primary school to try to meet the growing needs and demands for science, technology, engineering, and mathematics (STEM) competencies. One way of introducing children to programming and STEM competences is through robotics (González and Muñoz-Repiso 2018; Bers 2012) and several different robots exists created for this purpose.

While most of these experiments take place during school hours there is also a huge potential in looking at out of school activities that foster STEM competences as children spend most of their time in out-of-school environments (Stevens and Bransford 2007). A study by Sheehan and colleagues (2019) have shown a positive effect on children's learning when parents engage in programming activities and according to Vygotsky

E. Brooks et al. (Eds.): DLI 2022, LNICST 493, pp. 55–67, 2023.
https://doi.org/10.1007/978-3-031-31392-9_5

(1978), parents play an important role in the scaffolding of children's learning, but is it also possible that children can influence parents' learning through social interaction? According to Bers (2019) the early introduction to STEM and CT should not be made to meet the requirement of the future workforce, but instead the future citizenry. Although a need to strengthen children's STEM competences still exists, there is an increased focus on learning STEM competencies in primary school, this does however, not help parents in becoming digital literate.

In this paper we report from a study where families (children and parents) work together in their own homes on programming tasks with an educational robot Robomaster S1 (DJI 2022). For the study, we developed a home kit for the families consisting of the robot, an iPad, a booklet with tasks, and different materials needed for the tasks. For each task, the families were asked to answer a number of questions to evaluate the process. In this paper, we present and evaluate the method used along with preliminary results about their collaboration and learning potential regarding STEM and CT for parents and children.

2 Background

The term CT was first used by Seymour Papert (1980) and later used by Jeanette Wings (2006), stating that CT is thinking like a computer scientist to solve problems, design systems and understanding human behavior, however, it a skill for everyone and not just fundamental for computer scientists. Later she defined it as: *"the thought processes involved in formulating problems and their solutions so that the solutions are represented in a form that can be effectively carried out by an information-processing agent"* (Wings 2011; p. 1). To uniform CT teaching in K-12 Barr and Stephenson (2011) identified a number of core computational thinking concepts including: Data collection, Data analysis, Data representation, Problem Decomposition, Abstraction, Algorithms & Procedures, Automation, Parallelization, Simulation.

According to Grover and Pea (2013) a good programming tool for learning about programming and CT in K-12 is one that provide "a low floor" and a "high ceiling" meaning a programming tool that is easy for beginners to start using and is powerful enough to satisfy advanced programmers. One way of providing the low floor is through graphical programming environments (e.g., block-based programming), allowing the user to focus on design and content creation rather than the syntax. One of the most widely used graphical programming environments is Scratch (Zhang and Nouri 2019; Brennan and Resnick 2012). Brennan and Resnick (2012) developed a framework for studying and assessing the development of CT with students programming in Scratch. The framework was divided into computational concepts that students engage with when they program (such as sequences, loops, and conditions), practices that students develop as they engage with the concept (e.g., Abstracting and modularizing, and testing and debugging) and computational thinking perspectives of how they understand themselves, their relationships to others, and the technological world around them.

While science, engineering, mathematics, and programming/CT are seen as distinct disciplines they are also intertwined and often borrow from each other's methods and approaches (Denning and Freeman 2009). It can be beneficial to keep the disciplines intertwined when teaching as e.g., CT and mathematics builds a reciprocal relation for learning between the two domains and because this way of teaching is closer to the professional practices (Weintrop et al. 2016). Likewise, the use of educational robots can foster learning within all the STEM disciplines as children engage in activities where they design, construct, program and interact with robots and in the process learn about gears, actuators, sensors, and programming. Furthermore, robotics projects can support other skills such as: collaborative work, creativity, self-esteem, and leadership (González and Muñoz-Repiso 2018). According to Bers (2012; p. 8) *"Children engage in social interactions and negotiations while playing to learn and learning to play (…) When making robots, children become engineers exploring with gears, levers, motors, sensors, and programming concepts".*

Children's engineering interest, engineering knowledge and engineering abilities can also increase in out-of-school environments (Ehsan and Cardella 2017). In the study Ehsan and Cardella (2017) showed how children and their families engage in engineering design tasks and found that children can enact competencies such as: abstraction, algorithms, and procedures, debugging, problem decomposition, parallelization, pattern recognition, and simulation.

Studies of collaborative problem-solving have e.g., shown that students acquire more abstract knowledge when working collaboratively compared to working individually (Scwartz 1995). Studies of children and parents collaborating or doing things together have also shown positive effects on children's learning, such as co-viewing (Strouse et al. 2018) and co-reading (Lauricella et al. 2014) or programming together (Sheehan et al. 2019). Overall, there seem to be great benefits for children learning in collaborative settings with their parents but how about the parents learning potential?

According to Ploetzner and colleagues (1999), explaining things lead to the acquisition of new knowledge as the learner identifies missing information needed to explain things. When explaining or teaching others, the listeners will often point out missing information and inconsistencies or ask for clarification that will help the explainer to identify these (Ploetzner et al. 1999).

Thus, we presume that the parents also learn something in the process of working together with the children. As robotic programming is an unfamiliar domain for most children and parents, we do not expect the parents to only explain things, but rather to be part of a collaboration where the roles can change during the activities.

3 Method

In our research, we wanted to study how children aged 10–15 years and their parents in collaboration learn about STEM with a focus on mathematics and CT. For the study, the families received a package with the robot, an iPad and different materials needed for the tasks such as cones, tape, practice targets and a folding rule. The families were also asked to self-assess the process of solving the tasks using an approach inspired by a cultural probe approach (Gaver et al. 1999). In this section we first describe the Robomaster robot followed by a description of how we developed the tasks and finally the evaluation method and how we collected the data.

3.1 Robomaster Robot

The Robomaster S1 is a programmable educational robot created to support STEM-oriented activities. The robot is developed by DJI (DJI 2022). Robomaster's design resemble a tank (Fig. 1). It consists of four omnidirectional wheels, a chassis with build-in touch sensors and LED's. A gimbal-based cannon with a camera mounted on the chassis. The cannon can be used to shoot water pearls and laser. Robomaster can be remotely controlled using an app installed on a tablet or mobile phone. The app includes options for programming Robomaster either by using a block-based programming language (Scratch 3.0) or text-based programming language (Python). It can e.g., be programmed to drive in different directions, rotate the cannon, or change the color of the built-in LEDs. In addition, it can detect and follow various objects such as people, targets objects, and colored tape paths on the ground. It can also play and respond to sounds.

Fig. 1. Picture of the Robomaster S1 educational robot from DJI homepage: https://www.dji.com/dk/robomaster-s1.

3.2 Development of the Content

We invited three mathematics teachers to individual sessions to help us design age-appropriate tasks and support the teaching curriculum. We also received input on how they designed tasks for specific learning objectives as well as didactic and pedagogical considerations in relation to how we design and scaffold the different tasks. The teachers all had experience with teaching at primary school and experience with educational robots and block-based programming.

In the design sessions we first introduced Robomaster and gave a short demonstration of how you control it and the various options for programming it and the teachers were invited to try the robot themselves.

After introducing Robomaster we interviewed them about their teaching experience. We asked them to first list what their students were required to learn and to provide examples of how they teach, including their didactic and pedagogical considerations.

We then proceeded to a brainstorming phase with the teachers on how we could design tasks using the Robomaster that supported the learning objectives elicited in the previous phase. The authors discussed the input from the workshops and incorporated the input into 8 different tasks. Although the tasks were built around the input we received from the workshops, it has also been necessary for us to adapt the content and add subtasks to ensure a proper scaffolding of the content. One of the participants from the workshop reviewed the content and send us feedback on the tasks. The feedback was incorporated into the final version of the booklet. Most of it was suggestions for different wordings and a few misconceptions.

3.3 Tasks

In the following we provide a short overview of how each of the tasks are designed to give insights into how the programming and math concepts are incorporated into the tasks.

Task 1

The purpose of this task is to introduce the programming environment and block-based programming (see Fig. 2). To complete the first task an example from the booklet must be copied by connecting the correct coding blocks and afterward change the parameters in the code. The robot can be programmed to translate in X and Y directions (Fig. 3) and rotate left and right (Fig. 4). In the coding example the robot must be programmed to translate in a given direction and later to rotate. The purpose of this coding example is to introduce to mathematical concepts such as coordinate systems, translation, and rotation.

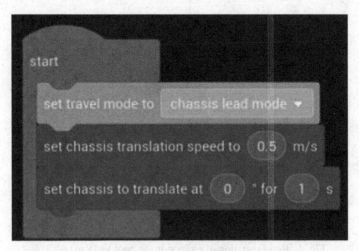

Fig. 2. Coding example from task 1.

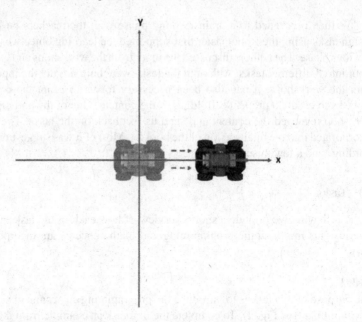

Fig. 3. Representation of translation in the booklet from task 1.

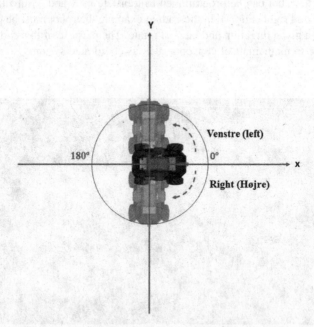

Fig. 4. Representation of rotation in the booklet from task 1.

Task 2

This task built on what was learned in the introduction of the programming environment and coding. In this task more blocks of codes have to be combined and loops are introduced in order to change the color of the LEDs.

Task 3

In this task the robot must be programmed to move in different geometric shapes (squares and rectangles) with and without using loops (see Fig. 5). This again include combining more blocks of code and use what was learned in task 1 and 2.

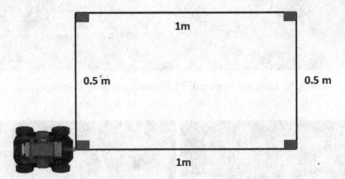

Fig. 5. Example from the booklet from task 3. The robot has to be programmed to move in a rectangle using a loop.

Task 4

In this task different sensors and events are introduced e.g., changing the color of the LEDs when the robot drives into a wall, when it registers the sound of a clap or when the camera detects a person.

Task 5

Task 5 involves using the gimbal cannon. First part of the task is to manually control the robot to shoot down practice targets with water pearls (Fig. 6). In the second part of the task the robot must be programmed to shoot down the practice targets using yaw and pitch degrees to turn the gimbal cannon (Fig. 7).

Task 6

In this task a slalom track must be built using cones. In the first part of the task the robot has to be manually controlled to complete the track and afterwards programmed to automatically complete the track. The same was repeated with another track, this time built using tape. The next step is to add practice targets and make the robot shoot them as it moves through the track. In the process different coding concepts are introduced such as conditions.

Fig. 6. Example from task 5 taken with the build-in camera.

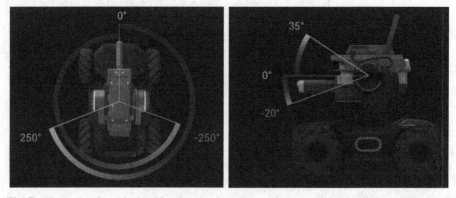

Fig. 7. Illustration from the booklet showing how the gimbal cannon can rotate in pitch and yaw axis.

Task 7

This task is inspired by the game battleship (Fig. 8). First, a coordinate system must be built on the floor using tape and each player picked a square (without telling the other player). Each turn the player has to program the robot to move from one square to another. The player who first move the robot to the other players square wins the game. In this task variables and coordinate systems are introduced.

Task 8

The last task is an open task where the families must come up with an idea of their own and try to program it. The purpose of this task is to assess what they have learned in the previous tasks and how they use it to program their own program with no guidance.

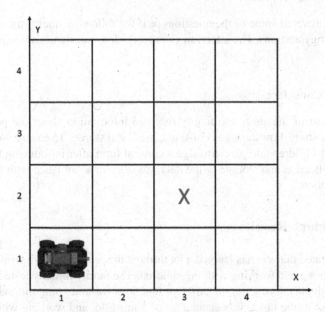

Fig. 8. Overview of the battleship game.

3.4 Data Collection

In this study we report the preliminary results from one family (a mother and her two boys aged 14 and 15) who tested the robot at home for a period of six weeks. In this period, they could complete the tasks in the booklet or explore the robot on their own. We collected preliminary data from the families' work with the robot. After every task, the family answered five questions about their work with Robomaster and how they collaborated. The approach was inspired by a cultural probe approach (Gaver et al. 1999). For each task they completed there was an envelope with questions written on postcard sized cardboards. The cardboards contained both rating- and open questions. They were e.g., asked to review the task and described how it were supposed to work and what challenges they had. In the process they were asked to discuss both mathematic, CT, and robotics-related content and how they collaborated during the tasks.

During each task, the family used a screencast on the iPad that recorded data about how the family programmed Robomaster. We intended for the screencaster to collect sound as well, but the family forgot to push the button.

The robot had a built-in camera that could live-record from the robot's point of view and the family was asked to use the recording function when using the robot.

We also had planned that the family should record their solution to every task on a video camera, however, the boys of the family found it too intimidating.

The authors conducted an individual semi-structured interview with the mother. The interview lasted 45 min. The interview guide was jointly developed by both authors. To structure the interview guide, three general themes were identified: Cultural Probe Approach, family collaboration, CT, and mathematics. A flexible approach was taken to the use of the interview guides. As an example, the order of the questions changed if she had already answered some of the questions or if the follow-up question covered some of the following questions. The interviews were recorded, and significant segments were transcribed.

3.5 Ethical Considerations

Before the start of the study the family received information about the purpose and process of the study, how data was collected, used, and stored. To ensure voluntariness we asked both children and parent to sign a consent form after introducing them to the study. The collection and storage of the data was done in accordance with the existing GDPR legislation.

4 Preliminary Results

The mother stated that she has learned a lot through the project, both in terms of coding and programming and working with the children. The family initially tested the Robo-master through play, trying out the different functions without going through the tasks. When they got to the tasks, it became a bit of a must-do, and working with the robot was not the same joy. The robot testing took place in the evening after the family had been to school and work, as this was the only time the mother had time to participate. The two children had different approaches to the tasks; one was very competitive and wanted to finish quickly, and the other was more interested in constructing and creating something with the robot.

Along the way, the family took on different roles, with one acting as the expert, one programming, and one reading the tasks aloud. Often the mother read aloud and asked them to stop and reflect along the way. Their roles also changed along the way, so everyone had a chance to chime in and be the programmer. Here, the mother felt that the more they worked with the robot, the more she dared to be inspired by the children; she learned a lot by observing them and then trying it herself.

The youngest of the boys tended at times to withdraw from the tasks and lie down on the bed, and if the tasks became too difficult, they both gave up. The older brother became preoccupied and persistent in working with the robot, perhaps because the difficulty level was too easy in the first of the tasks. By working with the robot, the family gained a deeper understanding of technology regarding Robomaster as well as other technologies and programming. The mother, in particular, was unsure of the mathematical content and found it challenging. Here she had to be helped by her sons, who had to explain how to do it along the way. There was, therefore, a strong focus on how they could solve the individual tasks together.

In the interview, the mother explained that it worked well with the instructions in the booklet. They were detailed and guided them well through the tasks. It was also a great help to see the correct solution for each task. They got through the first tasks easily, however, the mother reported that it became very difficult around task four which could also be deducted from the rating of the difficulty for the task, and they were also unsure if they had completed the task correctly.

According to the mother it could have been helpful with more tasks that built up their skills and prepared them more before task four. As the difficulty increased, the motivation would also drastically drop especially for the youngest child. This also led to a change in engagement, where the youngest child in the beginning was the most active the roles changed. As the tasks became more difficult, it was the eldest who stuck to the task until it was solved. It was also requested that more open task was implemented to simply play with the robot.

5 Discussion and Conclusion

In this paper, we have presented the method, including tasks where children and their parents work in collaboration with robotic programming with the purpose of learning about STEM and CT. The preliminary results show that both the mother and the children participated actively in the collaboration to solve the tasks and with changing roles. The mother indicated that she struggled with the mathematics content but received help from the children who explained it to her. From her statements, it seems as if she in the beginning took on a role as a facilitator but engaged more in the task when the children started having trouble trying to solve it together.

From the ratings and the statements in the interview, we noticed that it became difficult around tasks 3 and 4. One explanation for the perceived level of difficulty could be that in the first tasks, the family could follow the instructions step by step. Still, for each task they completed the tasks would progressively require that they combined the things they have already learned in new ways. This could indicate that the family may not have a sufficient understanding of the programming concepts to use them in new ways this is what Brennan and Resnick (2012) refers to as the intersection between concepts and practices and can be seen as a literate understanding of the programming concepts. To achieve this, we may need to add more sub-task to better scaffold the understanding. The perceived difficulty could also partly explain why the family went from feeling joy when during the task but later felt it as a must-do as the challenges in the beginning better matched their abilities (Nakamura and Csikszentmihalyi 2014). Other factors could be due to the time of the day and fatigue. The mother felt she had insufficient time and thus started to feel like it was an obligation instead of a fun activity. It was also mentioned how the free-play activities were more fun and that the family would have liked to see more open tasks. We did encourage the family to play around and experiment with the robot but perhaps this should be more explicit in the booklet and incorporated into the tasks.

Despite the difficulties the family managed to complete all the tasks in the booklet except for one task that was not solved correctly. In the process the family have worked with different programming and mathematic concepts and applied these to solve the task. Furthermore, the tasks would require a basic understanding of how the robot works and practical issues regarding the robot such as connecting it to the tablet, understanding how the robot received input from the sensors loading the cannon etc.

While the mother only to a limited extend articulated the learning and use of the STEM and CT competencies, the completion of the tasks indicate that there has been a development.

From the data collection, we gained insights into their experience with working with the robot. The cardboard questions informed us about the instant experience of working with the robot, which could later be elaborated in an interview, The screen recordings helped us understand some of the issues they had while programming the robot. However, while the data collection provided insights into their collaboration and how they interacted with the robot there we also a few issues. One was due to an error where the voice-recording was not activated. Thus, we were able to use the screen-recordings to see the process of programming the robot but unable to hear the ongoing discussion while they did it. Secondly, the family did not use the video-camera due to privacy reasons. We wanted the family to use the camera to document what they did and use it for creating a walk-through video.

In the preliminary results we have presented in this paper, we have only interviewed the mother, but for future studies we want to include the children as well. The interview will be based on the data we collect from the self-assessment and recordings so we can ask concretely about specific episodes and working relationships.

The preliminary results have shown how one family interacts with the robot and have given us insight into how the family has collaborated to complete the tasks. Based on the preliminary results, we only saw limited indications of STEM and CT learning potentials but expect that the future results will help develop our understanding of these collaborative learning outcomes and interactions that can support the development of STEM and CT competences for children and their parents.

References

Schwab, K.: The Fourth Industrial Revolution. Currency (2017)

Stevens, R., Bransford, J.: The LIFE center's lifelong and lifewide diagram. In: Learning in and Out of School in Diverse Environments: Life-Long, Life-Wide, Life-Deep. University of Washington Center for Multicultural, Seattle, WA (2007)

Strouse, G.A., Troseth, G.L., O'Doherty, K.D., Saylor, M.M.: Co-viewing supports toddlers' word learning from contingent and noncontingent video. J. Exp. Child Psychol. **166**, 310–326 (2018)

Lauricella, A.R., Barr, R., Calvert, S.L.: Parent–child interactions during traditional and computer storybook reading for children's comprehension: implications for electronic storybook design. Int. J. Child Comput. Interact. **2**(1), 17–25 (2014)

Sheehan, K.J., Pila, S., Lauricella, A.R., Wartella, E.A.: Parent-child interaction and children's learning from a coding application. Comput. Educ. **140**, 103601 (2019)

Weintrop, D., et al.: Defining computational thinking for mathematics and science classrooms. J. Sci. Educ. Technol. **25**(1), 127–147 (2016)

Ehsan, H., Cardella, M.E.: Capturing the computational thinking of families with young children in out-of-school environments. In: 2017 ASEE Annual Conference and Exposition (2017)

Murcia, K.J., Tang, K.S.: Exploring the multimodality of young children's coding. Aust. Educ. Comput. **34**(1) (2019)

González, Y.A.C., Muñoz-Repiso, A.G.V.: A robotics-based approach to foster programming skills and computational thinking: pilot experience in the classroom of early childhood education. In: Proceedings of the Sixth International Conference on Technological Ecosystems for Enhancing Multiculturality, pp. 41–45 (2018)

Bers, M.U.: Designing digital experiences for positive youth development: from playpen to playground. OUP USA (2012)

Wing, J.: Research notebook: Computational thinking—what and why? The Link Magazine, Spring. Carnegie Mellon University, Pittsburgh (2011). http://link.cs.cmu.edu/article.php?a=600

Barr, V., Stephenson, C.: Bringing computational thinking to K-12: what is involved and what is the role of the computer science education community? ACM Inroads **2**, 48–54 (2011)

Zhang, L., Nouri, J.: A systematic review of learning computational thinking through Scratch in K-9. Comput. Educ. **141**, 103607 (2019)

Denning, P.J., Freeman, P.A.: The profession of IT computing's paradigm. Commun. ACM **52**(12), 28–30 (2009)

Brennan, K., Resnick, M.: New frameworks for studying and assessing the development of computational thinking. In: Proceedings of the 2012 Annual Meeting of the American Educational Research Association, Vancouver, Canada, vol. 1, p. 25 (2012)

Gaver, B., Dunne, T., Pacenti, E.: Design: cultural probes. Interactions **6**(1), 21–29 (1999)

Vygotsky, L.S., Cole, M.: Mind in Society: Development of Higher Psychological Processes. Harvard University Press, Cambridge (1978)

Papert, S.: "Mindstorms" Children. Computers and Powerful Ideas (1980)

Grover, S., Pea, R.: Computational thinking in K-12: a review of the state of the field. Educ. Res. **42**(1), 38–43 (2013)

Wing, J.M.: Computational thinking. Commun. ACM **49**(3), 33–35 (2006)

Ploetzner, R., Dillenbourg, P., Preier, M., Traum, D.: Learning by explaining to oneself and to others. Collab Learn.: Cognit. Comput. Approaches **1**, 103–121 (1999)

Schwartz, D.L.: The emergence of abstract representations in dyad problem solving. J. Learn. Sci. **4**(3), 321–354 (1995)

DJI: https://www.dji.com/dk/robomaster-s1. Accessed 21 Oct 2022

Wing, J.: Research notebook: Computational thinking—what and why. The Link Magazine 6 (2011)

Nakamura, J., Csikszentmihalyi, M.: The concept of flow. In: Flow and the Foundations of Positive Psychology, pp. 239–263. Springer, Dordrecht (2014). https://doi.org/10.1007/978-94-017-9088-8_16

Bers, M.U.: Coding as another language: a pedagogical approach for teaching computer science in early childhood. J. Comput. Educ. **6**(4), 499–528 (2019)

Interactive Design Process for Enhancing Digital Literacy Among Children: A Systematic Literature Review

Kaiqing Chen[1,2](✉) ⓘD, Dominique Falla[1]ⓘD, and Dale Patterson[1]ⓘD

[1] Queensland College of Art, Griffith University, Nathan, Australia
kaiqing.chen@griffithuni.edu.au
[2] Design Art College, Xiamen University of Technology, Xiamen, China

Abstract. In the field of education, there is a significant amount of literature that focuses on how children's age and cognitive research can improve children's digital literacy. However, little work based has been undertaken exploring the combination of children's digital product design and digital literacy. Although involving children in the design process can improve design quality, it is unclear how participating in the design process affects children's digital literacy. The current study conducted a systematic review of the literature published between 2011 and 2021 on the design process, and found 20 studies that met the inclusion criteria, extracting factors that attach importance to children's values and that enhance their digital literacy in the design process. The majority of the reviewed studies revealed two common ways in which children are included in the interaction design process and influence design decisions; this is usually in the early stage of the design as a provider of design intent and as a tester for product use after the product is completed. But since 2000, there has been a trend to focus on the development of children's digital literacy, and that children are not just consumers of technology. Rather, their role as creators has also received more research attention. The current review aims to provide new insights and suggestions on how to improve children's digital literacy.

Keywords: Digital literacy · Children · Interactive design · Design process

1 Introduction

In today's society, which increasingly communicates and accesses information through digital technologies such as internet platforms, social media, and mobile devices, digital technology brings convenience and benefits to everyone. Digital literacy means possessing the skills and abilities to find meaning from digital information, which means understanding the technology and using it appropriately [1]. To date, much research on information literacy has focused on middle school students, college students, or adults, but the use of digital technology

© ICST Institute for Computer Sciences, Social Informatics and Telecommunications Engineering 2023
Published by Springer Nature Switzerland AG 2023. All Rights Reserved
E. Brooks et al. (Eds.): DLI 2022, LNICST 493, pp. 68–76, 2023.
https://doi.org/10.1007/978-3-031-31392-9_6

in early education has increased. Toddlers are increasingly using technology and popular media, and they are starting to use this technology at a younger age. Digital book reading among parents and young children has dramatically increased, and parents and children are increasingly using personal portable devices such as iPads to read stories together. Educating children in digital literacy enables them to understand the technology so that they can use it safely and effectively. A study of digital literacy practices in schools and at home for children in Sweden, Norway, and Australia states that digital literacy is reflected in "activities that encompass verbal, embodied, and social competencies", such as the ability of children to guide each other and solve problems [2–4]. Almost any industry that children will move into as adults will require some form of digital literacy, and these skills will best assist them in their further studies and careers.

Research on interaction design such as for touch screens includes the ability of users to understand digital content in a sociocultural context; for example, the ability to understand the meaning of symbols, the haptic ability to touch and click, and the ability to take actions based on audio instructions and prompts [2]. In terms of use by children, their cognition affects their touch-based interactions, and children's understanding of the interface is based on their skills at specific stages of their development [5]. In the field of children's digital products, much research has been conducted on children's cognitive and design uses. For example, designers and researchers often incorporate an interpretation of what a child is and how children learn. However, children's involvement in the design process has been little explored. Despite the strong evidence regarding children's products that user experience must be centred on children's needs, how to obtain, quantify and evaluate children's user needs is one of the least discussed and most ambiguous aspects of the design research on user experience. Many children's digital product designs are modelled on the values and needs of adults, not children. In order to enhance children's digital literacy, more research in children's digital product design is needed, especially that which could result in better quality apps for enhancing children's creative activities. The current article provides a review of design research centred on enhancing children's digital literacy from the perspective of interactive design.

This research aims to explore the assumptions related to the concept of digital literacy present in the area of designing for children, how these influence design decisions, and the impact that children make by participating in the design process. The current review covers common interactive design methods and recent research developments. This study hopes to explore the following questions:

- How does including children in the interaction design process relate to improving children's digital literacy?
- What are some common ways of including children in the design process and influencing design decisions?

2 Method

Published literature pertaining to children's digital literacy was retrieved from two databases, Web of Science and Scopus. A systematic search was performed using a comprehensive combination of keywords, employing a search string containing three main parts: (1) keywords related to children's digital literacy; (2) keywords related to design; and (3) subject area specifications. Articles may have multiple subject areas in Web of Science and Scopus. To avoid a large number of false positives, we excluded natural sciences and medical sciences.

The search targeted the metadata (title, abstract and keywords) of the paper, not the entire text, and it yielded 1,586 entries. This research tabulated individual programs and systematically coded for quality to review the evidence base, based on the scope and nature of the data report. The complete search string is provided in Table 1.

We identified the following inclusion criteria for the articles. They needed to be

- written in English;
- research on or evaluations of the user experience of children using digital products;
- related to primary school-aged children (3 to 12 years);
- concerned with outcomes related to children's digital literacy; and
- published between 2011 and 2021; SCI\SSCI\A & HCI.

Table 1. Search syntaxes

Database	Search terms
Web of Science	**Search #1** ("digital literacy" [Topic]) AND (child* [Topic])
	Search #2 ("digital literacy" [Topic]) AND (*design* [Topic])
	Search #3 ("digital literacy" [Topic]) AND (interact* [Topic])
	Search #4 ("digital literacy" [Topic]) AND (creat* [Topic])
Scopus	**Search #1** intitle: ("digital literacy" AND "child")
	Search #2 intitle: ("digital literacy" [Topic]) AND (*design* [Topic])
	Search #3 intitle: ("digital literacy") AND (interact* [Topic])
	Search #4 intitle: ("digital literacy") AND (creat* [Topic])

3   Results

This section describes the results of the review. As described in the Method section, a manual search was conducted in the selected journals. Figure 1 shows the steps of the literature searches of a total of 1,586 articles that mentioned digital literacy. Duplicated articles and articles unrelated to this topic were excluded, and 164 articles were identified that engaged with children and mentioned design. We then excluded 119 records based on their abstracts and 25 papers based on their full-text articles, following the exclusion criteria. Of the 18 studies that discussed empirical research on children's interaction with technology, five were found to be studies discussing the involvement of children in the design process and 13 were found to be studies of the effects of technology on children's lives and development. These were the ones included in the qualitative synthesis.

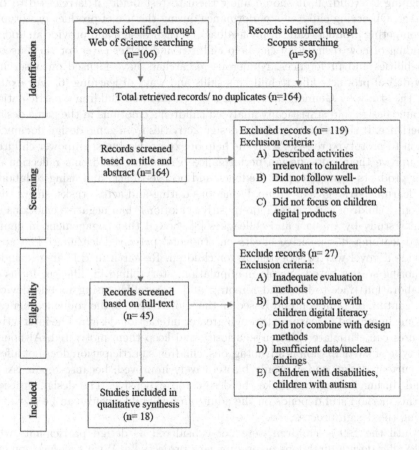

Fig. 1. Flowchart for article selection process

4   Discussion

Since the mid-1990s, digital researchers have developed a user-centric approach, where children are more challenging than adults. Over time, researchers have developed and implemented methods and activities that allow children to participate in the design process, from determining needs to assessing technology [6].

Studies include recent research developments that describe how the views and assumptions about children and interaction design were constructed, and how children influenced the design process and the interaction design regarding how to impact children's digital literacy. To better discuss children's involvement in the design process, the review on this issue with examples of studies and an analysis of relevant interaction design for children's perspectives and strategies are provided below.

Literature prior to the 1990s discussed children informing the design process, primarily as users for observation or as testers of users. If a design team is designing for children, it should allow them to test before it is released to the market. Observing children's performance during the use of product prototypes or competing products can supply feedback on their design and provide an understanding of how technology can help children and better cater for their needs, capabilities and preferences. Numerous researchers have focused on observing how digital products affect children's skills and ways of learning [6]. For example, the study by Gennari and colleagues [7] evaluated children's participation in game design and statistically analysed children's emotions in the game design experience. It shows that children's design activities from game design documentation to prototype release, with the help of expert designers, empower children to improve their game design performance. Promoting children's reflection on their products through expert feedback and peer feedback, and using collaborative learning strategies or group discussions during and across tasks, shows that engaging children can trigger more positive emotions than negative emotions. A similar study by Hamari and colleagues [8] showed that engagement in game-based learning has positive effects on students' perceived learning. The apps provide a novel way of storytelling for children. Research in this area includes authoring stories based on role manipulation, storytelling in different forms of collaboration (face-to-face and remote), and storytelling using mobile devices that capture relevant content. Based on the above research, the young learner can become immersed in learning through greater interaction design. The interactive features can stimulate children's curiosity and keep them motivated. Although this type of participation is advantageous, children's participation does not affect the current design and can only be iteratively improved, because repair issues found during testing can make the design too expensive. The design decision for this method still depends on the adult, and no child's voice can be provided during the design process.

Until the 1990s, children were not considered as design participants who could offer design directions or prompt new projects [9]. With the development of prototypes and design ideas, if a design team has questions about the progress of the design, they can work with children who can provide their ideas. Children can express their opinions through focus groups, personal interviews or written questionnaires. Hourcade (2015) argued that before design begins, children can share ideas and interests, and it is necessary to carry out activities to understand children who may use the technology and its background. Key stakeholders (e.g., parents, teachers) can often provide useful information to the team before directly working with the children. Often, activities include observing and gathering ideas from a group of children. Understanding and observing children's thoughts or interests from the beginning of a project can make its design more targeted. However, there are not enough studies to show that children can make progress in improving their digital literacy when being used purely to provide information.

Since 2002, researchers have begun to focus on how to include children as design partners in the design process. When children participate in the design process as design partners, they become part of the design team. Children can be equal partners in promoting design development and implementing decisions [6]. In this partnership, design ideas come from collaboration between adults and children. The advantage of children joining as design partners is that they will provide more information during the design process, which may lead to technology that can better meet children's own needs, interests and abilities. Studies have shown that including children in the design process is not only conducive to the development of a design but that participatory design can also be used as a means of children's cognitive development [10]. It can also be used as a tool for capacity development by promoting critical thinking in children [11] and have a beneficial impact on children involved throughout the design process [12]. Including children on the team is not only about letting them express their thoughts and opinions, so that adults can better understand the cultural differences between generations; it can also develop children's ability to analyse and solve problems. Collaborative design thinking creates the best way for children to collaborate, allowing them to explore and define problems [13]. The study by Yarosh and colleagues [14] used a participatory design study to support child wellbeing. In teaching the invention process, children's ideas and prototypes reveal how they understand gratitude, mindfulness and problem-solving, such as preventing making wrong decisions and finding alternative solutions. When considering game design interventions on design skills for young children, Kalmpourtzis [15] claimed children could brainstorm and collectively synthesise their proposals to create joint game proposals. Allsop (2016) used mind maps and videos of group discussions to record children's thinking processes when making computer games. Participatory design is beneficial to children involved in the design process and can be used as a method of cognitive development. The process by which children design and change the games that provide this experience can address issues that both consider children's values and help them build an understanding of broader social values [16]. In a study by Qing Li [17], children claimed to experience excitement and pride when building and completing games; these positive emotions can help long-term memory and enhance creative problem-solving ability. In addition to problem-solving skills, the ability to tell and create stories is also a popular theme in children's digital literacy. Storytelling is a teaching method suitable for children. According to Hourcade (2015), "If you put facts together in one story, it is easier to remember them than in lists". Interactive technology plays an essential role in storytelling. It helps children develop communication skills, express themselves, and develop their imagination by allowing them to store and copy, share, and edit stories. In a study by Robertson and Good [18], a virtual environment created using a game engine enabled children to participate in stories in the form of characters, allowing them to tell stories in a new way that inspired children to program. Similarly, recent research by Aliagas and colleagues (2017) showed that interactive elements increase children's autonomy, making them co-authors or storytellers of story creation. Interactive elements can trigger a child's response to digital text, help them create a new story, or help stories emotionally resonate with them.

Challenges are involved in making children a design partner, and it takes time to build a design team because most children do not immediately become inventors or designers. They need time to build confidence and understand what they should do in design activities [19]. Another challenge is to include children in the design team's location. Usually, schools are the best place for design activities, but the authority of teachers will also, to some extent, help children to challenge adult opinions and cooperate in equal part [6].

5   Conclusion

In the field of interaction design, ensuring the user's needs and focusing on the user's capabilities and preferences are at the core of the design process. Children who participate as design partners can positively impact the development of design while also improve children's digital literacy. Because the design process needs to consider children's digital literacy-that is, the skills and abilities that young children need to use technology, as well as their perceptions of technology use. In comparison with the traditional views of literacy, this new form of literacy emphasises children's ability to understand and create multimodal digital texts in order to communicate with texts or others. Young children are able to use multimodal cues to understand meaning in the context of digital text. Such multimodal cues include pictures, symbols, sounds, images, and gestures, and the process of interaction design is to use them in the design of touchscreens such as mobile tablets and phones. In addition to focusing on the skills and abilities children need to use technology, there is a need to focus on children's perceptions of technology use. Specifically, much research has focused on how to develop children's observations and insights into "critical thinking" through interactive design. For example, teaching children the boundaries between advertising and product content as soon as they can distinguish between the two can help children develop critical thinking skills to differentiate between media and messages as they grow up. Designers want to make the experience of "failing" or "making mistakes" more interesting for children in the design of digital products. The concept of "fun failure experience" can help children build a quality of resilience and bravery. By including children in the design process and extending the goal from digital product design to digital literacy development, children can move beyond the design process and prepare for future challenges.

The majority of the reviewed studies revealed three common ways in which children are included in the interaction design process and influence design decisions. Usually, they are involved in the early stage of the design as a provider of design intent and as a tester for product use after the product is completed. But since 2000, there has been a trend to focus on the development of children's digital literacy, and that they are not just consumers of technology, but also creators. The role of children as creators of technology not only helps with design decisions, but also helps improve children's digital literacy. Specifically, including social function design, feedback information, and exploration of innovation need to provide opportunities to child users to express themselves. If parents are used as children's spokespersons or taking parents' needs as a benchmark for measuring family needs will not reflect the complex interaction between family members effectively. Parents and children are obviously different in motivation, goals and description of the same scene, and thereby resulting in missing information. It is very challenging for children to participate in user research activities and for children to be used as interviewees. Although the language comprehension abilities of school-age children is still at the stage of development, it is still difficult for them to understand the rhetorical devices such as abstract or metaphor. Lastly, the next step of the research is to expand the methods of children's participation in design, and to study the specific methods of how to better involve children's users in the design process.

References

1. Druin, A.: The role of children in the design of new technology. Behav. Inf. Technol. **21**(1), 1–25 (2002)
2. Aarsand, P.: Categorization activities in Norwegian preschools: digital tools in identifying, articulating, and assessing. Front. Psychol. **10**, 973 (2019)
3. Danby, S., Evaldsson, A.C., Melander, H., Aarsand, P.: Situated collaboration and problem solving in young children's digital gameplay. Br. J. Edu. Technol. **49**(5), 959–972 (2018). https://doi.org/10.1111/bjet.12636
4. Björk-Willén, P., Aronsson, K.: Preschoolers' "animation" of computer games. Mind Cult. Act. **21**(4), 318–336 (2014). https://doi.org/10.1080/10749039.2014.952314.1
5. Nacher, V., Jaen, J., Navarro, E., Catala, A., González, P.: Multi-touch gestures for pre-kindergarten children. Int. J. Hum. Comput. Stud. **73**, 37–51 (2015)
6. Hourcade, J.P.: Child-Computer Interaction. Self, Iowa City (2015)
7. Gennari, R., et al.: Children's emotions and quality of products in participatory game design. Int. J. Hum. Comput. Stud. **101**, 45–61 (2017)
8. Hamari, J., Shernoff, D.J., Rowe, E., Coller, B., Asbell-Clarke, J., Edwards, T.: Challenging games help students learn: an empirical study on engagement, flow and immersion in game-based learning. Comput. Hum. Behav. **54**, 170–179 (2016)
9. Aliagas, C., Margallo, A.M.: Children's responses to the interactivity of storybook apps in family shared reading events involving the iPad. Literacy **51**(1), 44–52 (2017)
10. Allsop, Y.: A reflective study into children's cognition when making computer games. Br. J. Edu. Technol. **47**(4), 665–679 (2016)

11. Checa-Romero, M.: Developing skills in digital contexts: video games and films as learning tools at primary school. Games Cult. **11**(5), 463–488 (2016)
12. Burgos, D., Tattersall, C., Koper, R.: Re-purposing existing generic games and simulations for e-learning. Comput. Hum. Behav. **23**(6), 2656–2667 (2007)
13. Van Mechelen, M., Laenen, A., Zaman, B., Willems, B., Abeele, V.V.: Collaborative design thinking (CoDeT): a co-design approach for high child-to-adult ratios. Int. J. Hum Comput Stud. **130**, 179–195 (2019). https://doi.org/10.1016/j.ijhcs.2019.06.013.3
14. Yarosh, S., Schueller, S.M., et al.: "Happiness inventors": informing positive computing technologies through participatory design with children. J. Med. Internet Res. **19**(1), e6822 (2017)
15. Kalmpourtzis, G.: Developing kindergarten students' game design skills by teaching game design through organized game design interventions. Multimed. Tools Appl. **78**(14), 20485–20510 (2019)
16. Kynigos, C., Yiannoutsou, N.: Children challenging the design of half-baked games: expressing values through the process of game modding. Int. J. Child-Comput. Interact. **17**, 16–27 (2018)
17. Li, Q.: Digital game building: learning in a participatory culture. Educ. Res. **52**(4), 427–443 (2010)
18. Robertson, J., Good, J.: Using a collaborative virtual role-play environment to foster characterisation in stories. J. Interact. Learn. Res. **14**(1), 5–29 (2003)
19. Endsley, M.R., Bolté, B., Jones, D.G.: Designing for Situation Awareness: An Approach to User-Centered Design. CRC Press, Boca Raton (2003)

Designs for Innovative Learning
with Digital Technology

Purposeful Prototyping with Children to Generate Design Ideas

Annie Aggarwal(✉) and Mathieu Gielen

TU Delft, Faculty of Industrial Design Engineering, 2628 CE Delft, The Netherlands
annie.aggarwal17@gmail.com

Abstract. Prototyping to generate ideas, as part of the design process offers various learning opportunities to sharpen young novice designers' design and making skills. This study situates itself within the landscape of Makerspaces and co-design with children as emerging opportunities of learning and skill building for children. From experiences of co-design with children it is often observed that children engage with outcome and object-focused model making or plain crafting with no intent of iterative prototyping for ideation. This paper describes the case of design prototyping sessions conducted with children aged 8–11 years old as a classroom activity. The sessions were investigated and analysed to reveal enablers and limitations to purposeful prototyping with children. Defining and contextualising the design problem with the children, the variety of prototyping materials for flexible building, interpretation and expression, and mid-prototyping discussions were all found supportive to children's purposeful prototyping.

Keywords: Prototyping · Children · Ideation

1 Introduction

Design processes offer various learning opportunities for young novice designers. Design activities enable children to shape design skills such as thinking in all directions, making productive mistakes, deciding on a direction, sharing ideas, bringing ideas to life and developing empathy [1]. Prototyping activity of building or crafting low-fidelity physical forms for ideation is explored in this study as one such design activity within a design cycle [2].

Prototyping is an integral part of the design process, also in its relevance to hone designers' skills. Prototyping can enable child designers to 'think by making' [3] as they frame and re-frame design problems while making. Designers often inform and develop design ideas through iterative cycles of reflection and action, where prototyping enables ideation in material forms.

The current landscape of the Maker Movement, dedicated to hands-on making and technological innovation [4] has paved the way for exploration of Makerspaces as alternate learning environments. As prototyping activities cater to the development of makers' crafting, making and building skills. Thus, prototyping within primary education

E. Brooks et al. (Eds.): DLI 2022, LNICST 493, pp. 79–86, 2023.
https://doi.org/10.1007/978-3-031-31392-9_7

has the potential to both teach children valuable 21st century skills while also producing innovative ideas [5].

However, novice designers oftentimes lack intentionality during the prototyping process, especially during the early stages of design [6]. From co-design experiences of prototyping activities with children, 7 to 12 years of age, it is often observed that children do not engage in iterative prototyping, nor do they employ divergent/convergent design ideation processes. Rather, they tend to be outcome focused, as they prototype to build a single object rather than develop ideas through prototyping. Children also tend to get lost in abundant material, often picking the most good-looking materials. As a result, time is wasted on irrelevant elements or prototyping does not yield a lot of information to forward the design idea [2]. Children's making capabilities may encourage object-oriented prototypes and ideation rather than those to do with different types of interactions, sounds or organisation of the space. Both the educational yield and innovation outcomes of children's involvement in design would benefit from knowing what supports children in finding and maintaining a focus on ideation during prototyping; for the purpose of this study, we refer to this as purposeful prototyping [2].

In the context of an evidence-based lesson series and accompanying toolkit for co-design with children at primary schools called 'Your Turn' [5], several activities were developed to foster children's understanding of the purpose of prototyping and train their prototyping skills [2, 7]. These activities interrupt the primary design process, leading to the question if the organisation of the prototyping session within a design project itself could also bring about more purposeful prototyping.

2   Research Theme and Methodology

This research sets out to explore what activities, materials and interactions enable or limit purposeful prototyping for ideation amongst children. A real-life design project proposed by the librarians at school was selected for the qualitative exploration of children's prototyping activities. The library at school faced various challenges and needed re-design ideas for the given space. Children participated as designers to generate design ideas by prototyping.

2.1   Session Activities and Materials

In the pilot case study reported here, design prototyping sessions with a group of 20 children aged 8–11 years old and following an International Baccalaureate, Primary Years Programme (IB, PYP), were held as classroom activities. A brief 20-min sensitisation to introduce and define the design challenge was conducted a day prior to the first 45-min design prototyping session with children. A second 45-min prototyping session was held a week later with the same group of children in continuation. Two librarians from the school participated as co-researchers and the class teacher as facilitator. A round of interview post each session, enabled the researcher to gather co-researcher and facilitator experiences and feedback of the sessions.

The following three specific focal points for supporting purposeful prototyping were identified from literature and previous experiences; these were considered during session set-up and analyzed afterwards.

Definition and Situation of Design Problem: A study of intentional prototyping with children for testing and evaluation purposes [2] promotes the formulation of sound goals to enable novice designers and children to focus on the right things while prototyping. Re-design of the library space was explored in its capacity to enable sound goals for children to prototype purposefully. It was selected as a design problem that the children would be familiar with, that would be relevant and motivating for them to engage with, and one with possibilities of multiple directions of exploration and many ideas.

The context of the design project was defined with children during the sensitisation by recollecting experiences of use and challenges in the given space, followed by brainstorming initial ideas for re-design. Once established, the design problem was presented on the screen throughout the first prototyping session with children.

Prototyping Materials: Materials were selected to generate quick low-fidelity and flexible prototypes for ideation. The prototyping materials such as basic shapes and small pieces were inspired by Doll's House Make Toolkit to encourage focused applications and scaled models [8] in the given context. Basic and generic materials instead of fancy materials such as glitters or stickers or specific materials such as scaled furniture or puppets were provided for prototyping. These were chosen for their low-level meaning and capacity to build, think and express with. A variety of material and tactile characteristics were provided to offer inspiration for ideation. These ranged from base materials such as paper, cardboard, foam sheets, fabric pieces, shoe boxes to foam pieces of different shapes, plastic cups, odd objects and knick-knacks; material often used for design prototyping. Tinkering material such as needle and thread, beads, buttons and sticks along with crafting material to join, combine, paste or modify prototypes was available for prototyping.

Design Communication: Co-researchers interviewed children during the prototyping activity, 15–20 min after the start of each session. The interviews were intended to engage children in reflective discussions and audio-recorded for documentation. The questions addressed the prototyping activity in terms of what, why and how children were building, development or change in ideas and next steps of prototyping.

Additionally, discussion cones were available for children to raise on their table to call teachers in case of doubts or for any other discussion points. Reflection templates to be filled in by the children, were collected at the end of the first session. The template was prepared to encourage children to reflect in words or drawing, on what materials they picked and why, what they prototyped and their next steps. The second and last session closed with video-recorded presentations of built prototypes by the children.

2.2 Analysis

Qualitative analysis of the data was applied, following the principles of mostly deductive thematic analysis [9]. Session audio recordings were transcribed, visual design output (such as photographs of mid-prototyping activity and of built prototypes) annotated with key statements. The gathered data of 20 children's prototyping activity was organized as 12 prototyping trajectories (Fig. 1 shows an example). The prototyping trajectories were supported by researcher's observation notes and any other filled in reflection templates and 2D sketches and drawings created by the children. Then low-level statements pertaining to the research theme and sub-themes were formulated, clustered, and relations between clusters formed to map the elements and processes under research. Two main researchers performed a round of mapping, after which results were discussed and refined.

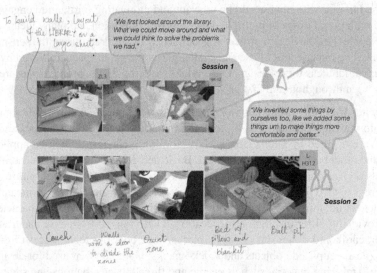

Fig. 1. Participant Z & L, and H & K's prototyping from session one, evolved into H and L's group prototyping during second session, while K joined another group for session 2.

3 Results

Children's prototyping outcomes and experiences are described to reveal enablers/limitations which include the definition and situation of design problem, prototyping material and mid-prototyping discussions.

Definition and Situation of Design Problem: The introduction of the design problem through a sensitisation activity where children identified the current use and challenges of the space, enabled children to take ownership of the design problem and supported their problem framing while prototyping. As one child reflected on how they, *"thought about all the problems and how to solve them!"*, and another child stated, *"I thought about the......different problems we talked about and I thought maybe...we could actually umm do the things, if we add some more things."*

The reflection on challenges in a familiar space, also enabled children to come up with both ego-centric and user-centric ideas. As they claimed how *"some people like loud reading, but others want to read silently"*, or why, *"We placed this table here, so teachers can keep their coffee mugs when they are called by some children."* Children also prototyped experiential and detail-oriented ideas based on their needs of the space, such as *"fuzzy and soft couches for a calm, cozy and comfortable space."*

The familiarity with and presence of the context encouraged children to formulate a mental or create a physical 'base'. As one child explained how they started their prototyping, *"We first (looked) around the library. What we could move around and what we could think to solve the problems we had."* Children's 'base' ranged from floor plans sketched and traced with 3D objects to physically stepping in and out of the space to trace the floor plan in 2D and with 3D materials. The prototyping 'base' provided sufficient grounding for further ideation of spatial elements and organisation. 3D prototypes were created with awareness of scale and size, and spatial reasoning. As some children described how, *"In the prototype we only have two, but we're going to use really more. Cause it's going to be big in real life"* or how, *"This moves here, so we have more space there."*

The spatial nature of the design project enabled children to use collections of small objects to represent and quickly change spatial arrangements. Though, the familiarity with the problems and the present restrictions of the space, hampered children from exploring distant concepts for a library, beyond the defined context and challenges.

Prototyping materials: The generic and basic materials with low-level meaning encouraged children to attribute specific meanings to forms of organisation and elements. Materials like cardboard, boxes, sheets of paper, foam pieces, plastic pieces and sticks were all employed in a variety of ways; to develop a scaled physical base, organise spatial layouts and craft furniture pieces including couches, bookshelves, signage, books and more.

Varying textures, forms and material characteristics such as soft fabrics and foam sheets, shapes of stiff foam pieces, hard plastics or cork supported and triggered children's diverse design ideas of space and furniture. While discussing their prototypes one child mentioned picking fabric to represent qualities such as *"soft, fuzzy or comfortable"*, or a *"curved piece of foam to act as a sound reflecting ceiling."*

A child described their initial plan to re-organise the entire library into zones, their prototypes and subsequent ideas were both inspired and limited by the materials in the form of *"11 chairs/couches as various options for seating"*. While the materials limited children's big ideas into those they could make, the restriction inspired children to tackle sub-problems and explore detailed solutions and ideas through prototyping.

In certain instances, materials were explored without explicit relation to the design problem. Craft explorations allowed tinkering with ideas through making. Reflection questions on how they came up with this idea, triggered children to adapt their crafting explorations to design ideas. As one child describe, *"first I was in lunchtime I was playing with some sticky notes and I tried to make a puppet and...I made this, it is a puppet, and I thought it would be nice if we make bookshelves out of these"*. The adaptations of material forms into design solutions thus exhibited a sense of flexibility in ideating as opportunities emerged.

Another child describes during the second session, *"I changed everything, so last week I drew the plan, before I wasn't in partners (in a team), but then today I chose to be in partners.... I'm making these lights over the bookshelves now."* Children also started with low-fidelity, flexible and adaptive pencil lines, placed and assembled pieces to accommodate changing ideas. Though these were replaced with firm lines, stuck pieces and fixed elements of organisation towards the end of the sessions.

Design Communication: The discussion cones to encourage children to initiate discussions, were quickly forgotten as children engaged with building their ideas. Mid-prototyping interview questions of what and why children were prototyping, triggered children to describe their simply built, low-fidelity prototypes with lots of functional details and reasoning supporting their ideas. As one child described a (robot-like) machine they built out of small blocks of foam pieces, when asked what they were making, *"they have chime and they can also make some buttons so the machine can deliver some books and...the machine can also have some sensors and then there's some button that 'to library', so if you press the button to 'library' the machine can take the, the machine can automatically take the book to the library and can give it to the librarian."* A lot of the ideas were not (yet) captured in the prototypes, and only surfaced in mid-prototyping interviews.

Only the question regarding their next steps elicited some speculative responses, when children expressed how their ideas might change or they might add some things or explore more activities and areas within the space. Other reflection questions and the closing presentation, however, triggered static descriptions rather than allow for further speculation.

Very few children filled in their reflection templates. Furthermore, the filled in templates comprised of only sparse details and incomplete descriptions of children's prototyping activities.

4 Discussion

Design prototyping sessions with children aged 8–11 years revealed activities, materials and interactions that enabled and limited children to purposefully ideate through prototyping. The identified enablers/limitations include the activities to define and contexualise the design problem, prototyping material provided and design communication.

The activities to define and contextualize the design problem engaged children in experiential reflections, enabling an in-depth exploration of specific problems and emergence of ideas based on personal needs. It can thus be argued that the sensitisation activities enabled children to formulate *sound goals* [2] for creative problem-solving while prototyping. The design problem and familiarity with context enabled children to express user centric and experiential ideas informed by spatial reasoning. The spatial nature of the context encouraged children to develop a mental or physical base for scaled explorations. While relevant anchors to children's problem-oriented explorations, the close-to-home definition and situation of the problem limited children from engaging with divergent thought processes beyond the scope of the identified concrete problems.

The generic quality of materials with low-level meaning encouraged tinkering, iteration, and individual expression to generate specific forms and ideas. The basic materials allowed children to start with low-fidelity prototypes which were flexible and adaptive, assembled or drawn rather than fixed; expressing awareness of the intent of prototyping to accommodate changing and developing ideas. The basic material also enabled children to easily attribute specific meanings and functions to lowly-defined elements (e.g. chairs, light fixtures) within the organisation of their prototyping base. A variety of material properties appeared to support diversity in solutions. In some cases, the prototyping material restricted children's 'grand' ideas into 'buildable' ones and subsequently steered children towards sub-problem and detailed explorations. The prototyping materials provided in this case study enabled children to ideate purposefully and, in some cases, random tinkering and crafting were adapted to design solutions in response to mid-prototyping reflection questions.

Children's built prototypes were representations of rich details and functional aspects, only communicated during mid-prototyping discussions triggered by co-researchers. Children expressed no interest or motivation in initiating a discussion with co-researchers while prototyping, nor in writing about their activity. Mid-prototyping reflection questions on what and why children were prototyping along with discussion of their next steps and goals stimulated children to describe and reason their prototyping and prototypes in depth. It was observed that the discussions were more descriptive than speculative. The mid-prototyping questions encouraged only some speculative responses and the questions were found lacking with respect to prompting speculation on follow-up steps or ideas. Instances of exchanges with peers triggered new inspiration and iterations, even after they indicated saturation.

Further to the three identified focal points of purposeful prototyping, awareness of session closing in relation to children's ideation, further opportunities of research and limitations of the study are discussed.

Children's flexible and adaptive prototyping trajectories took a turn towards representative 'final' models, and speculative responses turned into descriptive presentations. Both indicate that the awareness of number of sessions and a closing presentation of built prototypes prompted children to converge to their final ideas.

Specific activities to define and contextualize the design project should be further explored in different contexts such as products or services. Choice of prototyping materials and making left up to children, or materials more representational of the design context offer scope of further research on purposeful prototyping with children. Further iteration of in-process reflection prompts, also in the context of collective group discussions should be explored for purposeful prototyping to enable reflection and speculation. Principles for constructive design feedback dialogues amongst young novice designers [10] are proposed as guidelines for future exploration of prototyping dialogues with and amongst children.

The current curriculum of this specific school engages the children in inquiry-based explorations to shape and create their own individual projects, which in many aspects resemble design projects. Having worked on such projects in groups or by themselves before, the children were able to recognise and manage their own group dynamics for purposeful prototyping, given the choice.

5   Conclusions

Based upon this pilot case we propose four pillars for purposeful prototyping. Firstly, the design problem is co-defined in close collaboration with the participating children to foster ownership towards the problem. Prototyping materials that have a large variety of (visual/tactile/material) characteristics and only low-level meaning will allow for flexible interpretation and expression. Informal conversations with reflective and speculative prompts can actively engage children in ideation while prototyping. Lastly, we propose both, prototyping and ideas are captured as rich stories that transcend the visually apparent characteristics of the prototypes.

Ethical Considerations

The design project was carried out within the primary school's regular design curriculum. Children and parents were informed what research was conducted during the project, after which children were free to opt in (or out and participate in alternative educational activities). A real-life design problem was chosen, and the solutions produced by the participants were communicated to the school team for inclusion in their innovation plans. Children were informed before the start of the project that some, not all, solutions might be implemented. The researchers thank the teachers and children of the participating school class for their contributions.

References

1. Klapwijk, R.: Creativity in design. In: Benson, C., Lawson, S. (eds.) Teaching Design and Technology Creatively, pp. 51–72. Routeledge (2017)
2. Klapwijk, R., Rodewijk, N.: Purposeful prototyping through a discussion game in primary education. Proc. FabLearn Netherlands **2018**, 50–61 (2018)
3. Looijenga, A., Klapwijk, R., de Vries, M.J.: The effect of iteration on the design performance of primary school children. Int. J. Technol. Des. Educ. **25**(1), 1–23 (2014). https://doi.org/10. 1007/s10798-014-9271-2
4. Peppler, K., Kafai, Y.B., Halverson, E.: Makeology: Makerspaces as Learning Environments, 1st edn., vol. 1. Routledge (2016)
5. Klapwijk, R.M., Gielen, M.A., Schut, A., van Mechelen, M.P.P.: Your turn for the teacher: guidebook to develop real-life design lessons for use with 8–14 years old pupils (2021)
6. Deininger, M., Daly, S.R., Sienko, K.H., Lee, J.C.: Novice designers' use of prototypes in engineering design. Des. Stud. **51**, 25–65 (2017)
7. Rattink, I.: Meaningful prototyping in primary education. Master Graduation Report. TU Delft (2020)
8. Sanders, L., Stappers, P.J.: Convivial Toolbox: Generative Research for the Front End of Design (Illustrated ed.). Laurence King Publishing (2013)
9. Clarke, V., Braun, V., Hayfield, N.: Thematic analysis. Qual. Psychol.: Pract. Guide Res. Methods **222**(2015), 248 (2015)
10. Schut, A., van Mechelen, M., Klapwijk, R.M., Gielen, M., de Vries, M.J.: Towards constructive design feedback dialogues: guiding peer and client feedback to stimulate children's creative thinking. Int. J. Technol. Des. Educ. **32**(1), 99–127 (2020). https://doi.org/10.1007/ s10798-020-09612-y

The Use of Adaptive VR Environments to Foster Students Learning in Multilingual Study Guidance

Emma Edstrand(✉) ⓘ, Jeanette Sjöberg ⓘ, and Sylvana Sofkova Hashemi ⓘ

Halmstad University, Kristian IV:S Väg 3, 301 18 Halmstad, Sweden
{emma.edstrand,jeanette.sjoberg,sylvana_sofkova.hashemi}@hh.se

Abstract. Recently, the use of immersive technology has gained an increasingly interest in teaching. Virtual reality (VR) is an example of a resource offering prominent potentials for students' learning. The purpose of the study is to investigate the ways adaptive VR environments can foster students learning in multilingual study guidance. There are large differences at a national level in how multilingual study guidance is designed. Based on a co-design approach, combining methods of action research and design-based research, this study seeks answers to how to didactically design multilingual study guidance for promoting the development of students' conceptual knowledge with adaptive VR environments. Expected outcomes of the study can be related to the development of a didactically adaptive multilingual study guidance with the purpose to promote students' conceptual knowledge by means of adaptive VR environment. These results will be based on the development process leading to a didactical design of multilingual study guidance with adaptive VR environments, which will be tested in collaboration between teachers, students, VR designer and researchers.

Keywords: Co-design · Design-based research · Learning · Multilingual study guidance · Virtual reality

1 Introduction

In recent years, the use of digital resources has gained increasingly prominence in schools and teaching [1]. The rapid development of digital tools has resulted in a situation where information and knowledge are available in new manners and our learning and reasoning to an increasing extent takes place in interaction with such external tools [1]. This development has resulted in new arenas for research and raises questions about how teachers and students can best be supported in discovering meaningful ways to use digital resources in learning activities. Virtual reality (VR) is a technology that offers virtual experiences which the user can perceive as real [2]. Through three-dimensional (3D) systems in combination with interface devices, users become immersed in a virtual environment [3]. Features such as sound, visualizations and haptic feedback create a sense of being there [4, 5]. In this way, VR constitutes an example of a technology that

© ICST Institute for Computer Sciences, Social Informatics and Telecommunications Engineering 2023
Published by Springer Nature Switzerland AG 2023. All Rights Reserved
E. Brooks et al. (Eds.): DLI 2022, LNICST 493, pp. 87–94, 2023.
https://doi.org/10.1007/978-3-031-31392-9_8

invites new conditions for how to organize learning activities. However, research points to the need for more studies in this developing field [6].

Currently, we have a large group of multilingual students in Swedish schools. Every fifth student in compulsory school has basic knowledge of a language other than Swedish [7]. Multilingual study guidance in students' first language is a support that exists in Swedish schools to enhance the development of students' learning [7]. Research demonstrates that the development of students' knowledge benefits from the fact that concepts and content related to a specific subject are consolidated both in the students' first language and in Swedish [8, 9]. There are large differences at a national level in how multilingual study guidance is designed [10, 11]. The Swedish Schools Inspectorate has for many years pointed out shortcomings in how schools organize multilingual study guidance [11]. For example, multilingual study guidance is in general not designed grounded in the students' individual needs [12]. Knowledge and research on multilingual study guidance is limited and this study therefore focuses on the need for new arenas and resources that can be adapted and developed to meet student's need. VR can be used as a resource to meet individualized study guidance designs. Through VR environments, the teacher can create interactive environments based on subject-specific content suitable for the student's needs [13]. In this work-in-progress paper, we describe a study which is in initial phase where the data collection will start in autumn of year 2022. The purpose of the study is to investigate the ways adaptive VR environments can foster students learning in multilingual study guidance. The research question addresses how to didactically design multilingual study guidance for promoting the development of students' conceptual knowledge with adaptive VR environments.

This study is a cross-disciplinary collaboration between researchers, teachers, students, and an external consultant bringing in expertise in developing adaptive VR environments (VR-designer). All parties will engage in creating context-sensitive knowledge, which is based on local theories of teaching and learning in VR environments [14]. Considering this, the study will go beyond issues that only concern implementation and development of digital technology in school settings, which has central contributions in the form of a cross-disciplinary grounded model for practice-based research.

2   Related Work

Interacting in a multidimensional environment with realistic representations of everyday phenomena makes it possible for students to overcome physical separation and feel immersed in a new way of learning [15]. VR simulates physical presence and the illusion of being on site can increase students' engagement [16] as well as lead to improved communication and cultural skills [17]. In a literature review on the use of VR head-mounted display in education and training, Jensen and Konradsen [18], identify research which points to that users of VR environments based on a highly immersive system are more engaged, take the VR simulation more seriously and spend more time on a learning task (see e.g., [19]). In their study, Makransky, Terkildsen and Mayer [6] found that students learned more in low-immersive environments compared to high-immersive environments. However, since this research points to divided results [see e.g., [19], Makransky et al. [6] argue for the need of more research. Furthermore, research shows that in virtual environments, students can actively participate in meaningful activities and take responsibility and regulate their learning through, for instance, progression at their own pace, selection of support functions and repetition [15]. Students' stress and affective filters have been shown to decrease [20], such as social anxiety and modesty, which generates greater self-confidence and more willingness and motivation to learn [21]. Some known limitations for the use of immersive technologies are, for example, pedagogical framing and individual diversity [22] and technical distraction [23].

Developing conceptual knowledge in all school subjects is an all-encompassing goal for students in Swedish primary and lower secondary school [24]. Subject knowledge and language are developed in an integrated process, which means that subject teaching, not only in Swedish, becomes important for students' language development [25]. Developing a language in parallel with learning a specific school subject presupposes that, within the framework of subject teaching, students are given conditions to acquire the language that characterizes the respective school subject. The student develops subject literacy, which includes both subject-specific concepts and linguistic resources for reading, interpreting and producing texts [26].

Research argues that an important aspect for newly arrived students to reach academic success is to offer access to all subject areas and take advantage of their first language [27, 28]. This implies that teachers need to not only focus on newly arrived students learning the Swedish language but to focus on the development of students' subject-specific knowledge at first hand [29]. In Swedish schools, teachers in multilingual study guidance should, as Dávila and Bunar [30, p. 109] put it: act "as a bridge between children's first language and the subject area content" [see also 31, 32]. The few research studies that exist in the field of multilingual study guidance highlight collaboration between teachers giving study guidance and subject teachers as to best develop study guidance in line with the knowledge goals in the curriculum [e.g., 32, 33]. Other important aspects for a successful multilingual study guidance are to offer teachers more time to plan teaching activities but also offer them arenas for competence development so that they can design activities with high quality [29].

In a review of multilingual study guidance in the Swedish school in grades 7–9, the Swedish Schools Inspectorate [10] shows that study guidance does not always provide the expected support that students need to be able to meet the knowledge requirements of the curriculum. Rosén, Straszer & Wedin [34] argue that several teachers in multilingual study guidance use digital resources of various kinds during the study guidance. For instance, teachers and students use the teacher's phone to go online and search for information or to search for YouTube clips to support students' development of knowledge. When it comes to research studies on how multilingual study guidance with digital resources is didactically designed, the literature review has not identified any relevant studies. Thus, research is needed on how multilingual study guidance is conducted in schools [32] since there are only a handful empirical studies that are undertaken in classrooms where multilingual study guidance takes place [examples of studies: 31, 33].

3   Theoretical Framework

The study is underpinned by a co-design approach combining methods of action research [35, 36] and design-based research [14, 37]. This will provide the study with a practitioner-empowering and theoretical lens successfully combined in the past [38] to examine educational designs "in a holistic, systematic, principled and sustainable way, taking into account the complexity of the contemporary learning environments" [39]. This entails involving researchers, teachers, students, and VR designer in equally legitimate opportunities of systematic, iterative and reflective development [40] of concrete educational activities in real classroom situations [e.g., 41].

Teaching in these new forms of educational environments in which learners engage with different digital tools (e.g., VR environments) is recognized as moving away from delivering content to students towards a creative process of design for learning of new practices, activities, resources, and tools that underpin particular learning objectives in a given educational context in a continuous dialogue with the learners in practice [42]. Hence, the learning process concerns then an activity-centered design of emergent learning situations with teachers designing for learning tasks where students have opportunities to create their own learning paths, previously more controlled by a teacher who, for example, would provide a specific material [43]. Designing for learning and teaching concerns supporting students in using and expressing their knowledge and skills through and with multimodal resources which also implies recognizing expressions as signs for learning [44, 45].

Here, the fundamental parts of teaching regarding what should students learn (content), how they should learn it (methodology) and why this content and this method for these specific students (purpose and goal) need to be addressed together with a new knowledge domain that entails not only which technology to use but also a larger context based on questions concerning interactivity in the physical and virtual spaces, when to teach and where [46]. This entails awareness of the relationships that arise between technology, student, and context. The content-technology relationship is brought to the fore as a question of design and which technology to be used, also considering questions such as why and how. In the student-technology relationship, the focus shifts to the use of digital resources and the interaction. Considering these relationships, the primary role of the teacher is then related to the design and layout of teaching situations and learning activities [43, 47].

We will use a previously developed and tested Design Dice framework for didactical design [46, 48]. In this study, didactical design (DD) refers to the design of teaching sequences targeting a specific learning objective and subject content that includes a preplanned sequence of lessons, with a detailed teaching plan, including how to implement and conduct the task. Researchers, teachers, students and VR designer will work in a cyclic process which contains initial problem identification, contribution with new design ideas that is jointly discussed and reflected upon during workshops and team-meetings informing the development of subsequent didactical designs (i.e., re-designs) then implemented and tested in classroom settings. This complex change in teaching requires time, careful planning, and a gradual as well as systematic incorporation of what proves to become successful. This is where this study of, iterative, and systematic co-design work will contribute analyzing concrete educational activities in real learning situations over time.

4   Methodology

The research team has already established collaboration and agreement with three schools, two teachers in multilingual study guidance and the VR designer. The teachers and the VR designer have started an initial collaboration regarding the development of VR environments in teaching activities. Approximately eight students (aged 9 to 13) from three schools will participate in the study. In this study, multilingual study guidance teachers, students, VR designer and researchers together plan for and carry out workshops and implement DDs in order to develop teaching practices. Throughout the design phases, we will continuously gather empirical material, which includes a) documentation of interviews with teachers working with multilingual study guidance, students and VR designer, b) documentation of collaborative work in workshops, c) documentation of teaching activities in the adaptive VR environments, and d) documentation of stimulated recall interviews with teachers, students, and VR designer. Audio recordings of interviews and video recordings of activities in the VR environment constitute the main method for documenting communication and interaction between teachers, students, and VR designer. Recordings of activities in the VR environments will be used to analyze how teachers and students interact in the VR environment. The video recordings of VR activities will also be used as props in stimulated recall interviews for teachers, students and VR designer to reflect on opportunities and challenges with the study guidance carried out in the adapted VR environments [49].

Different analytical tools will be used to make comparisons between different types of DDs of multilingual study guidance activities and between different schools. We have made a preliminary planning of which analysis tools to use but depending on the nature of data some flexibility is required. One of the methods used is workshops. The workshop format leans on highly dialogic and iterative processes and supports collaborative learning and partnership between teachers, students, developer, and researchers in the project [50]. According to Ørngreen & Levinsen [50], research on the workshop method is limited. With this study we contribute to a growing knowledge using innovative methods in collaboration between teachers, students, VR designer and researchers with a special focus on DD involving adaptive VR environments to foster students conceptual learning. The audio recordings and stimulated recall interviews will be analyzed using thematic analysis [51] where we identify patterns in the empirical material which in turn are organized into themes. The study will derive from a three-year, iterative, and systematic co-design work where concrete educational activities in real learning situations over time will be analyzed.

5   Expected Outcomes

As already mentioned, we have not yet collected the data and thus not carried out any analyses. However, results from the authors' previous studies on the use of digital technologies in school settings demonstrate that digital tools have the potential to reconfigure learning activities that support students' learning. However, it is not enough to add technology to enhance learning but rather, it must be embedded in a systematic pedagogical arrangement that focuses on specific educational goals [e.g., 52, 53]. Furthermore, previous results indicate a diversity of experiences on the effect on digital technology in school settings which is important to consider [e.g., 54, 55].

Expected outcomes of the study can be related to the development of a didactically adaptive multilingual study guidance with the purpose to promote students' conceptual knowledge by means of adaptive VR environment. These results will be based on the development process leading to a didactic design of multilingual study guidance with adaptive VR environments, which will be tested in collaboration between teachers, students, VR designer and researchers.

References

1. Säljö, R.: Medier i skola och undervisning – om våra kunskapers medieberoende. In: Godhe, A.-L., Hashemi, S.S. (eds.) Digital Kompetens för Lärare, Malmö, Gleerups, pp. 17–35 (2019)
2. Blascovich, J., Bailenson, J.: Infinite Reality. HarperCollins, New York (2011)
3. Huang, H.M., Rauch, U., Liaw, S.S.: Investigating learners' attitudes toward virtual reality learning environments: based on a constructivist approach. Comput. Educ. **55**(3), 1171–1182 (2010)
4. Slater, M.: Immersion and the illusion of presence in virtual reality. Br. J. Psychol. **109**(3), 431 (2018)
5. Mikropoulos, T.A., Natsis, A.: Educational virtual environments: a ten-year review of empirical research (1999–2009). Comput. Educ. **56**(3), 769–780 (2011)
6. Makransky, G., Terkildsen, T., Mayer, R.: Adding immersive virtual reality to a science lab simulation causes more presence but less learning. Learn. Instr. **60**, 225–236 (2019)
7. Skolverket: Studiehandledning på modersmålet: att stödja kunskapsutvecklingen hos flerspråkiga elever. Stockholm, Skolverket (2019)
8. Cummins, J.: Urban multilingualism and educational achievement: identifying and implementing evidence-based strategies for school improvement. In: Van Avermaet, P., Slembrouck, S., Van Gorp, K., Sierens, S., Maryns, K. (eds.) The Multilingual Edge of Education, pp. 67–90. Palgrave Macmillan UK, London (2018). https://doi.org/10.1057/978-1-137-54856-6_4
9. García, O.: Bilingual Education in the 21st Century: A Global Perspective. Wiley-Blackwell, Malden, MA (2009)
10. Skolinspektionen: Studiehandledning på modersmålet i årskurs, 7–9. Skolinspektionen (2017)
11. SOU 2019:18: För flerspråkighet, kunskapsutveckling och inkludering. Modersmålsundervisning och studiehandledning på modersmål. https://regeringen.se/rattsliga-dokument/statens-offentliga-utredningar/2019/05/sou-201918/. Accessed 10 June 2022
12. Avery, H.: Teaching in the 'edgelands' of the school day: the organization of mother tongue studies in a highly diverse Swedish primary school. Power Educ. **7**(2), 239–254 (2015)
13. Garshi, A., Jakobsen, M.W., Nyborg-Cristiensen, J., Ostnes, D., Ovchinnikova, M.: Smart technology in the classroom: a systematic review. In: Porspects for Algorithmic Accountability (2020)
14. McKenney, S., Reeves, T.C.: Conducting Educational Design Research. NY, Routledge, New York (2012)
15. Meril-Yilan, S.: A constructivist desktop virtual reality-based approach to learning in a higher education institution. In: Becnel, K. (ed). Emerging Technologies in Virtual Learning Environments. IGI Global (2019)
16. Fryer, L.K., Coniam, D., Carpenter, R., Lăpușneanu, D.: Bots for language learning now: current and future directions. Lang. Learn. Technol. **24**(2), 8–22 (2020)

17. Cheng, A., Yang, L., Andersen, E.: Teaching language and culture with a virtual reality game. In: Proceedings of the 2017 Chi Conference on Human Factors in Computing Systems, pp. 541–549 (2017)
18. Jensen, L., Konradsen, F.: A review of the use of virtual reality head-mounted displays in education and training. Educ. Inf. Technol. **23**(4), 1515–1529 (2017). https://doi.org/10.1007/s10639-017-9676-0
19. Alhalabi, W.S.: Virtual reality systems enhance students' achievements in engineering education. Behav. Inf. Technol. **35**(11), 919–925 (2016)
20. Lin, T.J., Lan, Y.J.: Language learning in virtual reality environments: past, present, and future. Educ. Technol. Soc. **18**(4), 486–497 (2015)
21. Papin, K.: Can 360 virtual reality tasks impact L2 willingness to communicate? In: Future-proof CALL: Language Learning as Exploration and Encounters – Short Papers from EURO-CALL 2018, pp. 243–248. Research-publishing.net (2018). https://doi.org/10.14705/rpnet.2018.26.844
22. Parmaxi, A.: Virtual reality in language learning: a systematic review and implications for research and practice. Interact. Learn. Environ. (2020). https://doi.org/10.1080/10494820.2020.1765392
23. Berti, M.: Immersions for the Language Classroom. Italian Open Education: Virtual Reality Immersions for the Language Classroom, pp. 37–47 (2019)
24. Schleppegrell, M.J.: Academic language in teaching and learning. Elem. Sch. J. **112**(3), 409–418 (2012)
25. Rubin, M.: Språkliga redskap - Språklig beredskap: en praktiknära studie om elevers ämnesspråkliga deltagande i ljuset av inkluderande undervisning. Malmö universitet, Fakulteten för lärande och samhälle (2019)
26. Shanahan, T., Shanahan, C.: What is disciplinary literacy and why does it matter? Top. Lang. Disord. **32**(1), 7–18 (2012)
27. Cummins, J.: Teaching minoritized students: Are additive approaches legitimate? Harv. Educ. Rev. **87**(3), 404–425 (2017)
28. Valdés, G.: Entry visa denied: the construction of ideological language borders in educational settings. In: Garcia, O., Nelson, F. (eds.), The Oxford Handbook of Language and Society, pp. 321–348. Oxford University Press, New York, USA (2017)
29. Vogel, D., Stock, E.: Opportunities and Hope Through Education: How German schools Include Refugees. Education International Research, Brussels (2017)
30. Dávila, L., Bunar, N.: Translanguaging through an advocacy lens: the roles of multilingual classroom assistants in Sweden. Eur. J. Appl. Linguist. **8**(1), 107–126 (2020)
31. Reath Warren, A.: Developing multilingual literacies in Sweden and Australia: Opportunities and Challenges in Mother Tongue Instruction and Multilingual Study Guidance in Sweden and Community Language Education in Australia. Stockholms universitet, Stockholm (2017)
32. Engblom, C., och Fallberg, K.: Nyanländas lärande och språkutvecklande arbetssätt. Rapport från en forskningscirkel. Uppsala, Uppsala universitet (2018)
33. Duek, S.: Med andra ord. Karlstads universitet, Samspel och villkor för litteracitet bland nyanlända barn. Karlstad (2017)
34. Rosén, J., Straszer, B., Wedin, Å.: Transspråkande i studiehandledning som pedagogisk praktik. Lisetten **1**, 16–19 (2017)
35. Elliott, J.: Principles and methods for the conduct of case studies in school-based educational action research. In: Anderberg, E. (ed.) Skolnära forskningsmetoder, pp. 111– 141. Lund, Studentlitteratur (2020)
36. Adelman, C.: Kurt lewin and the origins of action research. Educ. Action Res. **1**(1), 7–24 (1993)
37. Design-Based Research Collective.: Desing-Based Research: An Emerging Paradigm for Educational Inquiry. Educational Researcher, **32**(1), 5–8 (2003)

38. Majgaard, G., Misfeldt, M., Nielsen, J.: How design-based research and action research contribute to the development of a new design for learning. Des. Learn. **4**(2), 8–27 (2011). https://doi.org/10.16993/dfl.38

39. Sun, Y.H.: Design for CALL – possible synergies between CALL and design for learning. Comput. Assist. Lang. Learn. **30**(6), 575–599 (2017). https://doi.org/10.1080/09588221.2017.1329216

40. Schön, D.A.: Educating the reflective practitioner: toward a new design for teaching and learning in the professions, vol. 1. San Francisco, Jossey-Bass (1987)

41. Cviko, A., McKenney, S., Voogt, J.: Teachers as co-designers of technology-rich learning activities for early literacy. Technol. Pedagog. Educ. **24**(4), 443–459 (2015)

42. Mor, Y., Craft, B.: Learning design: reflections upon the current landscape. Res. Learn. Technol. **20**, 85–94 (2012). https://doi.org/10.3402/rlt.v20i0.19196

43. Selander, S., Kress, G.: Design för lärande - ett multimodalt perspektiv. Stockholm, Norstedts (2010)

44. Bezemer, J., Kress, G.: Multimodality, Learning and Communication: A Social Semiotic Frame. Routledge, London (2016)

45. Selander, S.: Didaktiken efter Vygotskij: design för lärande. (Första upplagan). Stockholm, Liber (2017)

46. Sofkova Hashemi, S., Spante, M.: Den didaktiska designens betydelse: IT-didaktiska modeller och ramvillkor. In: Sofkova Hashemi, S., Spante, M. (eds.) Kollaborativ undervisning i digital skolmiljö. Malmö, Gleerups (2016)

47. Boistrup, L.B., Selander, S.: Designs for Research, Teaching and Learning: A Framework for Future Education. Routledge, New York (2022)

48. Sofkova Hashemi, S.: Exploring educational designs by schematic models: visualizing educational value and critical issues of recognition and socio-material frames. Des. Learn. **14**(1), 14–28 (2022). https://doi.org/10.16993/dfl.171

49. Calderhead, J.: Teachers' beliefs and knowledge. In: Berliner, D.C., Calfee, R.C. (eds.) Handbook of Educational Psychology. Simon & Schuster Macmillan, New York (1996)

50. Ørngreen, R., Levinsen, K.: Workshops as a research methodology. Electron. J. e-Learn. **15**(1), 70–81 (2017)

51. Braun, V., Clarke, V.: Using thematic analysis in psychology. Qual. Res. Psychol. **3**(2), 77–101 (2006)

52. Edstrand, E.: Learning to reason in environmental education. Digital tools, access points to knowledge and science literacy, (Diss.) Studies in Educational Sciences, University of Gothenburg (2017)

53. Sjöberg, J., Brooks, E.: Genusrelaterade dilemman i kollaborativa aktiviteter när elever utvecklar speldesign - villkor för aktörskap. In: Kontio, J., Lundmark, S. (eds.) Digitala didaktiska dilemman. Stockholm, Natur & Kultur (2022)

54. Roumbanis Viberg, A., Forslund Frykedal, K., Sofkova Hashemi, S.: Teacher educators' perceptions of their profession in relation to the digitalization of society. J. Praxis High. Educ. **1**(1), 87–110 (2019)

55. Spante, M., Sofkova Hashemi, S., Lundin, M., Algers, A.: Digital competence and digital literacy in higher education research: systematic review of concept use. Cogn. Educ. **5**(1), 1–21 (2018). https://doi.org/10.1080/2331186X.2018.1519143

Bringing Computational Thinking to Life Through Play

Camilla Finsterbach Kaup[1,2]([✉]) [iD], Anders Kalsgaard Møller[2] [iD], and Eva Brooks[2] [iD]

[1] University College of Northern Denmark, Hjørring, Denmark
cmf@ucn.dk
[2] Aalborg University, 9220 Aalborg, Denmark
{ankm,eb}@ikl.aau.dk

Abstract. Digital tools and solutions are increasingly used in society, creating a need for more digital skills in the workplace and everyday life. As society becomes increasingly digital, computational thinking becomes a fundamental skill for the 21st century. This paper examines play's role in young children's CT development in early childhood education. This paper presents a narrative review and uses forward snowballing to extend the search result. Twenty-two articles met the criteria and were manually collected. The publications were categorized into five categories: programming tools, robotics, unplugged activities, making and exploring, and guided vs. free play. For CT activities to be social and communicative, concepts such as mutuality and scaffolding must be incorporated into operational pedagogical CT frameworks. As such, CT can be designed as a play-oriented activity in that children coordinate and develop themselves, with or without educators' guidance. As a co-creator, an educator can mediate CT and support the children in guiding activities forward.

Keywords: Computational play · Computational thinking · Early Childhood Education · digital artefacts

1 Introduction

The increasing use of computational tools and digital solutions in society has created an increasing need for digital skills both in terms of employment capabilities but also in relation to citizen life. The increasing digitization in society makes Computational Thinking (CT) a fundamental skill for the 21st century where people are required to become digital literate.

CT was first introduced by Seymour Papert (1980) but is more commonly linked with Jeanette Wing's (2006) definition saying that CT is *"solving problems, designing systems, and understanding human behavior, by drawing on the concepts fundamental to computer science"* She also state that CT is a fundamental skill for everyone, not just for computer scientists and that *"we should add computational thinking to every child's analytical ability"*.

E. Brooks et al. (Eds.): DLI 2022, LNICST 493, pp. 95–112, 2023.
https://doi.org/10.1007/978-3-031-31392-9_9

Until recently computer programming was seen as a skill for mathematicians, scientists, and engineers, and the benefits for everyone to learn how to code was not yet perceived. Henceforth, the pedagogical approaches in the field of computer science drew from the Science, Technology, Engineering, and Mathematics- (STEM) disciplines (Bers, 2019). Due to the growing technical requirement in society CT and related fields have been introduced as early as preschool or kindergarten curriculums in several countries. Consequently, new pedagogical approaches in teaching CT must be developed and the content need to be adapted to better support the children in their development and understanding of CT. This has led to many different experiments where attempts have been made to introduce children to digital technology and CT through play and play-based learning activities. Different tools and software programs have been developed to support these activities such as block-based programming software, tangible coding objects and button-based programming robots.

In the same way, this movement has also led to new ways of framing CT. Barr & Stephenson (2011) aimed at developing an operational definition of CT for K-12 education and in the process came up with several core computational thinking concepts and capabilities to teach the students including: data collection, data analysis, data representation, problem decomposition, abstraction, algorithms & procedures, automation, parallelization. They also attempted to define a classroom culture that included strategies such as: Increased use of computational vocabulary, group work with explicit use of computational processes such as decomposition, abstraction, negotiation and consensus building, and a mindset that accepted failed solution attempts. A child's computational vocabulary can be seen when they begin to employ the processes of CT, such as sorting building blocks by color to decompose or make sequencing.

Brennan and Resnick (2012) presented a framework based on the aspects learned when young people engage with digital technology and programming with three different dimensions of CT - computational concepts (the concepts designers engage with as they program), computational practices (the practices designers develop as they engage with the concepts, and computational perspectives (the perspectives designers form about the world around them and about themselves). In Brennan and Resnick (2012) children learn how to program using the block-based programming software Scratch which has been widely used as a tool for children to initially start learning about programming and CT. In a systematic review by Zhang and Nouri (2019), they examine the CT skills that can be obtained through working with Scratch in K-9. While the study concludes that it is possible for children in kindergarten to learn certain CT skills the research in this area is very limited. The authors suggest that their findings can help teachers and researchers with "what to teach" and "what can be learned" by providing them with an overview of the mental abilities of the students but they should also start exploring if other methods are better suited to teach certain CT skills that are challenging to learn for children. Murcia and Tang (2019) examine CT in early childhood based on a social constructivist view of language and representation. They propose a parallel analogy in which coding might be equivalent to computational thinking. As an outward expression of computational thinking, coding is a visible manifestation of computational thinking (e.g., writing a program). Nevertheless, CT is only possible to develop and become

internalized (Vygotsky, 1986) for young children within a zone of proximal development through the interaction of coding (using symbols and other resources like tangible
coding technologies) with adults and peers within a social space. Coding, like every
language, consists of various representational modes, including mathematical symbols,
images, gestures and physical objects. In early childhood education (ECE), CT allows
children to share ideas, test their limits, and receive feedback with the help of information
they capture through their senses. In these actions, imagination and creativity play an
essential role in producing new knowledge (Buitrago et al., 2017). Moreover, CT skills
are developed through robotics by leveraging playful characteristics of the resource and
context, which represents a positive impact according to Froebel's approach to games
(Resnick & Rosenbaum, 2013).

In this review, we aim to identify and interpret the different applications of CT as
a starting point for discussing key areas of early childhood education with particular
emphasis on play and pedagogy. In this paper, we interpret existing literature from the
perspective of computational thinking and play. Through a narrative literature review,
we investigate CT in early childhood. However, because of the limited literature on
CT in early childhood education, we looked at how researchers cited other relevant
studies using forward snowballing. Taking a broader perspective on CT was crucial
to understand how CT could be applied in an ECE setting. This is further explained
in section three. How we methodically approached the narrative snowballing review.
This is followed by the outcome of the review divided into five thematic sections (CT
tools; Robotics; Unplugged activities; Making and exploring, and Guided play vs free
play). Then, we introduce a theoretical chapter based on Bruner's pedagogical theory
focusing on the concept of scaffolding and progression in learning followed by a note on
the relationship between play and learning. Finally, we present an analytical discussion
based on the outcome of the narrative snowballing review and the theoretical framing.

2 Pedagogical Perspectives

In this chapter, we describe pedagogical perspectives as a theoretical framing and analytical tool to discuss key issues of CT in relation to its application in early childhood
education specifically emphasizing play and learning. By this, the chapter is intended to
frame the concluding analytical discussion, which will end this article.

Becoming CT competent requires learning CT concepts, programming, coding, etc.
and working within the opportunities and limitations this offers. For children this means
to find out what can be done with different kinds of CT activities by trying them out in
different combinations and circumstances, which can enable children to develop competence from their experiences. This calls for sensitive educators to support children
to internalize and develop their CT understanding. In this regard, Bruner (1961) argues
for scaffolding, i.e., to actively support children when they start to learn new concepts.
Bruner's theory of scaffolding was particularly influenced by Vygotsky's zone of proximal development theory, where a child can learn from a more knowledgeable other (Wood
et al., 1976). However, for children to master such CT concepts and activities, they need
to continually deepen their understanding of CT. Problem-solving skills, abstractions,
and computational vocabulary are examples of some concepts covered in CT (Webb &

Rosson, 2013). Bruner (1977) termed such revisiting processes as a spiral curriculum in education, where each successive revision builds children's understanding and requires increasingly sophisticated cognitive strategies. According to Bruner (1977), CT learning hence should emerge from progressive practicing of CT through three stages, namely enactive, iconic, and symbolic (Lowe and Brophy, 2017):

- *Enactive*: children learn by engaging in active representations (i.e., through physical and manual activities).
- *Iconic*: children are confident in using an iconic mode of representation as they become more familiar with the content; they can perform tasks by imagining concrete pictures.
- *Symbolic*: As a result, children develop the ability to represent abstract, symbolic ideas without the need for physical manipulation or mental imagery.

To develop a pedagogical structure that reflects this kind of progressive learning when dealing with CT in teaching activities requires that educators have a fundamental knowledge of the field. Bruner (1977) emphasizes the necessity of clarifying the broader structure of a field of knowledge as it otherwise becomes difficult for children to generalize from what has been learnt. Here, building on children's interest and to make knowledge usable beyond the situation in which the learning has occurred. Taking departure in children's interest implies considering children's acts of learning. Depending on the children's age, this interest can have different directions. Kindergarten children tend to focus on establishing relationships between experience and action of trial-and-error character, i.e. by intuitive regulations rather than by symbolic operation. Schoolchildren, on the other hand, are more operational compared to younger children as they, for example, can transform data from the real world into the mind and from this use them selectively in solving problems (Bruner, 1977, 1990). In the context of CT activities, this would mean that young children are intuitive concrete actors being challenged in understanding basic ideas behind, for example, coding. Older children, on the other hand, can connect and transform concrete manipulation into abstract concepts and thereby grasp CT ideas of, for example, programming. Against this background, educators can be seen as limited in transmitting CT concepts to children in early childhood education, also when it comes to intuitive manners. To deal with such challenges, Bruner (1990, 1977) emphasized that meaning and processes involved in the making of meaning are central to individual's learning and development and require an active participation by the educators. One way of acknowledging these matters is through play.

Research on the topic of play describes it as an activity with its own values (Sutton-Smith, 2001), as an unpredictable process without a goal (Huizinga, 2004) or as identified rules of play such as mutuality, unity and turn-taking (Olofsson, 1987). However, in an educational context, play is often described as a resource for learning rather than an activity having its own value (Smith & Pellegrini, 2013). Describing play in terms of Sutton Smith (2001) can be described as having intrinsic values and diversity, which can raise questions about how play and learning can be seen as compatible with each other. This connection between play and learning is also acknowledged by Jonsson and Pramling Samuelsson (2017). While research argues that play as an unpredictable phenomenon cannot guarantee that adults can guide young children's learning towards a particular direction, Jonsson and Pramling Samuelsson (2017) argue that learning in fact has the same premises as play, in particular among younger children. Despite their different dimensions, play and its similarities with the premises of learning put forward creativity, joy, meaning making and children's opportunities to set their own goal as characteristics for play as well as learning (Pramling-Samuelsson & Johansson 2006). Based on this, it can be argued that teachers' scaffolding can become a basis for teaching young children. This as scaffolding can establish a relation between a child and teacher and thus direct their attention to the same object. Children's play ceases unless those involved succeed in establishing such a relationship, therefore teaching, learning and play are always of a social and communicative nature (Pramling, Doverborg, Pramling Samuelsson, 2017).

3   A Narrative Review with Snowballing

The narrative review aims to provide insight into the extant literature on CT play in early education. This type of review seeks to summarize or synthesize what has been written about a particular topic. The information presented is not intended to be generalized or to provide cumulative knowledge (Paré & Kitsiou, 2017). Green et al. (2006) argue that narrative overviews represent an excellent way to keep up with new research and to get a broader view of the field. However, the limitation of this approach concerns that it is not systematic enough to provide robust evidence such as in systematic reviews (Green et al., 2006). It is our intention to contribute to ongoing efforts in exploring CT in early childhood education. In this review, we aim to identify and interpret the different applications of CT as a starting point for discussing key areas of early childhood education with special emphasis on play and pedagogy. This will enable us to gain a deeper understanding of how CT can be embedded in research as well as how it can be introduced in early childhood education. The review question focused on: *How are CT and play utilized in early childhood education? How can computational play contribute to children's early childhood education?*

As Hart (1998) states, reviewing is the process of obtaining an overview of a diverse body of research to synthesize a unique approach to the subject matter. The literature search strategy we developed was intended to obtain an overview of the broad strands of research, not a comprehensive review of all existing literature.

3.1   Organizing the Review

The research articles we selected were selected from three main educational research sources, focusing on publications published between 2012 and 2022, both in Proquest, Education Database; Ebsco host, Academic Serch Premier and ERIC as well as SCOPUS with the phrase "computational thinking" AND "play" AND "early childhood". Table 1 below presents the inclusion and exclusion criteria that were used to determine the relevance of each research article.

The study was conducted in July 2022. In total, 23 articles were saved and classified as relevant or not for the review; 13 articles met the inclusion criteria defined in Fig. 1. Two authors decided on the inclusion status of titles and abstracts. The second screening of

Table 1. Inclusion and exclusion criteria

Inclusion	Exclusion
• Empirical investigation of CT play in early childhood education	• An empirical investigation of CT plays other than early childhood education
• The study should consider and discuss how CT play can be tangled in early childhood education	• Empirical investigation of programming excluding CT
• Peer-reviewed article	

full-text articles, again conducted by two independent research team members, ensured that the studies discussed CT play in early childhood education.

After screening the titles and abstracts of articles with potential relevance, full-text articles were obtained. Based on predetermined inclusion criteria, the full-text papers were analyzed. Our review process utilized forward snowballing to ensure that we included all relevant studies (Wohlin, 2014). The forward snowballing process is displayed in Fig. 1 as a step that identifies relevant articles based on those citing the article selected from the databases. Articles were sorted according to the same procedures as those identified using database searching. To identify each research question, we carefully read each article, considering the connection between CT and play and the relation to early childhood education. 9 articles were found during snowballing. We manually collected data from 22 articles that met the criteria. An overview of the 22 collected articles can be found in Appendix A.

All included publications were grouped into the following five categories: programming tools, robotics, unplugged activities, making and exploring, and guided vs free play.

In the following, the five categories are described.

3.2   CT Tools

Learning CT can take many forms, one of them can be through programming. Different programming languages have been developed, where children can create a program by putting together different pieces of code in sequences of commands. For example, it can take the form of blocks of code, such as in Scratch (Maloney et al., 2010) or ScratchJr (Flannery et al., 2013), or it can use other tangible representations of commands, such as icons, colors, or physical objects (Berson et al., 2019), for example, in a sequence (Wang et al., 2014) to code a program or object. In multiple studies with children, Scratch has been extensively used as a tool for teaching programming (Zhang & Nouri, 2019); however, other tools have been utilized in playful activities that engage children as early as preschool. Wang and colleagues (2021) have for example used a toy called code-a-pillar. With different joints added to the caterpillar's body, it is possible to program it to move in different directions. Using tangible coding blocks (wooden cubes), children aged 5–9 were able to build and escape mazes in an experiment based on a game-based design. Wang et al., (2014) claim that they in this way cultivated children's computational

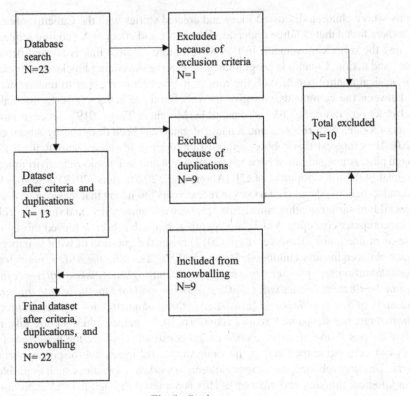

Fig. 1. Review process

thinking, as well as their awareness of abstraction, automation, problem decomposition and analysis.

3.3 Robotics

Multiple studies have indicated that robotic activities can foster CT in children (Angeli & Valanides, 2020), (González and Muñoz-Repiso, 2018), (Hall & McCormick, 2022) and (Bers, 2019). González and Muñoz-Repiso (2018) suggest that robot activities can be approached differently. The robots themselves can be used both as an object of learning where the objective is to learn about robotics. They can be used as means of learning, e.g., build a robot or program it to learn about CT or the robot can be used as support for other learning activities. Different educational robots exist that are easy to control or program for children from around 4–5 years of age. Bee-bots are for example robots that can be programmed to move in different directions by entering a sequence of movements using built-in pushbuttons (Angeli & Valanides, 2020).

According to Hall and McCormick (2022), when children play with robots, they begin the process of observing the robot, interpreting its actions, and responding to them. During this process, children will gain a better understanding of the different dimensions of CT. This is e.g., evident in a study by Murcia & Tang (2019). During an open-play activity where children discussed ideas and created stories with the Cubetto robot, the researchers found that children understood the cause and effect of the coding sequences directing the robot's movement. In this way, a more tangible link is created between "code" and action. Cubetto is programmed by placing the coding blocks in a sequence on a physical control panel. With the robots, it also becomes easier to understand the link between the commands you give the robot and the actions it performs making the abstract programming task more tangible (Murcia & Tang, 2019). An environment that incorporates both robotics and a nautical game has been designed by Abreu et al. (2020). They suggest that robots can assist children in learning computational skills through play. Among children between the ages of 4 and 8, a tactile-rich environment is beneficial to their development of CT (Abreu et al., 2020). Bers (2012) describes how the development of educational robots in recent years has meant that they can be used to teach children various mathematical concepts such as number, size, and shape as well as various computer concepts. Which, among other things, has been achieved through the above-mentioned tools. However, Bers (2012) raises the question of what is important to teach children in early childhood. She states that: *"Teaching the ABC's, numbers, or computational concepts earlier might be appealing but might not make a difference in the long run. While these are activities that can pave the road for later academic transition, the mastery of new practices and knowledge is the fundamental developmental task for the next stage, the elementary school years"* (p. 9). To achieve this, robotic kits need to offer the possibility of creative open-ended construction where the behavior of the robots can be programmed and at the same time offer interactive responses through sensors. This way robotics encourages children to work with practices such as problem-solving, logical thinking and creativity. This is achieved through playful explorations where children engage in social interactions and negotiations with parents and other children. In this setting children can e.g., become engineers that explore robotic and programming concepts as well as storytellers that instruct how a character (robot) acts in response to the environment (Bers, 2012).

3.4   Unplugged Activities

The use of CT in early childhood classrooms should consider the developmental stage of children. Studies have demonstrated that children between the ages of four and five learn effectively through concrete and hands-on activities (Bers, 2018; Lee et al., 2022). Unplugged activities are based on the approach of exposing children to CT without using computers (Olmo-Muñoz et al., 2020) or digital devices. The activities can involve logic games, cards, strings, or physical movements that are used to represent and understand CT concepts (Brackmann et al., 2017). Studies have shown that unplugged activities positively affect the development of CT skills (Brackmann et al., 2017) and that the combination of plugged and unplugged activities for the early years of primary education can have a positive effect on CT skill acquisition and motivation. (Olmo-Muñoz et al., 2020). This study also found a gender effect where females were more motivated. In Critten, Hagon and Messer (2022), an example of an unplugged activity is given, where children as young as two years old learn about sequences by describing in what different sequence steps occur with simple activities such as bathing a doll. The study showed that the children initially had difficulties thinking about sequences but developed this skill through discussions with other children and adults. Moreover, CT-related literature in early childhood suggests unplugged activities in which children integrate stories or learn literacy skills to tell the story sequentially (Lee et al., 2022).

3.5 Making and Exploring

Assessing the literature of how children in the early years engage and learn about technology there seems to be two different modes of interaction: Children can either explore technology e.g., see what happens if I do this – if I want it to do this what do I do? Or they can make/create with technology. Making is a learner-driven inquiry-based approach that allows children to use their ideas in a powerful and generative way that supports participation, learning and conceptual understanding (Vossoughi & Bevan, 2014). A special type of making activity is tinkering. Resnick and Rosenbaum (2013) explain that the *"tinkering approach is characterized by a playful, experimental, iterative style of engagement, in which makers are continually reassessing their goals, exploring new paths, and imagining new possibilities"*. It is a playful, explorative, and iterative approach where people are trying out new ideas and adjusting. Martinez & Stager (2013) makes a distinction between making and tinkering where they describe making as working on a planned project and tinkering as a mindset that involves a playful approach to solving problems through experimentation.

Opposite to planning tinkering is according to (Resnick and Rosenbaum 2013) a bottom-up process where they explore ideas by playing around with materials e.g., putting together LEGO bricks where they continually adapt their plans based on the interaction with the materials and people they are working with. They see tinkering as similar to play. Play is according to Resnick and Rosenbaum (2013) a way of engaging with the world where we test and experiment with new possibilities and that tinkering is a playful way of designing and making where children experiment and explore new ideas in the process of creation. Tinkering can be physical or virtual; a child can be tinkering when programming or writing a story. Tinkering is not defined by materials but the style of interaction (Resnick and Rosenbaum 2013). According to Vossoughi et al. (2013), it is essential to connect children's ideas with the significant sciences and STEM concepts and practices to support students in engaging in scientific activities. Children can participate in inquiry-based educational activities both inside and outside of school in settings that have been pedagogically transformed. The locations could be museums or libraries where they can work together on creating different artifacts to support their identity as makers and innovators. The activities typically build on children's prior experience and keep their identity as tinkers (Vossoughi et al., 2013). Similarly, it is important to create a connection between children's play, to engage them in CT supportive activities or ensure a transition from children's play to CT supporting activities.

3.6 Guided Play vs Free Play

There are different approaches to how play activities can be designed to support the development of CT. One of the discussions concerns how CT instructions could be designed regarding the degree of scaffolding, free play vs guided play, adults and children initiated (Bers, 2018, 2019). Most studies seem to suggest that the children need at least some level of guidance or scaffolding (Hall & McCormick, 2022; Critten, Hagon, & Messer, 2022; Wang et al., 2021; Stephen & Plowman, 2013). Stephen & Plowman (2013) argue that direct and indirect guidance are essential to support children's play and engagement with technology and according to Hall & McCormick (2022) dialogue, guidance and negotiation from adults are important to extend children's learning about CT. In their study the authors used a guided play approach that emphasized a specific CT learning goal that allowed the children to be explorative and self-directed in their play. Thus, they strived to balance openness, child-autonomy and scaffolding towards a learning goal.

As an example of guided play, Lee et al. (2022) identified that educators could create engaging scenarios to help children focus on relevant information. For example, children can play "Who am I?" by identifying the origin of footprints based on their shape, size, and imprint. By refining their observations, children eliminate the choices that do not match the attributes given. The footprint of a bare foot, for example, can be eliminated by removing everyone wearing shoes. The process of working through these scenarios develops abstraction skills in children. (p. 5).

In a study by Kotsopoulos and colleagues (2022), they explore to what extent CT is evident in children's free play in unplugged activities. Referring to Curzon (2013) the researchers claim that for unplugged free-play activities to lead to development of CT competencies, teachers need to perceive and capture situations where play activities can be linked to CT and nurture the children's thinking in that direction. The study concludes that a challenge is that teachers often do not have a sufficient understanding of CT to perceive and nurture CT elements, or conversely, they think they are observing an example of CT without these being present.

4   Analytical Discussion

The aim of this narrative review was to investigate existing literature on CT in ECE. Through the review, we found four perspectives related to CT, play and pedagogy.

(1) CT tools, (2) Unplugged CT, (3) Making and exploring, (4) Guided play vs free play. This chapter discusses the results of the review and identifies any gaps in the literature and is divided into two sections, *tool-mediated play activities* and *facilitating children's intentions*.

4.1   Tool-Mediated CT and Play Activities

The act of playing is an integral part of children's lives. Play helps a child to socialize, learn, think creatively, and feel intrinsically motivated. During the review, we discovered that many CT activities were created using CT tools. As one example of how these tools have been used to support children's CT development, Abreu et al. (2020) designed an environment that integrated both a nautical game and physical robots. In their study, they suggest that robots can be used to engage children in inclusive play experiments and to help them acquire computational skills through play. According to their study, children between the ages of four and eight benefit from playing in an environment that is tactile-rich. Nevertheless, Abreu et al., (2020) do not elaborate on what they consider as play. Tools, such as robots, fulfil a mediating function when it comes to children's development of CT. Hence, there exists an interplay between tools and CT activities, where CT is mediated by means of tools. In CT activities, CT can be considered as an abstract phenomenon, less concrete and real compared to physical tools and actions. Previously in this paper, the snowballing review has identified CT tools, robots, unplugged activities, and making and exploring as mediating tools contributing to children's CT play and knowledge creation.

The review shows that these different tools illustrate different kinds of mediation and thus mediate different perspectives of CT. We emphasize that it is pivotal that educators are aware of how different tools can mediate different understandings as these different forms of mediation can become effective resources for children to think with. This can create fruitful learning situations for children to appropriate knowledge about CT. Aligned with this, Bers (2018) argues that tools can become concrete and real by being considered as a playground where children can explore, create, imagine, interact socially, master skills, and solve problems together with each other. By using the metaphor of a playground, Bers (2018) emphasizes that children can choose among activities to do and use their imagination while making projects that they find meaningful. While engaging in computational thinking, children develop abstract, sequential thinking skills and problem-solving strategies (Bers, 2018, p. 2). Aligned with Abreu et al. (2020), Bers (2018) does not provide an explanation and definition of the phenomenon of play. It is crucial for CT development in ECE to foster a playground mindset in which children can express their creativity, joy, meaning, and play with things in an exploratory and open way. The educator must create a scaffolding relationship between children so that play does not cease. In this way connections are created between children, play, tools, educators, and computational play (Bers, 2018).

Despite the fact that the papers in the narrative review emphasize the role of CT in ECE, we argue that CT should benefit from being part of a pedagogical strategy that supports the role of play with children in ECE. As stated, play as an activity (Sutton-Smith, 2001) can involve different dimensions of unpredictability as well mutuality (Huizinga, 2004; Olofsson, 1987), which optimally contribute to children's meaning making processes. This means that play as such is children's own activity with a fruitful connection to learning and development. Play, then, can be understood as important for children as it engages and motivates children. Relating this to the outcomes of the scoping review, it is possible to state that children learn and play by exploring through e.g., imagination and creativity. However, when play is related to a learning environment such as ECE, both play and learning take on a special character. This is discussed by Jonsson and Pramling Samuelsson (2017), who emphasize this as participating in a communicative activity. A communicative activity in ECE is about doing something together; children together and teacher and child/children together. Doing something together hence develops both the play and the learning, where the mutuality and scaffolding become a matter of negotiation of meaning. Wood et al. (1976) and Bruner (1961) underlined this kind of mutuality and scaffolding afford the participants attention to the same object. Therefore, we argue that a pedagogical perspective on CT requires an authentic relationship between a teacher and children and, also, that this forms a foundation for establishing CT activities as social and communicative, where teachers' scaffolding consider teaching, learning and play as a pedagogical unity.

4.2 Facilitating Children's Intentions

The field of computational thinking is complex and involves many highly integrated concepts. There is a variety of prior experiences for the CT concepts that each learner brings to CT. Some individuals have experience with programming, while others are new to the field of coding. Some individuals can have expertise in pattern recognition, testing, or design, while others may not have heard of any of these. A person's learning process is characterized by enactive representations (e.g. mental models of the world), iconic representations (e.g. rough drawings for demonstrating concepts), and symbolic representations (e.g. formal application of modelling languages) (Lowe and Brophy, 2017). In computational thinking education, Lowe and Brophy (2017) observe that iconic and even symbolic representations are often presented without explaining how computation works. Therefore, and as stated in the above-mentioned section, we emphasize that learners and educators may benefit from replacing concepts with an operational pedagogical CT framework. Such a framework should be based on CT activities as social and communicative as well as on the concepts of mutuality and scaffolding. In such a framework, it is pivotal for teachers to learn to identify children's intentions. As this is a prerequisite for being able to participate in a spiral of activities (Bruner, 1977) together with others and thus considering teaching, learning and play as a unity become at the center for teachers. In the context of CT, this would mean that CT activities could be designed as a play-oriented activity which continues over time, and which is coordinated and developed by the children, with or without a teacher's participation. Kultti and Pramling (2017) add to this that a child also needs to identify and become aware that he or she is seen by others as someone with intentions. Vygotsky (1978) explained this process through the concept of 'to point'. To point is however not something humans are born with or naturally develop.

In the context of this paper, it becomes important to consider not only what a child expresses verbally, visually or through coding, but also through his or her gestures. Expressed differently, considering the child's multimodal palette of expressions becomes crucial when it comes to developing young children's CT by means of the unity of play, learning and teaching. Vygotsky (1978) considered verbal and other kinds of expressions as being cultural tools and emphasized those as crucial for what kind of knowledge, understanding and ways of seeing that a child develops. This is also a reason to why CT as a social and communicative activity should point to and talk with children by conceptualizing, questioning and telling them what is going on. In this way, the teacher becomes co-creator by mediating the world of CT and recognizing the child as someone with intentions that need to be scaffolded to move the CT project forward.

4.3 Concluding Comments

In formal and informal learning environments, there have been very few studies looking at how CT can be explored with young children in early childhood education. By examining how CT is embedded in children's activities and play, this study provides an overview of the literature. According to the literature, educators are not equally comfortable providing support that enhances the ability of children to use CT skills.

Playing is an effective way for children to socialize, learn, and be creative. As discussed in the review, children explore CT through tools and activities, allowing them to tolerate and understand CT. However, as we argue, play can be a way for children to make CT more familiar to them. CT activities should be viewed as social and communicative and based on the concepts of mutuality and scaffolding in an operational pedagogical CT framework. CT activities can therefore be designed as play-oriented activity that continues over time, with or without educators' guidance, and is coordinated and developed by the children. In the role of co-creator, the educator mediates the CT world and recognizes the child's intentions, which need to be scaffolded to move the CT activities forward. Further, hands-on activities based on children's play can be used to develop children's CT, but there is still a need to develop and create materials that can give confidence to early childhood educators, such as work development, so they can handle such activities in ECE. In this paper, we align with Green et al. (2006) comments about a narrative review by emphasizing that more research is needed to investigate how children in ECE engage in play to develop CT and how educators can support children's CT development.

Appendix A

	Authors	Title	Journal
1	Abreu, Lucia & Pires, Ana & Guerreiro, Tiago. (2020)	TACTOPI: a Playful Approach to Promote Computational Thinking for Visually Impaired Children	The 22nd International ACM SIGACCESS Conference on Computers and Accessibility (pp. 1–3)
2	Angeli, C., & Valanides, N. (2020)	Developing young children's computational thinking with educational robotics: An interaction effect between gender and scaffolding strategy	Computers in Human Behavior, 105
3	Bers, M. U. (2012)	Designing digital experiences for positive youth development: From playpen to playground	OUP USA
4	Bers, M.U. (2018)	Coding and Computational Thinking in Early Childhood: The Impact of ScratchJr in Europe	European Journal of STEM Education

(continued)

(continued)

	Authors	Title	Journal
5	Bers, M.U. (2019)	Coding as another language: a pedagogical approach for teaching computer science in early childhood	Comput. Educ. 6, 499–528
6	Bers, Marina & Flannery, Louise & Kazakoff Myers, Elizabeth & Sullivan, Amanda. (2014)	Computational thinking and tinkering: Exploration of an early childhood robotics curriculum	Computers & Education. 72. 145–157
7	Brackmann, C. P., Román-González, M., Robles, G., Moreno-León, J., Casali, A., & Barone, D. (2017)	Development of computational thinking skills through unplugged activities in primary school	Proceedings of the 12th workshop on primary and secondary computing education (pp. 65–72)
8	Critten, V., Hagon, H. & Messer, D. Can (2022)	Pre-school Children Learn Programming and Coding Through Guided Play Activities? A Case Study in Computational Thinking	Early Childhood Educ J
9	Flannery, L. P., Silverman, B., Kazakoff, E. R., Bers, M. U., Bontá, P., & Resnick, M. (2013)	Designing ScratchJr: Support for early childhood learning through computer programming	Proceedings of the 12th international conference on interaction design and children (pp. 1–10)
10	González, Y.A., & Muñoz-Repiso, A.G. (2018)	A robotics-based approach to foster programming skills and computational thinking: Pilot experience in the classroom of early childhood education	Proceedings of the Sixth International Conference on Technological Ecosystems for Enhancing Multiculturality
11	Hall, J.A. & McCormick, K.I. (2022)	"My Cars don't Drive Themselves": Preschoolers' Guided Play Experiences with Button-Operated Robots	TechTrends 66, 510–526
12	Kotsopoulos, D., Floyd, L., Dickson, B.A. et al. (2022)	Noticing and Naming Computational Thinking During Play	Early Childhood Educ J. 50, 699–708
13	Lee, J., Joswick, C. & Pole, K. (2022)	Classroom Play and Activities to Support Computational Thinking Development in Early Childhood	Early Childhood Educ J
14	Maloney, J., Resnick, M., Rusk, N., Silverman, B., & Eastmond, E. (2010)	The scratch programming language and environment	ACM Transactions on Computing Education (TOCE), 10(4), 1–15

(continued)

(*continued*)

	Authors	Title	Journal
15	Martinez, S. L., & Stager, G. (2013)	Invent to learn. Making, Tinkering, and Engineering in the Classroom	Torrance, Canada: Construting Modern Knowledge
16	McCormick, K. I., & Hall, J. A. (2022)	Computational thinking learning experiences, outcomes, and research in preschool settings: a scoping review of literature	Education and Information Technologies, 27(3), 3777–3812
17	Murcia, K., & Tang, K.-S. (2019)	Exploring the multimodality of young children's coding	Australian Educational Computing, 34(1)
18	Olmo-Muñoz, J., Cózar-Gutiérrez, R., & González-Calero, J. A. (2020)	Computational thinking through unplugged activities in early years of Primary Education	Computers & Education, 150, 103832
19	Vossoughi, S., Escudé, M., Kong, F., & Hooper, P. (2013)	Tinkering, learning & equity in the after-school setting	FabLearn conference. Palo Alto, CA: Stanford University
20	Wang, D., Wang, T., & Liu, Z. (2014)	A Tangible Programming Tool for Children to Cultivate Computational Thinking	The Scientific World Journal
21	Zhang, L., & Nouri, J. (2019)	A systematic review of learning computational thinking through Scratch in K-9	Computers & Education, 141, 103607
22	Yang, Weipeng & Ng, Tsz Kit & Hongyu, Gao. (2022)	Robot programming versus block play in early childhood education: Effects on computational thinking, sequencing ability, and self-regulation	British Journal of Educational Technology. 1–25

References

Abreu, L., Pires, A., Guerreiro, T.: TACTOPI: a playful approach to promote computational thinking for visually impaired children (2020). https://doi.org/10.1145/3373625.3418003

Angeli, C., Valanides, N.: Developing young children's computational thinking with educational robotics: an interaction effect between gender and scaffolding strategy. Comput. Hum. Behav. **105** (2020). https://doi.org/10.1016/j.chb.2019.03.018

Barr, V., Stephenson, C.: Bringing computational thinking to K-12: what is involved and what is the role of the computer science education community? ACM Inroads **2**(1), 48–54 (2011)

Bers, M.U.: Designing Digital Experiences for Positive Youth Development: From Playpen to Playground. OUP, USA (2012)

Bers, M.: Coding and computational thinking in early childhood: the impact of scratchJr in Europe. Eur. J. STEM Educ. **3** (2018). https://doi.org/10.20897/ejsteme/3868

Bers, M., Flannery, L., Kazakoff, M.E., Sullivan, A.: Computational thinking and tinkering: exploration of an early childhood robotics curriculum. Comput. Educ. **72**, 145–157 (2014). https://doi.org/10.1016/j.compedu.2013.10.020

Bers, M.U.: Coding as another language: a pedagogical approach for teaching computer science in early childhood. J. Comput. Educ. **6**(4), 499–528 (2019)

Berson, I.R., Murcia, K., Berson, M.J., Damjanovic, V., McSporran, V.: Tangible digital play in Australian and US preschools. Kappa Delta Pi Rec. **55**(2), 78–84 (2019)

Brackmann, C.P., Román-González, M., Robles, G., Moreno-León, J., Casali, A., Barone, D.: Development of computational thinking skills through unplugged activities in primary school. In Proceedings of the 12th Workshop on Primary and Secondary Computing Education, pp. 65–72 (2017)

Brennan, K., Resnick, M.: New frameworks for studying and assessing the development of computational thinking. In: Proceedings of the 2012 Annual Meeting of the American Educational Research Association, Vancouver, Canada, vol. 1, p. 25 (2012)

Bruner, J.S.: The act of discovery. Harv. Educ. Rev. **31**, 21–32 (1961)

Bruner, J.: The Process of Education. A Landmark in Educational Theory. Harvard University Press (1977)

Bruner, J.: Culture and human development: a new look. Hum. Dev. **33**(6), 344–355 (1990)

Buitrago, F., Casallas, R., Hernández, M., Reyes, A., Restrepo, S., Danies, G.: Changing a generation's way of thinking: teaching computational thinking through programming. Rev. Educ. Res. **87**(4), 834–860 (2017). https://doi.org/10.3102/0034654317710096

Critten, V., Hagon, H., Messer, D.: Can pre-school children learn programming and coding through guided play activities? A case study in computational thinking. Early Childhood Educ. J. **50**(6), 969–981 (2022)

Curzon, P.: cs4fn and computational thinking unplugged. In: Proceedings of the 8th Workshop in Primary and Secondary Computing Education, pp. 47–50 (2013)

Flannery, L.P., Silverman, B., Kazakoff, E.R., Bers, M.U., Bontá, P., Resnick, M.: Designing ScratchJr: support for early childhood learning through computer programming. In: Proceedings of the 12th International Conference on Interaction Design and Children, pp. 1–10 (2013)

Green, B.N., Johnson, C.D., Adams, A.: Writing narrative literature reviews for peer-reviewed journals: secrets of the trade. J. Chiropr. Med. **5**(3):101–117 (2006). https://doi.org/10.1016/S0899-3467(07)60142-6

González, Y.A.C., Muñoz-Repiso, A.G.V.: A robotics-based approach to foster programming skills and computational thinking: pilot experience in the classroom of early childhood education. In: Proceedings of the Sixth International Conference on Technological Ecosystems for Enhancing Multiculturality, pp. 41–45 (2018)

Hall, J.A., McCormick, K.I.: "My cars don't drive themselves": preschoolers' guided play experiences with button-operated robots. TechTrends 1–17 (2022)

Hart, C.: Doing a Literature Review: Releasing the Social Science Research Imagination. Sage (1998)

Huizinga, J.: Den lekande måanniskan: Homo ludens. Natur och Kultur. Brandell var översättare inte författare (2004)

Jonsson, A., Pramling Samuelsson, I.: Lek, lärande och undervisning, hand i hand i arbetet med de yngsta barnen? In: Pramling Samuelsson, I., Jonsson, A. (eds.) Förskolans yngsta barn – Perpektiv på omsorg, lärande och lek, pp. 91–102. Liber (2017)

Kotsopoulos, D., Floyd, L., Dickson, B.A., Nelson, V., Makosz, S.: Noticing and naming computational thinking during play. Early Childhood Educ. J. **50**(4), 699–708 (2022)

Kultti, A., Samuelsson, I.P.: Toys and the creation of cultural play scripts. In: Lynch, S., Pike, D., à Beckett, C. (eds.) Multidisciplinary Perspectives on Play from Birth and Beyond. IPECED, vol. 18, pp. 217–230. Springer, Singapore (2017). https://doi.org/10.1007/978-981-10-2643-0_13

Lee, J., Joswick, C., Pole, K.: Classroom play and activities to support computational thinking development in early childhood. Early Childhood Educ J. (2022). https://doi.org/10.1007/s10643-022-01319-0

Lowe, T., Brophy, S.: An operationalized model for defining computational thinking. In: 2017 IEEE Frontiers in Education Conference (FIE), pp. 1–8. IEEE (2017)

Maloney, J., Resnick, M., Rusk, N., Silverman, B., Eastmond, E.: The scratch programming language and environment. ACM Trans. Comput. Educ. (TOCE) 10(4), 1–15 (2010)

Martinez, S.L., Stager, G.: Invent to Learn. Making, Tinkering, and Engineering in the Classroom. Construting Modern Knowledge, Torrance (2013)

McCormick, K.I., Hall, J.A.: Computational thinking learning experiences, outcomes, and research in preschool settings: a scoping review of literature. Educ. Inf. Technol. 27, 3777–3812 (2022). https://doi.org/10.1007/s10639-021-10765-z

Murcia, K.J., Tang, K.S.: Exploring the multimodality of young children's coding. Aust. Educ. Comput. 34(1) (2019)

del Olmo-Muñoz, J., Cózar-Gutiérrez, R., González-Calero, J.A.: Computational thinking through unplugged activities in early years of primary education. Comput. Educ. 150, 103832 (2020)

Olofsson, B.: Leg for livet: iagttagelser og forskning om 0–7. åriges leg. Børn & Unge (1987)

Paré, G., Kitsiou, S.: Methods for literature reviews. In: Lau, F., Kuziemsky, C. (eds.) Handbook of eHealth Evaluation: An Evidence-based Approach, Chapter 9. University of Victoria, Victoria (2017)

Papert, S.: "Mindstorms" Children. Computers and powerful ideas (1980)

Pramling-Samuelsson, I., Johansson, E.: Play and learning—inseparable dimensions in preschool practice. Early Child Dev. Care 176, 47–65 (2006). https://doi.org/10.1080/030044304200030 2654

Resnick, M., Rosenbaum, E.: Designing for tinkerability. In: Design, Make, Play, pp. 163–181. Routledge (2013)

Smith, P.K. Pellegrini, A.: Learning through play. Encyklopedia on Early Childhood Development (2013). https://www.child-encyclopedia.com/pdf/expert/play/according-experts/learning-through-play. Accessed 03 Oct 2022

Stephen, C., Plowman, L.: Digital play. In: Brooker, L., Blaise, M., Edwards, S. (eds.) Sage Handbook of Play and Learning in Early Childhood, pp. 330–341. Sage (2013)

Sutton-Smith, B.: The Ambiguity of Play. Harvard University Press (2001)

Vossoughi, S., Bevan, B.: Making and tinkering: a review of the literature. Natl. Res. Council Commit. Out School Time STEM 67, 1–55 (2014)

Vossoughi, S., Escudé, M., Kong, F., Hooper, P.: Tinkering, learning & equity in the after-school setting. In: Annual FabLearn Conference. Stanford University, Palo Alto (2013

Vygotsky, L.S.: Mind in Society: Development of Higher Psychological Processes. Harvard University Press (1978)

Vygotsky, L.S.: Thought and Language. MIT Press, Cambridge, MA (1986)

Wang, D., Wang, T., Liu, Z.: A tangible programming tool for children to cultivate computational thinking. Sci. World J. 2014 (2014)

Wang, X.C., Choi, Y., Benson, K., Eggleston, C., Weber, D.: Teacher's role in fostering preschoolers' computational thinking: An exploratory case study. Early Educ. Dev. 32(1), 26–48 (2021)

Webb, H., Rosson, M.B.: Using scaffolded examples to teach computational thinking concepts. In: Proceeding of the 44th ACM Technical Symposium on Computer Science Education, pp. 95–100 (2013)

Wing, J.M.: Computational thinking. Commun. ACM **49**(3), 33–35 (2006)

Wohlin, C.: Guidelines for snowballing in systematic literature studies and a replication in software engineering. In: ACM International Conference Proceeding Series (2014). https://doi.org/10.1145/2601248.2601268

Wood, D.J., Bruner, J.S., Ross, G.: The role of tutoring in problem solving. J. Child Psychiatry Psychol. **17**(2), 89–100 (1976)

Yang, W., Ng, T., Hongyu, G.: Robot programming versus block play in early childhood education: effects on computational thinking, sequencing ability, and self-regulation. Br. J. Educ. Technol. **53**, 1–25 (2022). https://doi.org/10.1111/bjet.13215

Zhang, L., Nouri, J.: A systematic review of learning computational thinking through Scratch in K-9. Comput. Educ. **141**, 103607 (2019)

Designerly Processes with Robots as a Framework for Children's Perspective-Taking

Eva Brooks[1]([⊠]) [iD] and Jeanette Sjöberg[2] [iD]

[1] Aalborg University, Kroghstræde 3, 9220 Aalborg, Denmark
eb@ikl.aau.dk
[2] Halmstad University, Kristian IVs Väg 3, 301 18 Halmstad, Sweden
jeanette.sjoberg@hh.se

Abstract. The use of robotics technology in school is renowned for providing children with opportunities to interact and collaborate in various school subjects, which raise questions of how to design learning activities that include robot technology in education. In this paper we explore how a designerly approach can foster children's perspective-taking while creatively collaborating in mixed analogue and digital learning environments including robots, creative material and classical fairytales. Based on a social semiotics analytical framework, the study draws from workshops carried out with third grade classes of Danish school children, aged 9–10 years old. Using video recordings and a thematic analysis, the unit of analysis focuses on the activities with a special interest on children's interactions with robots, creative materials, classical fairytales and with each other. The results of this study imply that by using a designerly approach with robotics in programming activities, conditions were created for children to engage in interactions and reasoning with each other, where the mixed learning environment reinforced children's abilities of perspective-taking.

Keywords: Designerly · Child-robot interaction · Fairytales · Creative material · Mixed learning environments · Video observation · Linking · School children

1 Introduction

The use of robotics technology in classroom settings is at the present time renowned for providing children with opportunities to interact and collaborate in non-technical subjects as well as technical including programming, and science, technology, engineering and mathematics (STEM) oriented activities (Benitti, 2012; Bertel et al., 2020; Bruni & Nisdeo, 2017; Mubin et al., 2013). In this regard, artefacts and a playful approach towards STEM are considered as vital (Ackerman, 2004; Fisher et al., 2011), in particular highlighting how robots by offering tactile manipulation can promote self-exploration (Lupetti et al., 2017) as well as social and cognitive processes (Yadollahi et al., 2020). When children are involved in playfully framed programming activities

E. Brooks et al. (Eds.): DLI 2022, LNICST 493, pp. 113–131, 2023.
https://doi.org/10.1007/978-3-031-31392-9_10

with robots, they are encouraged to reason and practice perspective-taking (Sjöberg & Brooks, 2022; Brooks & Sjöberg, 2021). Yadollahi et al. (2020) argue that perspective-taking is important when it comes to designing meaningful interaction and collaboration. In this regard, a key quality of a robot is that it is equipped with perception abilities, which means that the robot should be able to extract information to achieve its task, which is termed perception-action loop (Milliez et al. 2014). In order to integrate a perspective-taking model in a robotic platform, Yaddolahi et al. (2019) investigated how a robot's cognitive-affective state influenced children's actions, emotions and perceptions of the robot. Perspective-taking thus can be considered as a sociocognitive process enabling a person to be aware of and perceive others' point of view (Healey & Grossman, 2018) in perceptual, cognitive and affective dimensions (Yadollahi, 2020). Surtee et al. (2013) describe perspective-taking tasks to consist of three components, namely a perspective taker (self), a target perspective (other) and an object or circumstance (object). Perspective-taking can also be described in relation to domain-specific skills such as spatial ability, which are considered as an important educational target for instruction in the K-12 curriculum (Eilam & Alon, 2019). These matters are mostly dealt with from a cognitive perspective and/or technical (Healey & Grossman, 2018; Yadollahi et al. 2019; Yadollahi, 2020; Eilam & Alon, 2019) based on Piaget's terminology (Piaget & Inhelder, 1956; Piaget, 1997), or focusing on robots' capabilities to uphold reasoning and spatial interactive components (Healey & Grossman, 2018; Milliex et al., 2014; Trafton et al., 2005) in relation to people in general and not necessarily having primary school children as the target group. However, several aspects of robotics and perspective-taking are still underexplored.

Tangible digital tools such as robots have a potential to offer perspectives, concepts and ideas involved in designerly processes concrete and possible to transform into practicable forms (Brooks & Sjöberg, 2021; Sjöberg & Brooks, 2022b). By means of digital tools such as robots and children's own physical designs, children can simplify their creation of ideas and thus on perspective-taking. It is in this intersection between such concrete and abstract processes involved in design activities that we are interested in facilitating, to explore children's perspective-taking. In this study, we have used a combination of analogue material (e.g. foam clay, crayons, markers, and LEGO) together with Ozobots as robotic characters (Ozobots are small robots that are either controlled using drawn colour combinations that they run over or via simple application-based block programming). When we investigate perspective-taking within this combinational context, we do this from a social semiotics analytical perspective focusing on how groups of primary school children (7–9 years of age) apply different strategies of perspective-taking. Since most studies in this field of research primarily focus on robots' perspective-taking, we apply a reverse perspective, namely to investigate how a robot-child interaction can facilitate and/or challenge children's perspective-taking. In doing so, we consider the child's perspective and how a child can influence the interaction with the robot as a core aspect of it, rather than the other way around. In other words, it is our assumption that it is not so important that the robot delivers correct feedback, it is more crucial that it can invite children to different kinds of reasoning and perspective-takings. Based on this, we explore how designerly processes, i.e. using a combination of creative material and robotics, can support primary school children's perspective-taking. With such an approach, this study can contribute to improving robotic tasks, such as programming, by means of designerly processes in primary school teaching and learning, but also contribute to the area of technology design targeting this age group of children.

2 Related Work

2.1 Robots in Education

Robot technology is evolving at an ever faster pace with the emergence of Artificial Intelligence (AI) and the improvement of hardware features, advances that have contributed to that robots have become increasingly independent and efficient at performing tasks (e.g. Lytridis et al., 2019). This has in turn led to the introduction of robots in different areas in society, such as the educational field. In recent years, robot technology of various kinds has become an increasingly common feature in formal education, ranging from the early school years up to higher education (e.g. Benitti, 2012; Anwar et al., 2019; Athanasiou et al., 2019). Not least social robots have become popular to use as teachers or teaching assistants, where research shows several benefits with students interacting with the robot to achieve a specific pedagogical purpose (e.g. Vrochidou et al., 2018; Kaburlasos & Vrochidou, 2019). One of the advantages that is highlighted with social robots in particular is that they seem to create an increased engagement among the students, which have positive effects on learning (e.g. Lytridis et al., 2019). The most common area of use for robots in teaching however is in so-called STEM subjects (Science, Technology, Engineering and Mathematics) and more specifically in programming activities (e.g. Zhang et al, 2021; Çetin & Demircan, 2020). Various studies have shown that cooperation and problem-solving are promoted in the introduction of robots in pedagogical practice (e.g. Bers, 2018; Durak et al., 2019; Silva et al., 2020; Brooks & Sjöberg, 2021). One possible downside is that a lot of focus is placed on the technical aspects of the robot, rather than an extended learning. This often has its origins in how the actual teaching situation with the robot has been framed. Even though robots have become an integral educational technology in learning situations, robots in education are primarily used to provide STEM education and proposing how robots can be used as a tutor or peer in learning activities. Thus, there is a need for research focusing on learning implications of robots in education rather than investigating how the technology works.

2.2 Child-Robot Interaction

When it comes to research on children and robot interaction, it has often focused on specific groups of children, such as children with autism and children diagnosed with cognitive impairment (e.g. Ismail et al., 2020; Katsanis, & Moulianitis, 2021). Other areas of interest have been to explore various kinds of trust in interactions between children and robots (e.g. van Straten et al., 2018; Di Dio et al., 2020). In several of these studies, robots have successfully been used as teachers or teacher assistants, focusing on activities of child-robot interaction in order to achieve a certain educational or therapeutic goal (Belpaeme et. al., 2018). The main reason for the observed positive effect of robots in education is that when a robot is involved in the educational process children seem to be more engaged (Belpaeme et. al., 2018). Recently, more attention has been paid to how child-robot interaction can be studied in relation to children's playfulness and sense of exploration (Sjöberg & Brooks, 2022a), as well as their designerly ability (Brooks & Sjöberg, 2021). In these cases, the interaction between the children and the robots becomes part of the children's exploratory and creative activities, where the robot fulfils an important function for the children's knowledge making and learning. However, this is still an unexplored area of research.

In a literature review on the use of robotics construction kits in K-12 learning, Sullivan and Heffernan (2016) identified that children could learn programming concepts and engineering content while interacting with robotic construction kits. It was also identified that in child-robotic interaction, children improved their problem solving abilities; moving from trial-and-error to more sophisticated modelling approaches. The literature review concluded that robotics construction kits appeared to provide rich opportunities to learn STEM disciplines from direct hands-on learning as well as from analogical/modelling application. However, research about how children reason and use technologies to position themselves is limited. In the present study, we use a kit of analogue and digital material to explore how this can spark children's reasoning about perspective-taking. By combining the analogue and creative material with digital and robotic material in a design process, we address learning processes as designerly-framed (Cross, 1982).

3   Theoretical Framework

In this section we present the theoretical framework on which this study is based. The theories emerged from the empirical material and are thus inductively chosen. First, we introduce a theoretical framing to designerly-framed learning processes which is followed by a social semiotics approach to perspective-taking by linking.

3.1   Designerly-Framed Learning Processes

Designerly processes with robots play an important role in developing children's learning. When children design, they not only acquisite knowledge by materialising ideas, they also experiment with possible futures by confronting these ideas with the world (Stappers, 2007). Such confrontations lead to an exploration of different outcomes and perspectives as well as negotiating their meanings with others, which can widen people's sense of participation (Rogers, 2000). Exploration, i.e. the ways people make sense of what they are doing contributes to how design and learning develop and are sustained (Brooks & Sjöberg, 2019; Pramling Samuelsson & Carlsson, 2008). The traditional way of considering design as based on form and function as well as on aesthetics and usability of a product is challenged by contemporary collaborative and process-oriented perspectives focusing on meaning and function (Dorst, 2015). Thus, design can offer opportunities for children to practise perspective-taking, to process abstract concepts, and to make meaning between these different ideas. Inspired by Cross (1982; 2006), we term such processes as designerly.

In designerly-framed learning processes, materials and technology (tools) are central features. The activity as such and the social world of which these tools are part of can be reflected in different ways in their design and use. So, the use of these tools exist with respect to some purposes that are tied to cultural practices and social organisation with which they are meant to function (Lave & Wenger, 1991). Expressed differently and in relation to the context of the present study, creative material and robots cannot be considered as having features in themselves, but as a process that involves specific forms of participation by schoolchildren, where creative material and robots fulfil a mediating function when it comes to children's perspective-taking. Thus, there exists an interesting interplay between mediating tools and learning activities, where mediating tools in their non-transparent way are necessary for allowing focus on, and thus supporting transparency of the subject matter (e.g. perspective-taking). Conversely, transparency or salience of how the tools can be used is important for allowing its non-transparent use (Lave & Wenger, 1991). This makes the design of mediating tools key to provide a balance between transparency and non-transparency, in particular when it comes to their role in communicating social processes.

A designerly perspective to perspective-taking allows children to be able to link their ideas by producing their own signs as new combinations of form and meaning (Kress, 2003). By allowing children themselves to be part of a designerly activity, their engagement in the learning process will be strengthened and they will be more inclined to take active participation (Brooks & Sjöberg, 2020).

3.2 Perspective-Taking and Verbal Linking

In the present study children should use both analogue material and digital technology, which can be seen as offering 'bits' of perspectives (van Leeuwen, 2005). Each of these 'bits' has values in themselves. The goal of the study is to explore how the children link those items of perspectives and pack them into a reasoning about perspectives. Different communicative situations require different understanding and use of perspectives. For example, in this study the children should link materials such as foam clay, LEGO, cardboard, glue, and sharpies together with a classical fairytale and Ozobot robots - each of these items have some meaning of their own but this meaning only becomes relevant if they are linked in terms of the needs of the children who want to find out how to do something (in this case to create a representation of a fairytale by means of material and Ozobots). In order to explore how the children link these items and perspective, the category of verbal linking (van Leeuwen, 2005) becomes central. Van Leeuwen (2005) identifies elaboration or extension as concepts that make verbal linkings explicit (see Table 1). Elaboration as a type of verbal linking includes subtypes such as explanations, examples, specifications and corrections. Extension as another type of verbal linking can be an addition, temporal, spatial and/or logical link. An addition linking exists when an item introduces new perspectives or information which can be adversative or alternative. Temporal linking exists when something is, has or will occur. Logical linking occurs when perspectives give reason for a comparison of or condition of another item. Spatial linking forms a category where proximity and co-presence of items occur. (Table 1).

A designerly perspective to perspective-taking allows children to be able to link their ideas by producing their own signs as new combinations of form and meaning

Table 1. Overview of verbal linking (van Leeuwen, 2005, p. 225).

Type of connection	Subtypes	Typical explicit verbalisations	Typical environmental condition
Elaboration	Explanation Example Specification Summary Correction	'that is', 'in other words', 'example', 'to illustrate', 'in particular', 'more specifically', 'in fact', 'actually'	Argumentation Persuasion
Extension: addition	Addition Adversative Alternative	'and', 'moreover', 'but', 'however', 'or'	Description Argumentation Persuasion
Extension: temporal	Next event Simultaneous event Previous event Conclusive event	'then', 'next', 'finally', 'in the end', 'meanwhile'	Narrative Procedure
Extension: spatial	Proximity Co-presence	'behind', 'in front', 'there' etc	Description
Extension: logical	Similarity Contrast Reason Result Purpose Condition (positive) Condition (negative)	'likewise', 'similarly', 'conversely' 'therefore', 'as a result', 'in consequence' 'in that case', 'if', 'otherwise', 'if not'	Argumentation Persuasion

(Kress, 2003). By allowing children themselves to be part of the designerly activity, their engagement in the learning process will be strengthened and they will be more inclined to take active participation (Brooks & Sjöberg, 2020).

4 Methodology

Following a designerly approach, we have applied a workshop methodology (Ørngreen & Levinsen, 2017) to investigate children's perspective-taking, while programming robots in combination with representing a fairytale using creative material. Overall, this approach offers a structure and flexibility to plan and monitor an activity including complex challenges. Workshops based on a designerly approach adopt a range of tools to support participants' group activities and energise a sense of ownership, especially when children are included (Fails, Guha, Druin, 2012). The empirical study consists of schoolchildren from a primary school in Denmark, including one 3-grade class with children between the ages of 9 to 10, in total 26 children. The children were divided into groups of four to five children resulting in a total of six groups. The group division was carried out by the teachers beforehand. By dividing the children in groups, we targeted a participative and negotiating character of meaning making to take place in the workshop activity (Lave & Wenger, 1991). This kind of condition implied a rich, interactive, and divergent environment (Brown et al., 1993), where the workshop context provided a dynamic participation among the children with an inherent integration of perspectives and negotiations.

Our team comprised four people: the main researcher (first author) and three research assistants from the same university as the main researcher. Our role was to facilitate the workshop structure (see below) and to promote children's collaboration and dialogue during the workshop activity. In addition, the teachers of each class participated to support their children throughout the workshop process (in average two teachers per class). The teachers had been informed about the procedure beforehand and were also supported during the workshop if they had questions.

Data were generated by means of video observations, ethnographic note taking, and casual conversation with the children and the teachers. The six groups each had a designated design station (table) where they carried out the activity. A video camera was set up at each table to capture both the children and what was going on at each station table.

4.1 Setting and Procedure

The study was situated in a school setting. The researchers brought creative material and Ozobots robots and had planned for a design-oriented workshop setting based on a combination of digital and analogue materials (Fig. 1). The analogue material consisted of creative material and classical fairytales (see below).

In establishing a design-oriented workshop context, the children were introduced to coding by means of Ozobot robots. The coding activity was framed by a classic fairytale theme, which the children could elaborate on and transform to coding actions where Ozobot represented one or more of the main characters in a specific plot of the story. Each group had access to 2–4 Ozobots. The children used creative material, such as foam clay, LEGO, cardboard, glue, and sharpies/marker pens in combination with applying colour- and sequence coding of the Ozobots to move according to the fairytale plot. Ozobot is a versatile robot designed to enhance children's interest in programming and thus suitable for STEM (Science, Technology, Engineering, Mathematics) education. In the workshops the Ozobots were used to invite the participating children to re-enact a narrative composition by conceptualizing and reproducing the fairytale, using coding. The fairytales were selected by the researchers beforehand and included classical fairy tales, which were: (1) Crying wolf; (2) Little red riding hood; (3) What the old man does is always right; (4) The little match girl; and (5) There is no doubt about it. Through this, we targeted a digital component combined with analogue ones to foster children's participative engagement and perspective-taking (Fig. 2).

Our designerly take on the workshop methodology was based on a design development process (Sanders & Stappers, 2012, p. 26), which was divided into four different phases, each one with a specific purpose. The different phases unfolded sequentially. Table 2 illustrates the different phases and the activities that unfolded within each phase.

Fig. 1. Workshop setting in the school context.

Fig. 2. Children working with coding, Ozobot robots, creative material, and the fairytale

Table 2. Overview of workshop phases.

Phase 1: Setting the scene	The objective of the first phase is to introduce the children to the activity, their specific roles, the task definition, its purpose and different tools. This was done to all of the children and their teachers. By the end of this phase, the children were divided into groups. The teachers had done the group division beforehand. Each group was introduced to their specific fairytale. After this, the respective fairytale was read out loud, either by one of the group members, by a teacher/pedagogue, or by a research assistant. This was followed by a group discussion about the content of the fairytale to make sure that it made sense for the children. This included elaborations of, for example, the underlying moral message of the fairytale. Finally, the children were introduced to the Ozobots, including the coding possibilities, and the creative material. Setting the scene is about creating a climate of trust and empowering the children to act freely and creatively within the frame of the task
Phase 2: Discovery	Phase 2 takes place within each of the groups and aims to a shared understanding and definition of the task, including how to approach it. From a design perspective, this is about ideation, where ideas are generated as well as opportunity and challenge identified. This is also where the children start to translate the fairytale to coding, as well as how this could be represented by means of the creative material. This can be seen as a voyage of discovery where the children confront the knowledge embodied in the task, and begin to appropriate that knowledge to their own in an explorative and expansive way
Phase 3: Design and make	Phase 3 includes time for the children to iteratively reflect, explore and further develop their ideas from phase 2. This process is characterised by children's casual connections between their shared ideas, and preconditions relevant to the coding, design and materialisation of their visions and goals relative to the task. This is followed by hands-on initiatives of designing and making, where several discussions, reflections, and perspectives emerge. *Are the coding and creative representation of the fairytale relevant to convey our ideas and perspectives? How can we appropriately code Ozobot so that it in a trustworthy way represents the fairytale character's movement?*
Phase 4: Communication	The objective of phase 4 is to develop a conclusive scene for the children to present their solutions, choices, considerations, and perspectives for each other. This is followed by a plenary question and feedback moment from the audience including the groups of children, teachers, and research assistants. The phase ends with an evaluation, where the researcher and research assistants ask the children to give feedback on the activity

4.2 Ethical Considerations

The study was subject to common research-ethical principles of transparency in the research process and quality of documentation as well as the protection of sources and individuals (Danish Code of Conduct for Research Integrity, 2014; GDPR, 2016). Teachers and parents were informed about the study in writing. All parents confirmed that their child could participate in the study by signing informed consent forms, which included their approval for us to use videos and photos for scientific purposes. The United Nations convention on the rights of the child (1989) was fully respected and participating children were carefully informed before verbal consent was negotiated with them ahead and during every workshop.

4.3 Analytical Framework

The analysis was based on a thematic approach (Braun & Clarke, 2006; 2019) and comprised in total, 690 min (11,5 h) of video recordings. All video recordings were carefully scrutinised and selected samples were transcribed for further analysis. The transcripts were reviewed and coded by both authors to identify themes in verbal and non-verbal actions and interactions between the children and the digital and analogue activity. The initial themes were reviewed and defined by both authors. The performed analytical steps are illustrated in the below Table 3. This means that the paper's focus on perspective-taking emerged from an inductive approach to the data.

Table 3. Overview of the analysis process (based on Braun and Clarke, 2006).

Phases of the thematic analysis process	Description of the thematic analysis actions
Getting to know the data	Watching and re-watching the video data and field notes
Generating initial codes	Systematically coding interesting features of the data and identifying data relevant to each code
Searching for initial themes	Synthesising codes into initial themes and gathering relevant data to each initial theme
Reviewing themes	Checking if the themes work in relation to the coded data and the whole data set, generating a thematic map of the analysis
Defining themes	Iteration of the analysis to refine the details of each theme in relation to the research questions, generating definitions and names for each final theme

From this analysis we identified three overall themes: (1) Perspective-taking through elaboration spatial extensions; (2) Perspective-taking through elaboration, temporal and addition extensions; and (3) Perspective-taking through elaboration and logical extensions, which are presented in the next section.

5   Findings

The design-oriented activity was divided into four main phases: the setting of the scene phase; the discovery phase; the design and make phase; and the communication phase. Each phase of design activity included different types of perspective-takings that required some sort of choices to get closer to a solution. The groups approached the four phases in an engaged task-oriented way, and carefully wanted to accomplish the task. The analysis identified what the children considered as important and what was not when linking the materials and the different perspectives they offered. The analysis also showed that the content of the fairytales included in the study did not influence the kind of perspective-taking linking that emerged. The different linking of perspectives and choices were merely related to the children's interests, particularly addressing values related to aesthetics or functionality. All groups applied elaboration linking discussions where most of them were of an examplifying or specifying character rather than being persuasive. However, in one of the groups the elaboration linking was more of a correcting and explanatory character. Here, two of the group members wanted to keep up with a certain perspective and were thus arguing to persuade the other two group members to consider this perspective as the most relevant. In the following subsections, we present the outcomes of our analysis.

5.1   Perspective-Taking Through Elaboration Spatial Extensions

Perspective-taking through the linking-types of elaboration and spatial extension refers to how the children by linking all the perspectives (fairytale content, creative material and Ozobot robots) argued for a co-presence of the whole rather than focusing on parts of the different tools. The elaboration that was taking place within the group was discussive and argumentative in an agreeing manner. The different tools were put together in a cohesive manner, where the perspectives of each of them contributed to representing the core aspects of the fairytales that the group members jointly were agreeing upon. The argumentations were of a specifying or explanatory kind, where one group member specified, for example, what he or she meant by adding a prop to represent the fairytale or how Ozobot's character was in line with the content of the fairytale. In this way, the perspectives of the individuals' were listened to and accepted.

In this theme, the participants primarily applied spatial extension linking. The group who worked with the Crying wolf fairytale can exemplify this. This group's main focus was on how different props could be related to each other, for example the foam clay meadow and the Ozobot robot, or alternatively how Ozobot robots wayfinding could be connected to the props so that the co-presence of these aspects fitted into the core of the part of the fairytale they had chosen as key. The group divided tasks in pairs, where a girl and a boy worked with the creative material and another girl and boy focused on the pathway of the Ozobot robot. During all of the four phases, the group members were aligned with their individual understanding of the task as a whole and of the parts that together should form their cohesive design that communicated the perspectives that they through the different tools created. They agreed upon the moral of the story in such a way that it made sense "to speak the truth so that people in the long run would believe what you say".

The challenge the group dealt with was how this moral could be conveyed in a meaningful way. While they all discussed this, they focused on spatial dimensions. For example, they all found it crucial that the fairytale environment which they created with foam clay and the pathway that the Ozobot should 'walk through' were aligned. They discussed and described to each other how they thought that the Ozobot and the green grass where the shepherd and the lambs were located could demonstrate the "lazy shepherd who just wanted to lay in the grass and not take his task seriously". Jointly they concluded that Ozobot "needs to move slowly alongside the green grass" (representing the meadow where the lambs grazed grass) and stop in front of the huge grass plot. In other words, the ways the foam clay environment and the Ozobot alongside the pathway it was moving along should make connections and, thereby, when supporting each other extend the meaning of the moral perspective that they wanted to convey (Fig. 3).

Fig. 3. Children discussing how they can convey the message of a shepherd that did not take his work seriously (spatial extension linking).

With this background, perspective-taking was present in two ways. First, it communicated the children's shared point of view of the moral of the fairytale. Second, the groups' final representation of the fairytale showed how the different tools through their proximity appeared to signify a shepherd who by being lazy was not taking his job seriously.

5.2 Perspective-Taking Through Elaboration, Temporal and Addition Extensions

Perspective-taking through the linking-types of elaboration, addition and temporal extensions includes how the children by applying temporal linking put efforts into connecting the creative tools (foam clay and LEGO) with the pathway of the Ozobots to convey the context of the fairytale. As in the previous theme (Sect. 5.1), the elaboration type of linking within this theme were discussive and argumentative in an agreeing manner. The difference though was that within this theme the storyline was in focus in terms of how the different events of the narrative cohesively could be communicated. Another type of linking that was used within this theme was the addition extension. This was particularly shown when children added a perspective to an item, which will be exemplified in the below text.

This theme can be illustrated by examples from the groups working with the fairytales of The little red riding hood and What the old man does is always right. While the underlying moral message from The little red riding hood was clear for the children, it was less clear regarding What the old man does is always right. When the children elaborated on the latter, they specified details from the storyline regarding how the farmer's (the old man) every exchange of goods resulted in less money. From this, the children summarised the moral message by not understanding how the farmer's wife could hug and kiss her husband when he arrived home with a bag of rotten apples, after all he left the home with a horse. This resulted in an engaged moral discussion, where the children's perspectives were aligned, but not fully in agreement with the underlying perspective of the fairytale.

When the groups applied the temporal extension linking, they simply followed the storylines of the two fairytales. They started from the beginning, which was followed by what came 'after' that. These 'after' relations, i.e. what will follow next, were understood from the fairytale context. For example, when the children discussed a certain episode of the fairytale, they used words like 'next', 'after, or 'then'. When they arrived at the end of the storyline, they became procedural in their discussions by addressing the question of how to represent the end to adequately represent their perspective (i.e. how they considered the moral of the fairytale) (Fig. 4).

The children's application of the addition extension link can be exemplified by how they introduced new material in the form of foam clay to add to Ozobot. In doing so, they simply added, for example, a red hat to the little red riding hood to make it clear that Ozobot represented this character. While doing so, the child who added the material described for the other children in the group how this addition could make the Ozobot character more trustworthy.

Within this theme, perspective-taking was present primarily through the children's perspectives related to the narrative, which facilitated an elaborative discussion on perspectives related to how the group members looked at something, for example, the moral message of the What the old man does is always right.

Fig. 4. Children adding prop details following the narrative of The little red riding hood (addition extension linking).

5.3 Perspective-Taking Through Elaboration and Logical Extensions

Perspective-taking through the linking-types of elaboration and logical extensions refers to instances where the children did not agree on how the fairytale should be conveyed, in particular regarding in what order the different tools should be used; should they start with Ozobot and its wayfinding or start with establishing the fairytale context by means of the creative material. This can be exemplified by the group working with The little match girl. Here, the moral message was not in focus at all but rather which material, creative material or Ozobot robots, that should form the context of the fairytale. Throughout the second and third phases of the task, three members of the group applied the elaboration linking style by constantly arguing for the case of coding Ozobot's wayfinding as the most important feature to tell the story. The props that the other two children were making were considered as secondary. Through this arguing, the three group members tried hard to persuade the other two group members to agree with them.

This group applied a logical extension linking type when they were trying to convince each other about perspectives to take. This was applied in the forms of comparisons of the two conditions; to start with Ozobot or to start creating the fairytale environment. For example, the three group members who favoured Ozobots as the main components of the story expressed this by saying, "If we place this christmas tree here, the robot cannot pass by. It has to wait and be placed when we have finished the way Ozobot should move". Also, causal links were made such as 'because' or 'for that reason'. The comparative links most often indexed contrasts that should persuade the ones who had another perspective or, alternatively, make an argument by comparing aspects of the different perspectives that were discussed (Fig. 5).

This logical extension linking resulted in that the children created two parallel perspectives, which from both sides were considered as the most important. The two members who created props with LEGO and foam clay repeatedly tried to put these into the other three members' coding map. In doing so, they applied a positive condition subtype, such as "if doing this way…". However the three group members were not agreeing and constantly applied a negative condition subtype by saying, for example, "no, this would not work".

Fig. 5. Children representing the fairytale by logical extension linking type by designing Ozobot's wayfinding separated from the overall fairytale composition.

Within this theme, perspective-taking was present primarily through logical extension linking types, primarily based on contrasting and negative subtypes. Positive subtypes were included from one part of the group, but did not work to persuade the other part.

6   Conclusive Discussion

In this paper we set out to explore how a designerly approach can foster children's perspective-taking while creatively programming robots. Our findings have shown that by using a designerly approach with robotics in programming activities, conditions were created for children to engage in interactions and reasoning with each other, where the robots reinforced children's abilities of perspective-taking. In contrast to previous research, which mainly has studied perspective-taking from a cognitive or technical perspective, our study has shown that a designerly perspective offered opportunities for school children (9–10 years of age) to practise different strategies of perspective-taking. Thus, we argue that robots in education play a distinctive role by providing children extended learning opportunities. In this regard it was not important whether the robot gave adequate feedback or not. Instead, challenges in the child-robot interaction opened for children's reasoning about, for example, moral questioning. Additionally, child-robot interaction can also facilitate and/or challenge children's perspective-taking.

This implies that perspective-taking also pedagogically can be applied in relation to not only domain-specific skills but also transversal skills. Based on this, we emphasise that designerly framed child-robot interaction situations can create meaningful learning processes. This should be harnessed from yearly years where children are capable of displaying creative ideas and perspectives via designelrly experiences.

To answer our research question, we have explored how designerly processes, i.e. using a combination of creative material and robotics, can support primary school children's perspective-taking. Our results showed that perspective-taking was present in two ways. First, it communicated the children's shared point of view of the moral of the fairytale. Second, the groups' final representation of the fairytale showed how the different tools through their proximity appeared to signify a shepherd who by being lazy was not taking his job seriously. Furthermore, perspective-taking was present primarily through the children's perspectives related to the narrative, which facilitated an elaborative discussion on perspectives related to how the group members looked at something, for example, the moral message of the What the old man does is always right. Finally, perspective-taking was present primarily through logical extension linking types, primarily based on contrasting and negative subtypes. Positive subtypes were included from one part of the group, but did not work to persuade the other part. Just like bricoleurs, the children approached perspective-taking by arranging, rearranging, presenting, representing and by reasoning with bits of materials and technologies.

To conclude, perspective-taking is an important transversal as well as subject-specific skill. A designerly approach to perspective-taking, i.e. to combine different materials/modalities, can facilitate children to practise perspective-taking. Through such activities, the children could create complex perspective-taking reasoning with their peers that involved interaction between their own understandings of classical fairytales, their creative constructions and robot characters. The findings clearly showed how this invited the children to reason about consequences and implications of their arguments. However, this needs to be facilitated and verbalised by the teachers to make children aware of such matters. Our study suggests that children's engagement in perspective-taking activities in school settings augment their social, cultural and creative knowledge creation. With such an approach, this study can contribute to the field by improving robotic tasks, such as programming, by means of designerly processes in primary school teaching and learning, but also contribute to the area of technology design targeting this age group of children. In addition, another contribution is to have a design-oriented approach when implementing technology in teaching, i.e. robotics, as it helps to create situations where a teacher need to reason about and understand the technology in its context.

This study has presented results that augment previous research on children's perspective-taking. More studies will be useful to further investigate complexities and other framings of child-robot interaction in education that can support designerly ways of learning based on children's initiatives.

References

Ackerman, E.K.: Constructing knowledge and transforming the world. In: Tokoro, M., Steels, L. (eds.) A Learning Zone of One's Own: Sharing Representations and Flow in Collaborative Learning Environments, pp. 15–37. IOS Press (2004)

Anwar, S., Bascou, N.A., Menekse, M., Kardgar, A.: A systematic teview of studies on educational robotics. J. Pre-Coll. Eng. Educ. Res. (J-PEER) **9**(2), Article 2 (2019)

Athanasiou, L., Mikropoulos, T.A., Mavridis, D.: Robotics interventions for improving educational outcomes - a meta-analysis. In: Tsitouridou, M., A. Diniz, J., Mikropoulos, T.A. (eds.) TECH-EDU 2018. CCIS, vol. 993, pp. 91–102. Springer, Cham (2019). https://doi.org/10.1007/978-3-030-20954-4_7

Belpaeme, T., Kennedy, J., Ramachandran, A., Scassellati, B., Tanaka, F.: Social robots for education: a review. Sci. Robot. **3**(21), 1–9 (2018). https://doi.org/10.1126/scirobotics.aat5954

Benitti, F.B.V.: Exploring the educational potential of robotics in schools: a systematic review. Comput. Educ. **58**, 978–988 (2012)

Bers, M.U.: Coding as a Playground: Programming and Computational Thinking in the Early Childhood Classroom. Routledge Press (2018). https://doi.org/10.4324/9781315398945

Bertel, L.B., Dau, S., Brooks, E.: ROSIE: robot-supported inclusive education - a play- based approach to STEM education and inclusion in early childhood transitions. In: Levrini, O., Tasquier, G. (eds.) Electronic Proceedings of the ESERA 2019 Conference: The Beauty and Pleasure of Understanding: Engaging with Contemporary Challenges Through Science Education, pp. 1810–1817 (2020)

Braun, V., Clarke, V.: Reflecting on reflexive thematic analysis. Qual. Res. Sport Exerc. Health **11**(4), 589–597 (2019). https://doi.org/10.1080/2159676X.2019.1628806

Braun, V., Clarke, V.: Using thematic analysis in psychology. Qual. Anal. Psychol. **3**(2), 77–101 (2006). https://doi.org/10.1191/1478088706qp063oa

Brooks, E., Sjöberg, J.: Children's programming of robots by designing fairytales. In: Brooks, E., Dau, S., Selander, S. (eds.) Digital Learning and Collaborative Practices. Lessons from Inclusive and Empowering Participation with Emerging Technologies, pp. 158–174. Routledge (2021)

Brooks, E., Sjöberg, J.: A designerly approach as a foundation for school children's computational thinking skills while developing digital games. In: IDC 2020: Proceedings of the Interaction Design and Children Conference, June 2020, pp. 87–95. ACM (Association for Computing Machinery) (2020). https://doi.org/10.1145/3392063.3394402

Brooks, E., Sjöberg, J.: Evolving playful and creative activities when school children develop game-based designs. In: Brooks, A.L., Brooks, E., Sylla, C. (eds.) ArtsIT/DLI -2018. LNIC-SSITE, vol. 265, pp. 485–495. Springer, Cham (2019). https://doi.org/10.1007/978-3-030-06134-0_51

Brown, A.L., Ash, D., Rutherford, M., Nakagawa, K., Campione, J.C.: Distributed expertise in the classroom. In: Salomon, G. (ed.) Distributed cognitions: Psychological and Educational Considerations, pp. 188–228. Cambridge University Press, Cambridge (1993)

Bruni, F., Nisdeo, M.: Educational robots and children's imagery: a preliminary investigation in the first year of primary school. Res. Educ. Media **9**(1) (2017). https://doi.org/10.1515/rem-2017-0007. ISSN 2037–0830

Çetin, M., Demircan, H.Ö.: Empowering technology and engineering for STEM education through programming robots: a systematic literature review. Early Child Dev. Care **190**(9), 1323–1335 (2020). https://doi.org/10.1080/03004430.2018.1534844

Convention on the rights of the child: Treaty no. 27531. United Nations Treaty Series, 1577, pp. 3–178 (1989). https://treaties.un.org/doc/Treaties/1990/09/19900902%2003-14%20AM/Ch_IV_11p.pdf. Accessed 19 Apr 2022

Cross, N.: Designerly ways of knowing. Springer, Heidelberg (2006). https://doi.org/10.1007/1-84628-301-9

Cross, N.: Designerly ways of knowing. Des. Stud. **3**(4), 221–227 (1982). https://doi.org/10.1016/0142-694X(82)90040-0

Danish code of conduct for research integrity: Ministry of Higher Education and Research, Copenhagen, Denmark (2014). https://ufm.dk/en/publications/2014/files-2014-1/the-danish-code-of-conduct-for-research-integrity.pdf. Accessed 7 Mar 2021

Di Dio, C., et al.: Shall I trust you? From child–robot interaction to trusting relationships. Front. Psychol. **11**(469) (2020)

Dorst, K.: Frame Innovation. Create New Thinking by Design. The MIT Press, Cambridge (2015)

Durak, H.Y., Yilmaz, F.G.K., Yilmaz, R.: Computational thinking, programming self-efficacy, problem solving and experiences in the programming process conducted with robotic activities. Contemp. Educ. Technol. **10**(2), 173–197 (2019). https://doi.org/10.30935/cet.554493 - T

Eilam, B., Alon, U.: Children's object structure perspective-taking: Training and assessment. Int. J. Sci. Math. Educ. **17**, 1541–1562 (2019). https://doi.org/10.1007/s10763-018-9934-7

Fails, J.A., Guha, M.L., Druin, A.: Methods and techniques for involving children in the design of new technology for children. Found. Trends Hum.-Comput. Interact. **6**(2), 85–166 (2012). https://doi.org/10.1561/1100000018

Fisher, K., Hirsh-Pasek, K., Golinkoff, R.M., Singer, D.G., Berk, L.: Playing around in school: Implications for learning and educational policy. In: Nathan, P., Pellegrini, A.D. (eds.) The Oxford Handbook of the Development of Play, pp. 342–360. Oxford University Press, Oxford (2011)

General data protection regulations (GDPR) (2016/679). Official Journal of European Union. https://eur-lex.europa.eu/legal-content/EN/TXT/PDF/?uri=CELEX:32016R0679. Accessed 7 Mar 2021

Healey, M.L., Grossman, M.: Cognitive and affective perspective-taking: evidence for shared and dissociable anatomical substrates. Front. Neurol. **9**, 491 (2018)

Ismail, L.I., Hanapiah, F.A., Belpaeme, T., Dambre, J., Wyffels, F.: Analysis of attention in child–robot interaction among children diagnosed with cognitive impairment. Int. J. Soc. Robot. **13**(2), 141–152 (2020). https://doi.org/10.1007/s12369-020-00628-x

Kaburlasos, V., Vrochidou, E.: Social robots for pedagogical rehabilitation: Trends and novel modeling principles. In: Dimitrova, M., Wagatsuma, H. (eds.) Cyber-Physical Systems for Social Applications. Advances in Systems Analysis, Software Engineering, and High Performance Computing (ASASEHPC), pp. 1–21. IGI Global (2019)

Katsanis, I.A., Moulianitis, V.C.: An architecture for safe child–robot interactions in autism interventions. Robotics **10**, 20 (2021)

Kress, G.: Literacy in the New Media Age. Routledge, London (2003)

Lave, J., Wenger, E.: Situated Learning. Legitimate Peripheral Participation, Cambridge University Press, Cambridge (1991)

Lupetti, M.L., Yao, Y., Mi, H., Germak, C.: Design for children's playful learning with robots. Future Internet **9**(3), 1–20 (2017). https://doi.org/10.3390/fi9030052

Lytridis, C., Bazinas, C., Papakostas, G.A., Kaburlasos, V.G.: On measuring engagement level during child-robot interaction in education. Rob. Educ. (2019)

Milliez, G., Warnier, M., Clodic, A., Alami, R.: A framework for endowing an interactive robot with reasoning capabilities about perspective-taking and belief management. IEEE ROMAN, HAL Open Science (2014)

Mubin, O., Stevens, C.J., Shahid, S., Al Mahmud, A., Dong, J.-J.: A review of the applicability of robots in education. Technol. Educ. Learn. **1**, 13 (2013)

Piaget, J.: The Moral Judgement of the Child. Simon and Schuster, New York (1997)

Piaget, J., Inhelder, B.: The Child's Conception of Space. Routledge (1956)

Pramling Samuelsson, I., Carlsson, M.: The playing learning child: towards a pedagogy of early childhood. Scand. J. Educ. Res. **52**(6), 623–641 (2008). https://doi.org/10.1080/003138308 02497265

Rogers, N.: The Creative Connection: Expressive Arts as Healing. PCCS Books (2000)

Sanders, E., Stappers, P.: Convivial Toolbox. Generative Research for the Front End of Design. BIS Publishers, Amsterdam (2012)

Silva, L., Mendes, A.J., Gomes, A.: Computer-supported collaborative learning in programming education: a systematic literature review. In: IEEE Global Engineering Education Conference (EDUCON), pp. 1086–1095 (2020). https://doi.org/10.1109/EDUCON45650.2020.9125237

Sjöberg, J., Brooks, E.: Understanding school children's playful experiences through the use of educational robotics: the impact of open-ended designs. In: Fang, X. (ed.) HCI in Games, vol. 13334, pp. 456–468. Springer, Cham (2022a). https://doi.org/10.1007/978-3-031-05637-6_29

Sjöberg, J., Brooks, E.: Collaborative interactions in problem-solving activities: school children's orientations while developing digital game designs using smart mobile technology. Int. J. Child-Comput. Interact. 33, 100456 (2022b)

Stappers, P.J.: Doing design as a part of doing research. In: Michel, R. (ed.) Design Research Now. Board of International Research in Design, pp. 81–91. Birkhäuser (2007). https://doi.org/10.1007/978-3-7643-8472-2_6

Sullivan, F.R., Heffernan, J.: Robotic construction kits as computational manipulatives for learning in the STEM disciplines. J. Res. Technol. Educ. 48(2), 105–128 (2016). https://doi.org/10.1080/15391523.2016.1146563

Surtee, A., Apperly, I., Samson, D.: Similarities and differences in visual and spatial perspective-taking processes. Cognition 129(2), 426–438 (2013)

Trafton, J., Cassimatis, N., Bugajska, M., Brock, D., Mintz, F., Schultz, A.: Enabling effective human-robot interaction using perspective-taking in robots. IEEE Trans. Syst. Man Cybern. - Part A Syst. Hum. 35(4), 460–470 (2005)

van Leeuwen, T.: Introducing Social Semiotics. Routledge (2005)

van Straten, C.L., Peter, J., Kühne, R., de Jong, C., Barco, A.: Technological and interpersonal trust in child-robot interaction: an exploratory study. In: HAI 2018: Proceedings of the 6th International Conference on Human-Agent Interaction, pp. 253–259 (2018). https://doi.org/10.1145/3284432.3284440

Vrochidou, E., Najoua, A., Lytridis, C., Salonidis, M., Ferelis, V., Papakostas, G.: Social robot NAO as a self-regulating didactic mediator: A case study of teaching/learning numeracy. In: Proceedings of the 26th International Conference on Software, Telecommunications and Computer Networks (SoftCOM 2018), pp. 1–5 (2018)

Yadollahi, E., Couto, M., Dillenbourg, P., Paiva, A.: Can you guide me? Supporting children's spatial perspective taking through games with robots. In: Proceedings of Interaction Design and Children (IDC 2020 Extended Abstracts), ACM (2020). https://doi.org/10.1145/3397617.3397831

Yadollahi, E., Johal, W., Dias, J., Dillenbourg, P., Paiva, A.: Studying the effect of robot frustration on children's change of perspective. In: 8th International Conference on Affective Computing and Intelligent Interaction Workshops and Demos (ACIIW), pp. 381–387 (2019). https://doi.org/10.1109/ACIIW.2019.8925100

Zhang, Y., Luo, R., Zhu, Y., Yin, Y.: Educational robots improve K-12 students' computational thinking and STEM attitudes: systematic review. J. Educ. Comput. Res. 59(7), 1450–1481 (2021). https://doi.org/10.1177/0735633121994070

Ørngreen, R., Levinsen, K.: Workshops as a research methodology. Electron. J. e-Learn. 15(1), 70–81 (2017)

Digital Approaches Shaping Educational Practices

Navigating the Current "New World" of Teaching with Technology: A Glimpse into Our Teachers' Minds

Martin Cooney$^{(\boxtimes)}$ and Jeanette Sjöberg

Halmstad University, 301 18 Halmstad, Sweden
martin.cooney@hh.se
https://www.hh.se/english.html

Abstract. The COVID-19 pandemic helped spark a surge in innovative usages of technology in education, from robot-based remote graduation ceremonies to immersive learning through extended reality, meetings in fantastical game worlds, automatic examination methods, and flexible learning options such as hybrid classes. It's been said that we can't go back to "normal" because *this is* normal now–but what exactly is today's "new normal"? The current paper reports on the results of an anonymous online survey conducted with 42 teachers in business, IT, nursing, and education at our university in October 2021, to gain insight into where some teachers on the "front lines" currently stand on the use of technology in education. Some insights included that: More teachers than we had expected were using robotics and extended reality (XR), suggesting that silo effects can exist in education, even at small universities; furthermore, the rates of teachers who had seen such usage seemed close to the rates of teachers who had tried using them, suggesting the usefulness of raising awareness to promote professional digital competence (PDC). Rates for using games and exam tools were lower than expected, despite the availability of game platforms and a growing need to consider the threat of how technology can be misused to cheat in exams, possibly due to teachers' limited time for pedagogical development. Also, teachers appeared to have strong and differing opinions about learning formats, although a general preference was observed for physical classes and exams, and hybrid teacher meetings. Our aim is that these results will be used by our university's pedagogical center to support our teachers' PDC and uses of edtech in the near future.

Keywords: edtech · educational robotics · XR in education · gamification in education · hybrid learning · professional digital competence

1 Introduction

Teaching in contemporary higher education institutions (HEIs) is in a transformational phase, where the role of a university teacher is changing, also due to

We thank everyone who responded to our survey.

rapid and continual developments in educational technology (edtech). As well, the COVID-19 pandemic recently resulted in university teachers being more or less been forced into digital teaching. This combination of a natural trend toward increased use of technology in education, in conjunction with the temporary needs of "emergency teaching", has led to an emphasis on the importance for teachers to develop professional digital competence (PDC) (e.g., [5,14]): To compete and excel in a world in which digital literacy is vital and students have increasingly many choices of where and how to study, a fundamental goal of teachers should be to maintain some degree of awareness of the opportunities and challenges presented by the use of current technologies. For example, it's been said that a revolution in education is occurring due to incorporation of technological approaches related to robotics, extended reality (XR), and games, which can engage students and provide enriched experiences in various learning contexts [3,17,21]. Also, the pandemic-driven switch to online or hybrid learning required many teachers to learn how to use tools such as Zoom, that could meet basic safety requirements and also provide some enhanced flexibility [24]– conditions can change quickly, and we don't fully know what is waiting around the corner.

A downside is that PDC can be costly for busy teachers to develop: The e-learning landscape is vast, spanning many topics like robotics, XR, and gamification above, such that it could be time-consuming and difficult for regular teachers to maintain a picture of current developments that is both accurate and broad. Given that lack of time could also affect teachers' abilities to communicate about the methods they use, another danger could be that teachers might sometimes feel the need to develop solutions to problems that others have already faced or overcome; i.e., there might be educational silo effects. This could be also related to the "drawer effect" in statistics,[1] in which "non-significant" results are not published, leading others to repeat failed experiments and lose time and productivity. It's also not clear how much of a divide exists between researchers prototyping new systems, and teachers using them in practice, given also that academic organizations can differ in size, strategy, and resources allocated to teachers.

Thus, the goal of the current study was to gain some insight into the current state of how technology is being used in education at our university, by checking where some teachers on the "front lines" currently stand. After summarizing some related literature in Sect. 2, we report on an online survey in Sect. 3. We aim to use some insights regarding current opportunities and challenges in the area, which are discussed in Sect. 4, to better support our teachers, both by disseminating information at a workshop and identifying potentially useful research directions relevant to our long-term strategies.

---

[1] research.uh.edu/the-big-idea/what-went-wrong/behind-closed-drawers-the-file-draw er-effect.

2   Related Work

Various previous work describes ongoing efforts toward understanding the current state of edtech. For example, Laufer et al. conducted a multinational survey of HEI leaders from May to November 2020, finding that, although challenges exist–such as inequalities in access to technical resources and digital skills, and a need for strategies and leadership–some positive effects of edtech were seen in regard to improved access, individualized learning, and lifelong learning skills [20]. Williamson likewise reported musings in 2021 that new technologies like robot teachers capable of analyzing students' data could be the "future of education", and that there is great interest in the possibilities for AI to be used to 're-engineer the classroom' in post-COVID education; although various meta-edtech platforms are gradually springing up–such as *evidence intermediaries* that gather evidence on successful efforts and market intelligence groups that advise investments in the field, like the U.K.'s EdTech Impact site, the U.S.'s Edtech Evidence Exchange, and HolonIQ–there seems to be no *one* "go-to" place yet [29]. Thus, we believe there is still a benefit to probing teachers and gathering information on interesting use cases and insights, which is our goal in the current paper. Below, we further describe some work related to new technologies–robotics/XR, gamification, and exam tools–as well as perceptions of learning formats at the level of an individual class (campus-based, online, or hybrid). We note that this work is not limited to studies conducted at HEIs, given that work in some areas is still sparse due to the rapid pace of technological development, and our belief that insight can also be taken from other contexts such as children's education.

2.1   Engaging New Technologies

Robotics/XR. One technology intended to provide high feelings of engagement, immersion and social presence is robotics. Robots have been used in various roles: as learning materials for students to assemble and program, as remote attendance systems, as one-to-one tutors (e.g., intelligent tutoring systems and teachable agents), as class companions or mascots, and as teaching assistants; for example, the latter can read materials aloud, greet, help the teacher to avoid mistakes, provide complementary clarifications, and carry out physical tasks like handing out papers [8]. Recently, spurred by the pandemic, robots have also been used to conduct graduation ceremonies in Japan, Malaysia, and the Philippines.[2,3] Velinov et al. also reviewed recent studies on remote attendance robots, cataloguing benefits such as safety during a pandemic, and enhanced access for disabled, suspended, or remote students [28]. Yet, robots are still mostly rare in classrooms; Guggemos and colleagues, using a Pepper robot, targeted the

---

[2] businessinsider.com/philippines-sixth-graders-held-cyber-graduation-with-robots-20 20-6.

[3] breakingasia.com/gov/malaysian-university-using-robot-for-graduation-ceremonies-to-cut-virus-risk.

problem of how to design robots that will actually be accepted into real-world classrooms, identifying important characteristics such as adaptiveness, trustworthiness, social presence and appearance [15]. Halbach et al. also reported on the practical challenges of robust sound recognition when using Nao robots to facilitate language learning–also assisting staff and increasing engagement–in two trials over the duration of several weeks in some day-care centers [16]. Additionally, Trombly et al. investigated how to achieve effective group interactions, in implementing games with a teleoperated Pepper robot aimed to help children with Autism Spectrum Disorder (ASD), noting a positive trend of similar results when using human and robot instructors [27].

Robotics is also sometimes referred to in the "same breath" as XR, as in "Virtual, Augmented, Mixed Reality Human-Robot Interaction" (VAM-HRI); e.g., some interactions use both separately to get the best of both worlds, or use XR to add dynamic capabilities to robots [12,13]). XR encompasses a spectrum of applications which involve the real and virtual worlds to different degrees, such as Virtual Reality (VR; full, immersive simulations) and Augmented Reality (AR; digital entities are overlaid onto the real world), as expressed in Milgram's Continuum. Although software programs are typically less engaging than embodied learning with robots, a benefit is that they cost less to scale and can thus reach a wider audience. One recent interesting example is an AR app developed by Itamiya et al. to show kindergarten students what a fire or flash flood would be like in a memorable, immersive, safe, and engaging way, almost like they were "there"; e.g., by self-experimentation, the children were able to learn that moving close to the ground in a fire can be safer due to less smoke [18].[4] Various XR apps have been described that could also be used in education, such as Snap Camera with AR filters that can be used in Zoom, Sketchar which projects strokes onto a page step by step to help people to draw,[5] 3D Scanner App which allows scanning of arbitrary objects,[6] as well as magicplan[7] and ARki[8] which automatically measure rooms and allow architectural students to speculate about how a scene might look if it were designed differently (e.g., if a road had an overpass). XR applications are often written leveraging packages such as Apple's ARKit and Google's ARCore through game engines like Unreal Engine and Unity, where a hope is that standards like OpenXR and AR Foundation will help reduce "fragmentation", allowing teachers to more easily develop and port their ideas to a range of devices.[9]

On the other hand, new technologies also introduce new challenges, such as ethical concerns (e.g., [11,25]): For example, current robot and XR tools could be inaccessible to some (e.g., due to being costly, complex to use, or unable to

---

[4] youtube.com/watch?v=gWG-GXEZQtw.

[5] sketchar.io.

[6] 3dscannerapp.com.

[7] magicplan.app.

[8] darfdesign.com/arki.html.

[9] gmw3.com/2019/03/make-arkit-and-arcore-development-easier-with-unity-ar-foundation.

deal with vision or speech-related disabilities). Mental or physical harm could result (e.g., by enabling new kinds of abuse or trauma, or falling on someone). Also, a negative influence could otherwise be exerted (e.g., by reducing opportunities for student-teacher interactions). Some strategies to avoid such problems could include clear instructions on how robots and XR should be used; guidelines for detecting and handling abuse and a focus on safety; as well as more generally, incorporation of key values for responsible and sustainable design such as autonomy, justice, beneficence, and nonmaleficence. Given the vast space of possible learning interactions, what was unclear to us was how our teachers were experiencing the good and bad sides of these technologies.

Games and Gamification. Robotics and XR are also related to, and can be used for (serious) games and "gamification"–the use of engaging, game-inspired elements such as rewards like scores, virtual items, or achievement badges; progress tracking; competition; enjoyable narratives; and freedom to choose various ways to learn. For example, Parnes et al. have described an open platform, WalkAbout, which is a distributed virtual world application intended to engage and facilitate gamification in education (e.g. with points, activity tracking, and missions), that can act as an alternative to Zoom [22]. Also, various generic virtual worlds/game apps exist such as Decentraland, Second Life, Avakin Life, Roblox, World of Warcraft, Pokemon, and Minecraft. For example, the latter, although not free, was used to enable virtual graduation ceremonies by children in Japan, and meetings between teachers; other games such as Assassin's Creed have also allowed high school history students to explore and take quizzes related to Ancient Egypt.[10] Also of interest for education are "proximity chat" programs, such as Gather (Gather.town), Skittish, SpatialChat, Airmeet, Whereby, Rally, Daily, InSpace, Wonder, Kumospace, and Topia. Such programs make it easy for users themselves to dynamically form smaller groups for discussion, as in physical classes, which currently in Zoom would require effort for a host to coordinate.

At the same time, the literature also suggests the existence of a "dark side" of gamification [26]: Regarding the use of 12 game elements (denoted as Leaderboard, Badge, Point, Level, Progression, Social Status, Social Interaction, Instant Feedback, Avatar, Economy, Challenge and Narrative), Toda et al. reported negative effects included lack of interest or declining interest over time, demotivation due to being penalized, frustration due to not successfully fulfilling game goals, confusion about rules and complex game elements, distraction and transfer of focus to games rather than evaluation, and lingering worry that game activities could affect grades. Thus, as with robots and XR, appropriate design principles should be followed to realize the interesting opportunities that emerge from the use of such engaging tools and approaches, which we wished to learn more about.

---

[10] washingtonpost.com/video-games/2020/04/15/teachers-video-games-coronavirus-education-remote-learning.

Exam-Related Technologies. Various software programs are also being designed to help teachers to conduct exams, via proctoring, plagiarism detection, and automatic assessment and clustering. Tools like AutoProctor, e.g., with Google Forms, can be used to ensure that students complete tests within allotted times, there is no one else in view, and students do not switch to a different application; evidence such as trust scores and images can also be reviewed by human teachers afterwards.[11] Various plagiarism detection softwares also exist, such as Ouriginal, SafeAssign, Turnitin, and Copyscape, which match exam text with previous text in databases. Automatic assessment of English language ability has been conducted with the Duolingo English Test [23], and code has been automatically graded via nbgrader with JupyterHub[12], or CodeGrade.[13] As well, Overcode and interactive Bayesian Case Model (iBCM) seek to cluster students' programs in a way that helps teachers to understand the underlying quality of programming exam responses, which has been used in both on-campus or edX courses with thousands of students [19].

On the other hand, such new technologies also introduce new possibilities for misuse. For example, proctoring software can introduce privacy and security concerns in regard to surveillance of students and increased vulnerabilities [7]: Basically, room scans, checks, and monitoring could result in leakage of sensitive personal data, including audio; images and videos containing fingerprints, ID cards, or irises; or text representing addresses (IP, email, or home), names, phone numbers, ages, genders, passwords, medical conditions, or even keystroke cadence (e.g., for typed signatures). Furthermore, software can be hacked and used for malicious purposes, even after appearing to have been uninstalled.

Furthermore, it is also becoming increasingly easy to cheat on exams by using digital technologies [1]: In 2020, Brown et al. from OpenAI reported that their GPT-3 algorithm could automatically generate writing that humans couldn't easily identify as being machine-written [6]: Similarly, in spring 2022, 32 engineering teachers from our university were asked to guess which of 10 texts, representing answers to an engineering exam question, were authored by a human [10]: 5 of the texts were written by a human, and 5 generated by OpenAI's GPT-3 model Davinci (text-davinci-001). The resulting number of correct guesses was only marginally higher than random chance (58%), indicating that teachers mostly had no idea which answers were written by an AI or a human. Although a RoBERTa model fine-tuned to detect output from a related model, GPT-2, fared somewhat better, it also mistook one of the human answers as AI-generated, reporting a probability of only 0.02% that the human answer was real. Numerous other, similar services exist, such as Jasper.ai[14] and Contentbot.ai,[15] including some simple free demos that can be accessed online, as of fall 2022.[16]

---

[11] autoproctor.co.
[12] nbgrader.readthedocs.io/en/stable.
[13] codegrade.com.
[14] jasper.ai.
[15] contentbot.ai.
[16] app.inferkit.com/demo.

Various mitigation strategies could be followed: To avoid concerns arising from proctoring software, institutions can aim to communicate clear privacy and security standards (e.g., minimizing personal data and clarifying data retention periods), while also generally prioritizing ethical design in regard to justice, beneficence, non-maleficence, and autonomy. For exams, teachers could ask for figures in exam responses rather than only text, and conduct supervised written exams and oral exams in place of reports or programs. However, these are not perfect solutions. Exciting work is also being done now with automatic generation of images and videos, using tools like DALL-E, which can be tried out online in a reduced form.[17] Also, a challenge with requiring a higher degree of supervision is that teachers tend to have little time. One possibility for the future could be to use robots: e.g., as in the modified Kobuki robot designed by Al Tarabsheh and colleagues to proctor exams in a safe, contactless way, while navigating around a class, answering student questions, detecting cheating, and scanning exam papers at the end [2]. Similarly, oral exams can be time-consuming in large classes, and online oral exams might furthermore become susceptible to misuses of AI. For example, filters and DeepFakes can be used to change the appearance of a person, and the use of tools like Ecamm Live/Loopback to automate a person's behavior in meetings has been reported.[18] In short, there might be some "trouble brewing" in regard to the way the quality of learning is currently evaluated, suggesting the usefulness of raising the topic with our teachers. At the more general level, we wished to also obtain some additional insight into the kinds of new technologies that can help students to learn better and reduce teachers' workloads, based on our previous prototyping efforts [9].

2.2 Learning Formats

Academic institutions typically provide various guidelines and rules to teachers to support good learning. One concern is that administrators might not always hear all of the teachers' voices; for example, false consensus effect, or consensus bias, suggests that managers might sometimes assume that teachers who do not speak up share their beliefs [30].

In particular, the teaching environment is an important factor in learning that can be modified via technologies, where one scenario whose pros and cons have been weighed in previous work is remote learning–most often from the perspective of students: For example, a survey of 1224 university students in Ukraine conducted by Bakhov et al. suggested that remote learning offered important opportunities to study in comfort, work while studying, practice self-control and self-motivation, and engage with technologies; demerits for some included a perception of enhanced complexity, fatigue due to computer-based work, and a lack of required equipment and internet access [4]. In our previous work on digital socialization and AI in higher education, presented at a teachers' workshop, we also suggested some potential benefits and demerits exist from remote

---

[17] huggingface.co/spaces/dalle-mini/dalle-mini.

[18] cnet.com/tech/services-and-software/how-i-pre-recorded-myself-in-video-meetings-for-a-week.

teaching from a teacher's perspective:[19]: Some benefits of remote teaching can include wider access (people with disabilities, children, or who are sick or traveling), hygiene and safety (COVID-19), new opportunities for self-expression of roles, interests, and humor (e.g., the ability to send chat messages and use filters and backgrounds), more time with family at the "home office", greater ease of seeing/hearing/file-sharing, ability to turn off cameras and mics (to be free to periodically relax/exercise/hydrate/concentrate/talk with others), ease of generating recordings that students can pause, playback, and view at their own pace, and opportunities to test new possibilities for technology that could lead to enhanced educational experiences. Some demerits could include the difficulty in checking if people are engaged and understand what is being discussed (e.g. if students turn off cameras and mics), non-optimal home office setups (e.g., cramped, or in proximity to noisy neighbors, children or pets), possibly missing out on some communications due to disconnections/WiFi instability or sound troubles, embarrassing mishaps with some people not used to such technologies (e.g. appearing naked on camera), a lack of ability to sense touch, smell, or taste, difficulty in "going around the table", new possibilities for hacking vulnerabilities (e.g., snooping, "zoombombing", or identity fraud that could be related to deepfakes or "catfishing"), depression or sleep-reduction due to excessive screen time, and difficulty of closely monitoring others (which could help some managers to feel empowered and in control).

However, more options exist, such as blended and hybrid learning. Blended learning, which combines some physical and some remote classes, was considered outside of the scope of this paper due to the difficulty of obtaining feedback on the potentially infinite number of combinations that could arise. Rather here, we looked also toward hybrid learning, which provides teachers and students with more freedom over their own educational experiences–allowing them to participate physically or remotely, depending on what is perceived as best–albeit at the cost of some extra work required from teachers.

Although decisions in regard to learning format are often made by management, e.g., in regard to when to provide online learning throughout the pandemic period, it was unclear to us how teachers might currently feel about learning formats and technology, and the degree to which individuals should have a choice about how they learn; it seemed like some teachers might have strong opinions, given that such decisions can have a large effect on their daily teaching, which we wanted to check.

3   Methods

To gain insight into how teachers perceive current technologies, we conducted an online survey at our university in southern Sweden in October 2021.

---

[19] youtube.com/watch?v=V8uYLqqTmec.

3.1 Participants

Feedback was obtained from the employees of Halmstad University, a small university founded in 1983, with 12,039 students in total (approximately 500 international) and 607 employees, of whom 384 are academic staff, 59 are professors, and 88 are PhD students, as of 2021.[20] The turnover is 70% education and 30% research, and 50 study programs and 200 single subject courses are available, organized within four schools:

- **Business.** Business, Innovation, and Sustainability
- **IT.** Information Technology
- **Health.** Health and Welfare
- **Education.** Education, Humanities, and Social Sciences

The survey was sent via an email link to all employees at each school, of whom 42 responded, comprising 16 in Business, 11 in IT, 8 in Health, and 5 in Education; 2 respondents indicated they were not actively teaching. Thus, the response rate was approximately 11% (42/384).

3.2 Ethics

The principles described in the General Data Protection Regulation (GDPR, 2018) and Declaration of Helsinki (World Medical Association, 2018) were followed: the purpose of the study and basic approach were explained, informed consent was obtained in writing before beginning, and data security measures were followed.

3.3 Procedure

Participants were sent a link to a Google Forms survey, which took approximately 5–10 minutes to complete. The survey was roughly centered around the two themes described previously, new technologies and learning formats:

- **Usage of new technologies. First, teachers were asked to describe their use of technologies related to robots/XR, games, and exams (not just Zoom) in their lessons. Simple yes/no questions were used for convenience in tallying answers, along with text fields which the respondents could use to freely add explanations.**
- Preferences for learning formats. In the second half of the survey, teachers were asked, for each of three cases (regular classes, exams, and teacher meetings), to select one of three options: if everyone should have to meet physically or online, or have a choice to meet either physically or online. (Likert scale questions were also included in case more refined analysis might be required, but were

---

[20] hh.se/english/about-the-university/facts-about-halmstad-university/halmstad-univ
ersity-in-numbers.html.

not further analyzed in this study, since the results were felt to be sufficiently clear.) A yes/no question was used to check if teachers had ever conducted a hybrid class or meeting. Also, as before, text fields were used to collect any optional comments.

Our expectation was as follows:

- Usage of new technologies. Very few, or possibly none, of our teachers would have worked with robots or XR. Some might have tried exam tools, and more would have used games.
- Preferences for learning formats. Teachers would be split in opinion regarding the benefits of various teaching formats, and have little experience with hybrid teaching.

3.4   Results

Figure 1 shows some of the main quantitative results of the survey. Use of new technologies was generally low, as had been expected, and a difference was seen in preferences for learning formats based on the context.

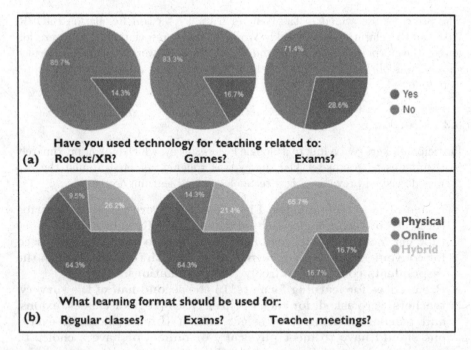

Fig. 1. Main results of the survey regarding: (a) use of technologies, (b) and preferences for learning formats.

Engaging New Technologies. About one in five respondents had witnessed some usage of robots and XR in the classroom, of which one in seven had themselves used robots or XR (21.4% vs. 14.3%). Specifically, participants described having used robots (3 participants), VR (3), and AR (1), with some indicating an intent to re-use (4). These tools were used to allow the students to learn about technology, to permit telepresence, and to enable learning experiences in a safe and easy manner that would not otherwise be possible (viz., to help students to see and learn about the aquatic world, large far-away ships, bullying at the workplace, and molecular shapes). Teachers who had not yet used such technologies indicated either interest (7), or lack of interest (3), in trying them. Some described lacking the competence needed (10), not being sure about benefits and what the technologies could be used for (8), having too much work and too little time and energy (5), or feeling that they had no access or opportunity (3).

Similarly, one in six had used some kind of game tools, including card games, simulation games, Quizizz (quizizz.com), Kahoot (kahoot.com), and physics and chemistry concept simulations and games (phet.colorado.edu). One teacher also mentioned incorporating game mechanics and having students develop their own games. Reasons for using game tools included to engage students, practice key concepts, and support interaction at workshop sessions.

As well, about one in three to four of the teachers had used some kind of tool to facilitate examinations, which included our learning management system BlackBoard (9), Moodle (to dynamically randomize multiple choice questions), GitHub (possibly also to check student involvement and activity in pushing commits during group work), and Safe Exam Browser (which locks a student's screen to deter academic dishonesty)–although one teacher noted potential dangers of using new digital tools given strict regulations regarding exams.

Teaching Formats. Some results are depicted in Fig. 2 and Table 1.

Almost all teachers (85.7%) indicated they had given a hybrid class or meeting. Teachers differed strongly in their experiences, with some saying hybrid classes went well and they would do it again (12), versus others who described it less favorably (7), even as a disaster, horrible experience, or worst-case scenario. There was some agreement from both sides that hybrid learning poses challenges (4) and that it helps to have assistance from others (2). Specific challenges mentioned included focusing attention (4), communicating with the online students (3), and treating students equally (2).

Relating to the kind of activity, our teachers preferred campus-based learning for both regular classes and exams, and a hybrid set-up for meetings between teachers (e.g., to discuss evaluations and plans for development within programmes and courses). Differences also appeared to exist between subject areas, as shown in Fig. 2: For example, some Business teachers felt online exams were acceptable, with fewer teachers choosing hybrid. As well, 100% of the IT respondents preferred hybrid meetings for teacher meetings. Online meetings were more popular among Health teachers than hybrid meetings, and physical teaching seemed to be most preferred among Education teachers.

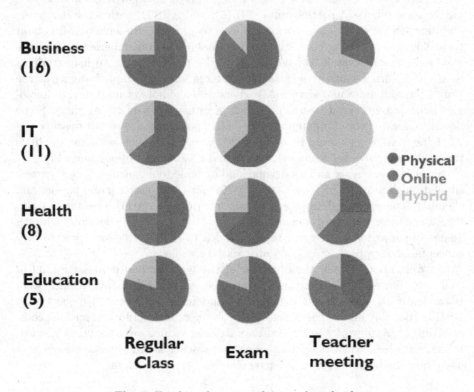

Fig. 2. Teaching format preferences by school.

Various free comments were also provided at the end of the survey, as shown in Table 1. Comments have been translated from Swedish when needed and paraphrased to remove specific details.

4   Discussion

In summary, the contribution of the current paper lies in reporting on some teachers' experiences with, and attitudes toward edtech, with responses obtained from all schools at our university:

New Technologies. Rates for usage of robots and XR, although low, were higher than we had expected, which felt promising; this appeared to support our idea that silo effects might exist in the communication of teachers' work, even at a small university, and raised the question of how such communication could be further facilitated. Another positive point was that applications covered

Table 1. Comments about teaching formats.

More participants attended when hybrid
The text messaging function online is nice because people who might not otherwise ask questions out loud feel like they can, also recording
My students appreciate very much being able to attend even if they cannot physically do so. It does cost me an extra 15–20 min of preparation before and after the teaching for preparation and packing but I reckon it is well worth it
During the pandemic, I built my "own" studio in a classroom where I lectured in front of a camera online. On one occasion I was "stormed" by a group of students who wanted to sit at the back of the classroom. That was quite a positive experience
I would like that online or hybrid is here to stay. I remember arguments with managers in the past about physical presence, and now it has been demonstrated that the world can keep rolling. I must also say that I have been much more productive during the pandemic than ever, and I can attribute it directly to remote work
I think that this new world (of teaching with technology) is very interesting. I would love to learn how to use and work with games, robots and VR. I think that courses for us teachers would be a golden opportunity to encourage new thinking about pedagogy and to make teaching more fun
Using technology and distance formats has helped a lot of students who need to travel longer distances. It has also opened up the opportunity to do small research and group discussion projects, or to engage with online simulators/teaching materials during lectures/classes. ... but I do like the familiarity of actually meeting people too. I feel you get more personal, meaningful responses in a real classroom (just a gut feeling). I intend therefore to use a hybrid format, trying to get the most out of each method
I think that hybrid is more productive, e.g. you can switch between tasks in seconds (don't have to move physically), you can attend if you are travelling, you can meet physically if you do not want to miss the social interaction, etc.
3D holograms in natural size would be ideal
I gave the message to the "online" people that they would not be focused on
Hybrid is not good for large classes, and is better for small ones
Hybrid format are limited by 1-mindset, 2-available technology, 3-a clear framework for hybrid meetings
It's hard to say how a teaching format should be, since it depends on the kind of class or exam, and the intended learning outcomes
Exceptions are okay (e.g., if ill, taking care of a sick child, or abroad) but to always cater to two options is useless
We should be consistent as teachers to avoid confusing students (all teachers should offer hybrid or not, at the programme level)
There can be concerns with copyrights and GDPR

a broad spectrum of subject areas, from physics and marine science to psychology, indicating such technologies can be generally useful. Furthermore, although correlation does not indicate causation, similar rates for awareness and usage, along with comments from some teachers, suggested the potential usefulness of spreading awareness of potential benefits and use cases. In contrast, the rate of game tool usage was lower than expected, suggesting that spreading information also about easy-to-use tools like Gather.town could be useful. The rate of using technology to facilitate examinations was low, as expected; furthermore, the majority of responses merely described using tools that all teachers at our university are obligated to use, and for simple functions like randomly ordering quiz questions. This felt interesting because there seems to currently be a mismatch in teachers' abilities to use technology for exams and the growing ease in which technology can be misused (e.g., in automatically writing reports in a manner that is difficult both for human teachers and computer programs to detect).

Teaching Formats. As expected, not all teachers agreed on teaching formats, but the rough pattern was that slightly over half of teachers favored forcing students to attend physical classes, while allowing teachers a choice in hybrid teacher meetings. The former result might have been in part because our university up until the pandemic had almost exclusively focused on campus-based education, which might have contributed to a conservative trend in thinking. Also, one potential explanation for why the preference for teachers and students was different was described by one teacher, who commented that there is a large difference in Zoom if faces can be seen or not, and that teachers often show their faces but students often turn off their cameras.

Regarding differences between schools, the preference for online exams among Business teachers might have been since some online education had been conducted there prior to the pandemic. The 100% preference in IT for hybrid meetings might have been due to various factors, including a positive attitude in engineers toward using technology, as well as some history of difficulty in finding sufficiently large, close-by physical spaces for school meetings that allow all attending to hear and see presentations easily. The preference for online meetings rather than hybrid among Health teachers might have arisen due to increased awareness of health concerns: a hybrid format, while offering more freedom and convenience, can also be unsafe like physical classes during a pandemic. The preference for physical classes among Education teachers might have emerged from such teachers having been drawn to our university, given the university's almost complete historic focus on physical teaching.

We had also not expected the high rate of teachers who reported having experience with hybrid activities. In line with this, teachers did not mention using the university's hybrid classrooms in the survey; e.g., one comment was "Do we have hybrid classrooms?" One possible explanation for the high self-reported rate was that the term "hybrid" might have seemed ambiguous; it's unclear if a positive answer might have meant that a teacher had connected a laptop or smartphone to Zoom, attended an online school meeting from their office, or even merely uploaded a recording of a classroom lecture. Likewise, this raised questions about what a hybrid classroom should look like, and what it means for a classroom to be considered "hybrid".

More teachers seemed to be for hybrid than against, but the ones who were against it seemed strongly so. The challenge of focus was mentioned, as more things to keep track of puts more extra work on the teacher, suggesting the benefit of finding ways to make the process easier (e.g., a feature to automatically read comments in the chat window could help solitary teachers who have their hands full managing presentations).

Interestingly as well, the free comments at the end of the survey mostly focused on learning format preferences and hybrid classes, possibly since this had been the last question beforehand in the survey, or because few teachers had experience with new technologies like robots but all teachers had experience with campus and online teaching, possibly leading to stronger feelings.

4.1   Limitations and Future Work

Our study is limited by the group of teachers who provided feedback, representing a small sample size from only one small university in Sweden engaged in only four subject areas. "Demand characteristics" might also have played a role; i.e., some teachers might have said what they thought we wanted to hear. Moreover, due to the exploratory nature of this study and the rapidly changing state of new technology, an existing survey with the questions we wanted to ask was not found, leading us to create our own survey; this leaves questions about the reliability and validity of the questionnaire items. To avoid survey fatigue, the number of questions was also limited; e.g., feedback was not obtained regarding blended learning. As two comments in the survey highlighted, the survey also did not probe teachers' perceptions of how meetings between students and stakeholders outside campus should take place. Also, although this was outside of the current scope, we acknowledge that technology is not just for teachers or teaching, in that teachers should strive to equip students with the tools they need to shape the world for themselves and become "agents of change".

Our next planned step is to conduct a workshop at our university. PDC will be scaffolded by providing some basic info and links to tutorials, which will also be used in courses for students on XR and robotics. As one comment in the survey mentioned, teachers can also be advised to start simple (e.g., H5P[21] to create HTML5 content like quizzes with Javascript) and then progress from there. Benefits and a list of specific examples of use cases will be discussed. Opportunities at our university will be clarified by sharing a list of tools available (first hardware, then potentially software). For exams, teachers will be shown automatic writing tools and mitigation strategies will be discussed (e.g., tools for detection and how to select exams to deter misuse of such technologies). Regarding teaching formats, we will spread knowledge of classrooms aimed to

---

[21] h5p.org.

support hybrid learning, and discuss experiences and strategies. Additionally, support will be sought at the organizational level, since time seems vital (as seemed to also be supported by a separate survey we had conducted previously on digital competences): e.g., how we can allocate time for teachers to take the leap into pedagogical development, since it is not enough just to have access to technologies. In addition to supporting awareness, we aim to also continue to explore how to design technological prototypes that can help teachers and students to achieve better learning.

Thus, the survey results seemed to suggest some interesting possibilities that will be explored in future work. By understanding the opportunities and challenges related to how our teachers are working with technology, our aim is that this line of research will hopefully help to support PDC and enriched educational experiences, within the ever-changing "new world" of teaching with technology.

References

1. Abd-Elaal, E.S., Gamage, S.H., Mills, J.E., et al.: Artificial intelligence is a tool for cheating academic integrity. In: 30th Annual Conference for the Australasian Association for Engineering Education (AAEE 2019): Educators Becoming Agents of Change: Innovate, Integrate, Motivate, pp. 397–403. Engineers Australia Brisbane, Queensland (2019)
2. Al Tarabsheh, A., et al.: Towards contactless learning activities during pandemics using autonomous service robots. Appl. Sci. **11**(21), 10449 (2021)
3. Almeida, F., Simoes, J.: The role of serious games, gamification and industry 4.0 tools in the education 4.0 paradigm. Contemp. Educ. Technol. **10**(2), 120–136 (2019)
4. Bakhov, I., Opolska, N., Bogus, M., Anishchenko, V., Biryukova, Y.: Emergency distance education in the conditions of COVID-19 pandemic: experience of Ukrainian universities. Educ. Sci. **11**(7), 364 (2021)
5. Brevik, L.M., Gudmundsdottir, G.B., Lund, A., Strømme Aanesland, T.: Transformative agency in teacher education: fostering professional digital competence. Teach. Teach. Educ. Int. J. Res. Stud. **86** (2019)
6. Brown, T., et al.: Language models are few-shot learners. Adv. Neural. Inf. Process. Syst. **33**, 1877–1901 (2020)
7. Coghlan, S., Miller, T., Paterson, J.: Good proctor or "big brother"? Ethics of online exam supervision technologies. Philos. Technol. **34**(4), 1581–1606 (2021)
8. Cooney, M., Leister, W.: Using the engagement profile to design an engaging robotic teaching assistant for students. Robotics **8**(1), 21 (2019)
9. Cooney, M., Sjöberg, J.: Playful AI prototypes to support creativity and emotions in learning. In: Sjöberg, J., Møller, A.K. (eds.) DLI 2021. Lecture Notes of the Institute for Computer Sciences, Social Informatics and Telecommunications Engineering, vol. 435, pp. 129–140. Springer, Cham (2022). https://doi.org/10.1007/978-3-031-06675-7_10
10. Engelbrektsson, O., Olsson, A.: A thesis that writes itself: on the threat of AI-generated essays within academia (2022)
11. Evans, J.: White paper-the IEEE global initiative on ethics of extended reality (XR) report-extended reality (XR) ethics in medicine. IEEE Standards Association (2022)

12. Goktan, I., Ly, K., Groechel, T.R., Mataric, M.J.: Augmented reality appendages for robots: design considerations and recommendations for maximizing social and functional perception. arXiv preprint arXiv:2205.06747 (2022)
13. Groechel, T., et al.: Kinesthetic curiosity: towards personalized embodied learning with a robot tutor teaching programming in mixed reality. In: Siciliano, B., Laschi, C., Khatib, O. (eds.) ISER 2020. SPAR, vol. 19, pp. 245–252. Springer, Cham (2021). https://doi.org/10.1007/978-3-030-71151-1_22
14. Gudmundsdottir, G.B., Hatlevik, O.E.: Newly qualified teachers' professional digital competence: implications for teacher education. Eur. J. Teach. Educ. **41**(2), 214–231 (2018)
15. Guggemos, J., Seufert, S., Sonderegger, S.: Humanoid robots in higher education: evaluating the acceptance of Pepper in the context of an academic writing course using the UTAUT. Br. J. Edu. Technol. **51**(5), 1864–1883 (2020)
16. Halbach, T., Schulz, T., Leister, W., Solheim, I.: Robot-enhanced language learning for children in norwegian day-care centers. Multimodal Technol. Interact. **5**(12), 74 (2021)
17. Hendler, J.: Designing systems "out of the box". In: Robots for Kids: Exploring New Technologies for Learning, p. 1 (2000)
18. Itamiya, T., Tohara, H., Nasuda, Y.: Augmented reality floods and smoke smartphone app disaster scope utilizing real-time occlusion. In: IEEE Conference on Virtual Reality and 3D User Interfaces (IEEE VR) (2019). https://ieeexplore.ieee.org/document/8798269
19. Kim, B., Glassman, E., Johnson, B., Shah, J.: iBCM: interactive Bayesian case model empowering humans via intuitive interaction. MIT CSAIL (Computer Science and Artificial Intelligence Laboratory) Technical report (2015)
20. Laufer, M., et al.: Digital higher education: a divider or bridge builder? Leadership perspectives on edtech in a COVID-19 reality. Int. J. Educ. Technol. High. Educ. **18**(1), 1–17 (2021)
21. Mourtzis, D., Angelopoulos, J., Panopoulos, N.: A teaching factory paradigm for personalized perception of education based on extended reality (XR). Available at SSRN 4071876 (2022)
22. Parnes, P., Backman, Y., Gardelli, V.: Walkabout-a net-based interactive multiuser 3D-environment for enhanced and engaging learning. In: 8: e utvecklingskonferensen för Sveriges ingenjörsutbildningar (2021)
23. Settles, B., T LaFlair, G., Hagiwara, M.: Machine learning-driven language assessment. Trans. Assoc. Comput. Linguist. **8**, 247–263 (2020)
24. Singh, J., Steele, K., Singh, L.: Combining the best of online and face-to-face learning: Hybrid and blended learning approach for COVID-19, post vaccine, & post-pandemic world. J. Educ. Technol. Syst. **50**(2), 140–171 (2021)
25. Slater, M., et al.: The ethics of realism in virtual and augmented reality. Front. Virtual Reality **1** (2020). https://doi.org/10.3389/frvir.2020.00001, https://www.frontiersin.org/articles/10.3389/frvir.2020.00001
26. Toda, A.M., Valle, P.H.D., Isotani, S.: The dark side of gamification: an overview of negative effects of gamification in education. In: Cristea, A.I., Bittencourt, I.I., Lima, F. (eds.) HEFA 2017. CCIS, vol. 832, pp. 143–156. Springer, Cham (2018). https://doi.org/10.1007/978-3-319-97934-2_9

27. Trombly, M., Shahverdi, P., Huang, N., Chen, Q., Korneder, J.: Robot-mediated group instruction for children with ASD: a pilot study. In: RO-MAN 2022 (2022)
28. Velinov, A., Koceski, S., Koceska, N.: A review of the usage of telepresence robots in education. Balkan J. Appl. Math. Inform. 4(1), 27–40 (2021)
29. Williamson, B.: Meta-edtech (2021)
30. Wilson, M.R., Corr, P.J.: Managing 'academic value': the 360-degree perspective. Perspect. Policy Pract. High. Educ. 22(1), 4–10 (2018)

Making Fiscal Policy Engaging for Students in Social Studies by Used Game-Based Learning

Mads Strømberg Petersen [ID], Niklas Lee Skjold Hansen, Gustav Jakobsen, Daniel Henriksen, and Thomas Bjørner[✉] [ID]

Department of Architecture, Design & Media Technology, Aalborg University, A. C. Meyersvænge 15, 2450 Copenhagen, SV, Denmark
tbj@create.aau.dk

Abstract. In this study, we present the effect of game-based learning within the fiscal policy subject in the Danish Gymnasium (upper secondary). The study included 51 students from two classes in social studies. One class with 31 students was included in the experimental study, which employed the game-based learning as part of reading about fiscal policy. One class with 20 students served as the control group and engaged only in an analog reading of fiscal policy. We based the evaluation criteria, which we assessed through a questionnaire, on items from the user engagement scale and a knowledge test. Further, the evaluation consisted of an interview with the teacher in social science and interviews with nine students. The findings revealed positive effects in favour of game-based learning, especially in students' interest in the learning material and being immersed while learning. The interviews revealed positive feedback toward the game-based learning, especially regarding the novelty and learning outcome. The results from the knowledge test were only slightly in favour for the experimental gaming group. Previous research has the same findings, but there is a lack of improved game design suggestions for how to make the perfect match between engagement and learning.

Keywords: Game-based learning · Serious games · Engagement · Fiscal policy · Students

1 Introduction

The Danish Gymnasium offers a 3-year upper secondary program. This qualifies a student for admission to higher education (e.g., universities or professional education). Internationally, there are reported various educational gender differences [1], which also refers to the Danish Gymnasium. The differences, among others, that need to be addressed concern differences in grade, reading engagement, dropout rate, and time use on video games. Danish female students overall score higher than Danish male students do with a 7.4 average versus the male students with a 6.9 average [2]. This gap has only

---

Research unit: Me-GA (Media Innovation & Game Research).

© ICST Institute for Computer Sciences, Social Informatics and Telecommunications Engineering 2023
Published by Springer Nature Switzerland AG 2023. All Rights Reserved
E. Brooks et al. (Eds.): DLI 2022, LNICST 493, pp. 153–167, 2023.
https://doi.org/10.1007/978-3-031-31392-9_12

increased in the last five years [2]. In subjects demanding more text reading, such as in social science, female students' grades are 1.4 points higher on average [2]. According to PISA [1], with an evaluation of the 15-year-old´s skills in reading, 10 other comparable countries scored significantly higher than the Danish students did. Almost no changes have been observed in the Danish students' reading skills since 2015, especially among the weak readers. One perspective into the problem could be to focus more on the reading engagement [3, 4] to provide further intrinsic and extrinsic motivation to start reading. Young males have scored the lowest in reading engagement [1], which could explain the lower grade for male students in the text-heavy subjects [2]. Male students also have a higher dropout rate than female students have, equal to around 20% for males and 15% for females [2]. Another difference between young males and females (aged 15) is that males play computer games more often and play for longer periods when playing [5]. For males, 28% played 2 h or more when playing, which was only 10% of the females. Furthermore, 28% of the males and 19% of the females played computer games several times daily.

In today's educational learning, game-based learning is becoming increasingly integrated as part of the teachers' didactic toolbox, in which games can supplement other types of learning materials [6, 7]. Others have already well documented how game-based learning can promote learning goals and stimulate reading engagement [7–13]. However, a continuing problem has understood the underlying design processes that govern the success of game-based learning. The research question for this study is as follows: Can game-based learning increase engagement in fiscal policies as part of the curriculum in social studies for Danish Gymnasium students?

2   Previous Research

Like other scholars [14, 15], we define a serious game as a one designed for a primary purpose other than pure entertainment. In this study, we used the term game-based learning [5, 16, 17] as a subgenre of serious games. However, it is worth mentioning that game-based learning has been practiced since at least the 20th century [15], and paper-based games became popular in the 1960s and 1970s. During the last decade, the use of digital game-based learning has gained popularity, along with computer gaming for various educational aspects. There is no consensus on what defines game-based learning, and it used in divergent ways, focusing on various perspectives depending on their purpose, the players' goals, and content [14, 18]. Furthermore, some categorical problems often exist within mixed terminologies (e.g., game-based learning, serious games, and gamification), and their connection to specific learning goals. Scholars have described multiple principles for game-based learning [5–8], including a focus on reading engagement [10, 19–24]. Important aspects of game-based learning and reading engagement include realism, feedback, discovery, repetition, guidance, flow, digital storytelling, social interaction, briefing, and debriefing [10, 19–24]. Furthermore, motivation is important. Reading engagement, both in game-based learning and in other media, including analog media, requires the reader's motivation [4, 20]. This involves aspects such as important elements within the text's content, text comprehension, knowledge acquisition, and social interactions that employ knowledge and lessons the text teaches [4, 20]. Scholars have also emphasized the specific aspects of intrinsic motivation as important when designing game-based learning for reading engagement [19–26]. These can include elements such as curiosity, a desire for a challenge, flow, involvement, and narrative engagement [25, 26]. The latter [27] seems important within game-based learning games that focus on reading engagement because of its relation to the story experienced while playing the game. Thus, it may result in imaginative immersion, narrative involvement, or narrative immersion. The desire to find the key to the office and adjustment the fiscal policy, or to obtain cheaper tickets to the music festival, might evoke curiosity, suspense, and narrative engagement, making the players want to continue playing [27]. Studies have also included transmedia storytelling as a gateway to reading engagement or educational purposes by combining analog reading with parts of the story included within game-based learning [23, 28]. There are still major challenges of how to measure the learning outcomes of game-based learning. The learning outcomes are often measured via self-report and knowledge tests [29]. Previous studies have reported that gamed-based learning has positive outcomes regarding being more engaging compared to traditional classroom instruction [7, 10, 24, 29, 30]. However, the effects of game-based learning on specific knowledge tests are more diverse and inconclusive [29].

3   Methods

3.1   Participants

This study is made in cooperation with a teacher in social science at a Danish Gymnasium. The Gymnasium is situated in the center of Copenhagen with 390 students across five lines of study, including science, languages, and social studies. This study included two classes consisting of 51 students in social science. Both classes had the same teacher. Class A consisted of 31 students with 13 males and 18 females. Class A functioned as the experimental group that used video games as a transmedia storytelling for the upcoming lecture about fiscal policy. Class B consisted of 20 students with 14 males and 5 females, and one student outside the gender dichotomy. Class B functioned as a control group for the evaluation, provided with the same reading and evaluation criteria, but without playing the game (only analog reading). The teacher in social science selected which of the classes would be in the experimental group and which would be the control group. Based on self-reporting, there was no difference between the two groups regarding time spent on computer gaming per week (Table 1). The groups were also similar in their interest in social studies, and their self-reported assessment for answering correctly to most questions in social studies (Table 1).

All participants gave informed consent and were informed that they could withdraw from the study at any time and their participation did not influence their grade. In addition, all participants were provided with anonymous ID numbers, and all data were labeled with these IDs. We applied special considerations when recruiting teenagers (ages 17–19) in accordance with Danish data law, the international code of conduct and ethical approval from the Gymnasium.

Table 1. Characteristics for Class A—the experimental gaming group (in grey); characteristics for Class B—the control group (in white) with analog reading only.

1=0-5 hrs weekly. 2=6-10 hrs weekly. 3=11-20 hrs weekly. 4=21-30 hrs weekly. 5=30+ hrs weekly	1	2	3	4	5	Total
How much time do you spend on video games on a weekly basis	15	3	7	2	0	27
	6	3	6	2	1	18
1=Strongly disagree. 2=Disagree. 3.=Neither agree or disagree. 4=Agree. 5=Strongly Agree.						
I am interested in social studies	0	0	4	9	7	20
	0	0	2	5	9	16
I can answer correctly to most questions in social studies	0	0	5	13	2	20
	1	0	7	6	2	16

3.2 Procedure

The procedure (Fig. 1) for Class A (Exp = the experimental gaming group) included first a written introduction from the teacher with instructions of what to read. This was followed by an instruction from the researchers of how to download the game. Students could ask some of the present researchers if there were any downloading problems. After gameplay, the students filled in a two-part questionnaire. The user engagement scale (short form) inspired Part 1 [31]. Part 2 consisted of questions regarding a knowledge check of fiscal policy, as provided within the game's learning content. After the gameplay session and filling in the questionnaire, nine students (seven females and two males) were interviewed. The interviews took place as friendship pairs, in which three students were interviewed simultaneously in three groups. As a method, friendship pairs can encourage the participants of this age group to feel more comfortable [32], thus facilitating a more open and deep discussion that might give the interview more spontaneity and surprising twists. Further, after two weeks, we interviewed the social studies teacher. The interview followed a semi-structured interview guide.

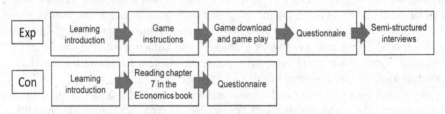

Fig. 1. The procedure for the experimental group (Exp) and the control group (Con).

Class B (the control group) received the same instructions from the teacher (Fig. 1), and had the same questions for the user engagement scale and knowledge check as Class A had. However, Class B did not play the game, but were only reading in the economics book.

3.3 Data Analysis

The items from the user engagement scale and the knowledge check were analyzed by a Shapiro–Wilk test for normality and Levene's test for homogeneity of variance. An independent samples t-test was performed in SPSS on parametric data and the Mann–Whitney U test for non-parametric data. Descriptive statistics was performed on the data from the user engagement scale reported via cumulative frequency. All the interviews were analyzed via traditional coding [33]. The coding followed four steps: organizing, recognizing, coding, and interpretation. Researchers transcribed the interviews and organized and prepared them for data. The codes in each interview were labelled in the predefined themes, although providing the possibility for additional themes. The data were analyzed via content analysis [33]. Intercoder reliability [34] was measured through Cohen's kappa for the friendship pair interviews. Intercoder reliability assesses the agreement among multiple coders for how they assign codes to text sections and can be used to assess consistency and validity among the codes [34]. The use of the Intercoder reliability resulted in a score of 0.86, which suggests a very strong agreement between the two coders for the codes applied based on the interview data.

4 Design and Implementation

The game was developed in the Unity Engine version 2021, utilizing asset packs from the Unity Store for the majority of the included 3D models. The in-game story takes places in the family home of the Minister for Finance. The home-alone teenage son (the main character) would like to join the Roskilde Festival in Denmark, which is one of Europe's largest music festivals. However, by fiscal policy, the teenage son would like to make an effect on the festival's prices. There are specific fiscal policy choices to make, as well to find the father's (the Minister for Finance) key to his home office. The home consists of five rooms, including the kitchen (Fig. 2), which opens to the living room, the office, the hallway, the bedroom, and the bathroom. At all times, in the upper right corner, there was information for the players regarding what to do next, for example, as in Fig. 2, "Explore the living room" (Udforsk stuen).

Before gameplay, the students were provided with the game controls in an introductory tutorial. The instructions appeared visually showing the keys (WASD, the arrows, or the mouse) to use for in-game controls and navigation. As the players discovered interactive objects, hints were shown, including which buttons to use for interaction (e.g., press E for interaction). To promote concentration, the game implemented visual and auditory stimuli using interactive objects that rewarded the player with a voiceover of the written text. The tasks (objects) needed to be completed in a specific order to ensure that the students received the story chronologically and followed the plot for adjusting the fiscal policy accordingly. To highlight the reading objects, a particle system (Fig. 3) was implemented on the objects. The particles made it easier for the players to identify the objects that needed to progress in the story. To avoid confusing players, the particles disappeared once activated.

To evoke further engagement, sound effects were added when picking up clues or keys, which simultaneously provided immediate feedback. At all times, it was possible

Fig. 2. The family home of the Minister for Finance. A particle system highlighted the reading objects

Fig. 3. A particle system highlighted the reading objects.

to read in the notebook "Press C to open or close the notebook" (Fig. 4, lower left corner), with the possibility off going back to re-read learnings about fiscal policy.

To provide reading engagement about fiscal policy, we provided the readings in different formats (Fig. 5), for example, as provided on the iPad (Fig. 5, left), in the notebook (Fig. 5, right), as text messages on the mobile phone, or stickers on the fridge.

Further, to provide engagement, we used an interactive push button system during the game to encourage the students to provide correct answers within the fiscal policy (Fig. 6).

Fig. 4. A notebook was present with possibilities to read about fiscal policy at all times.

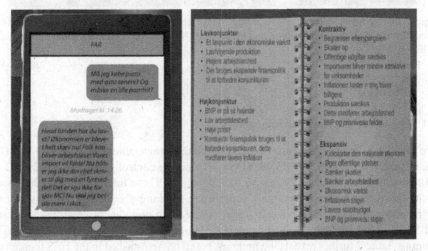

Fig. 5. The readings were present in different formats, e.g., on an Ipad or in a notebook.

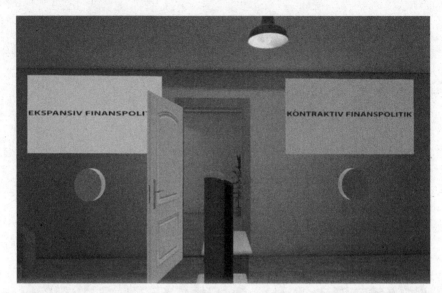

Fig. 6. Interactive push buttons for learning engagement in fiscal policy. Left (red) button is the choice of expansionary fiscal policy, and to the right (blue), is the choice of contractionary fiscal policy.

5 Findings

5.1 Game-Based Learning Engagement

We found significant difference by t-test in the user engagement scale (UES) between the experimental group (M = 3.68, SD = .50) and the control group (M = 3.29, SD = .40) conditions; t(34) = − 2.48, p = .018, (d = .46). These findings suggest that using game-based learning can positively supplement teaching about fiscal policies among Gymnasium students. These results reflect those from previous research based on the UES [7, 24], which also revealed an increased engagement in a learning context due to gaming. Table 2 further reveals the findings, based on items asked in the UES (perceived usability excluded).

The item from the UES that yielded the highest mean score (M = 4.00, SD = 0.68) was Q3.2 in the aesthetic appeal (Table 2), where 21 students in the experimental gaming group either totally agreed or agreed that the learning about fiscal policies was visually well communicated. In contrast, only nine students in the control group agreed on this. This means that the game was well designed, and it added further visual communication aspects. At the same time, and interestingly, the only item in the questionnaire (Table 2) where the control group had a higher mean score than the experimental group did was also within the aesthetic appeal. However, the mean difference is low, thus this finding comes with some uncertainties. Nevertheless, we were surprised that the score for the question "Learning about fiscal policies was interesting" (Q3.1) was not in more favor of the experimental gaming group. In the items for the focused attention in the UES, the experimental group had a small increase in the mean score (Q1.1: M = 3.42, SD = 0.72;

Table 2. Findings from the items in the User Engagement. The experimental gaming group (in grey), and the control group (in white) with analog reading only.

1=Strongly Disagree. 2=Disagree. 3=Neither Agree or Disagree. 4=Agree. 5=Strongly Agree.	1	2	3	4	5	n	Mean	SD	Mean diff.
Focused Attention:									
Q1.1: The time flew by while I	0	3	13	14	1	31	3.42	0.72	+0.37
learned about fiscal policies	0	4	11	5	0	20	3.05	0.69	
Q1.2: I was immersed while learning	0	5	10	12	2	29	3.38	0.86	+0.18
about fiscal policies	0	4	10	4	2	20	3.20	0.89	
Aesthetic Appeal:									
Q3.1: Learning about fiscal policies	0	2	7	18	1	28	3.64	0.68	-0.04
was interesting	0	0	8	9	2	19	3.68	0.67	
Q3.2: Learning about fiscal policies	0	0	6	15	6	27	4.00	0.68	+0.50
was visually well communicated	0	0	9	9	0	18	3.50	0.51	
Rewarding:									
Q4.1: Learning about fiscal policies	0	2	8	13	4	27	3.70	0.82	+0.14
was worthwhile	0	0	8	10	0	18	3.56	0.51	
Q4.2: It was a rewarding experience	0	0	9	17	1	27	3.70	0.54	+0.37
to learn about fiscal policies	0	2	9	6	1	18	3.33	0.77	
Q4.3: I became interested in the	0	0	9	16	2	27	3.74	0.59	+0.57
learning material	0	3	9	6	0	18	3.17	0.71	

Q2.2: M = 3.38, SD = 0.86) compared to the control group (Q1.1: M = 3.05, SD = 0.69; Q2.2: M = 3.20, SD = 0.89). The findings reveal that the game-based learning scored better regarding providing immersion about fiscal policy in contrast to the non-gaming control group. The experimental gaming group scored higher in the mean scores for all items related to "Rewarding." The highest difference observed between the experimental group and control group in the UES questionnaire (and in favor to the gaming group) was for the question Q4.3: "I became interested in the learning material" (M = 3.74, SD = 0.59), compared to the control group (control: M = 3.17, SD = 0.71). Findings from previous research can possibly explain the positive results in favor of the experimental gaming group [35], revealing that game-based learning significantly creates more flow experiences than does the non-game-based learning group, and game-based learning can provide significantly higher interest, based on students being able to control their learning [35].

5.2 Learning Goals

The participants were asked knowledge questions about fiscal policies in a questionnaire, immediately after the UES questionnaire. Table 3 reveals the percentage of correct answers for each question: Q1–Q5 for the experimental group and control group.

Table 3. Correct answers in % from the knowledge test.

	% Correct answers Eksperimental group	% Correct answers Control group
Q1: How do you lead an expansive fiscal policy?	45	56
Q2: What effect does an expansive fiscal policy have?	75	50
Q3: How do you lead a contractionary fiscal policy?	50	56
Q4: What effect does a contractionary fiscal policy have?	25	19
Q5: What is the gross domestic product (GDP)?	90	94
Mean	57	55

The experimental group answered correctly on 57% of the questions related to fiscal policy, while the control group answered 55% of the same questions correctly. These scores alone suggest that game-based learning has not provided a significant positive effect on students' learning capability beyond that of analog text reading. These relatively unexpected low scores for the experimental gaming group also stand in contrast to the findings of other studies that included knowledge tests in game-based learning [40]. One of the shortcomings in this study was the excess freedom it allowed for creating the game. Setting boundaries around the specific learning goals/success criteria for the fiscal policy theory to be implemented in the game could potentially have helped disseminate the theory and increase the number of correct answers from the game-based learning group.

However, from the interviews (Table 4), we found the comments about the game were very positive, also concerning the learning outcome, motivation, and novelty. Elements that could be improved in game are mainly based on the usability, with matching screen sizes for different playing formats. Some students were also missing further levels regarding more content within the game-based learning, as this was perceived as motivation for learning.

Table 4. Findings from the interviews based on content analysis.

Themes		Fre-quency	Quote examples
Feedback	Positive	7	It was manageable and easy to navigate and find out what you needed to do (ID1: M)
	Negative	1	There was a time where it said infiltrate your dad's office, and I didn't know what that meant (ID3: F)
Immersion	Positive	21	From the very start I was already deep in the game, so I found myself being easily immersed in the game. (ID1: M)
	Negative	4	There was a lot of walking back and forth which could get a bit homogeneous. (ID: 4 (Male))
Aesthetic Appeal	Positive	6	I feel that the graphics were realistic and were directed at us, opposed to if it had been cartoonish. (ID8 F)
	Negative	3	It would have been cool to see some of the characters in the story. (ID8: F)
Motivation	Positive	21	The requirement to answer correctly to progress in the game motivated me to learn. (ID6: Female)
	Negative	5	It could have been cool if when I finished, I was able to progress to further levels. (ID8: F)
Usability	Positive	12	I did not experience any bugs or inconsistencies in the game. (ID1: M)
	Negative	14	It was like the game was not tuned to my screen size. Sometimes text went out of the screen. (ID3: F).
Learning Outcome	Positive	27	The game related to what was taught in the class. Not too difficult, and no boredom (ID2: F).
	Negative	10	I don't think the game would yield the same return as from reading 10 pages The game comes with more fun, but less learning. (ID6: F).
Novelty	Positive	36	The game was a good introduction to the material instead of having to read it. It was a lot cooler to learn about it through the game. (ID8: F)
	Negative	0	
Relatability	Positive	11	I liked the in-game text. The game was target for us, which was nice. (ID4: M)
	Negative	0	

6   Discussion

6.1   Methodological Issues

In very specific contexts with real users, it can be difficult to conduct a perfect research evaluation. Logistics, time constraints, gatekeepers, legislation, lack of a proper posttest, technical issues, and resources can prevent perfect evaluations. In addition, randomization is often impractical for evaluating serious games in a fieldwork context. It could be unethical to randomize students in the same class, with some playing the game, and some not; this should also be avoided because of the potential learning effects. Research must also pay greater attention to evaluating serious games that target students in the Gymnasium. Moreover, some important challenges persist in increasing the validity and reliability of evaluations of game-based learning when students are the users, as well as which form of evaluation researchers should consider. Participants, including the teachers, should be motivated and want to participate—including in the evaluation phase itself. Further research must also consider the choice of method to be used and the way to ask the right type of questions in alignment with the students' capacities for reflectiveness in relation to their behavior and habits. There are also limitations in generating significant evidence and insights regarding students' learning of fiscal policy via game-based learning. First, a much higher number of participants is needed, and further experimental and control groups should be included in the research design. Second, further details on the participants' identities are needed (e.g., their confidence in gaming, game genre preferences, current knowledge, motivation, expectations, and technology acceptance).

6.2   The Importance of the Teacher and Collaborative Planning

A commonly used collaborative planning approach for including users in game-based learning projects emerged from participatory design methodologies [7, 24, 36, 37]. This approach includes, for example, co-creative tasks, collective iterations, consensus building, and problem solving. Much research has examined the collaborative planning approach via the pupils or students playing the games with intended learning outcomes, but less attention has been paid to the very important role of the teachers. Scholars have argued that teachers are key to the success of game-based learning as tool to motivate students and promote deep learning and, therefore, that it is important to provide the teachers with necessary gaming knowledge and skills so that they can integrate game-based learning effectively and efficiently in their classes [38, 40]. A teacher who does not find game-based learning useful will not implement it with the students. The teacher is the crucial gatekeeper, but is also the classroom figure who provides instructions and can include game-based learning within the progression of a class's content over a period of time, as well include the game content within specific, structured in-class discussions, and learning modules. An important aspect when designing game-based learning for teaching fiscal policy to students in upper secondary grades is the teacher's inclusion at an early stage. The teacher can provide valuable insight regarding students, specific learning outcomes, and content, while serving as the gatekeeper of information for the students and providing valuable evaluative information. It is also important to emphasize that this study was focused on teaching methods able to motivate all students. One aspect missing from a teacher's game was a competitive element that, according to the teacher, might have drawn more focus, especially from the male students.

Previous research [39] has already stated the importance of having the teacher(s) play the game themselves before presenting it to the students, as students are annoyed when the teacher does not know how the game works. The teacher's preparation within game-based learning needs to be minimal; for both the teacher and the students, it can often be beneficial to integrate the tutorial in the game. Further, this study benefits from an experienced teacher who can, e.g., mitigate risk or execute plan B when needed. However, it must also be emphasized that the teacher might not be skilled in how game-based learning can be optimally designed to meet learning outcomes. Among the prerequisites for successful collaborative planning with teachers are the creation of a common language [15, 36] and an efficient onboarding process, which could include visualization of game ideas, story ideas; and clear roles. The teacher is the expert in teaching the subject (in this case fiscal policy); we are the experts in games.

7 Conclusion

It is not an easy task to design a digital game for students with the intention of increasing their understanding of fiscal policy. We can conclude that the most important element in developing educational games may be engagement in good games that engage both pupils and teachers, and that the interplay between game play, students, and teachers can create some dynamic learning opportunities. However, a core foundation for making these learning opportunities possible is to have the right balance of skills and challenges for the participants; both within specific learning objectives, but also for control of gameplay.

The game-based learning about fiscal policy developed in this study was engaging for the students. Based on participants' responses, the game was well-fabricated visually, increased students' attention, and was a more rewarding experience than reading the textbook would have been. However, the results from the knowledge test only slightly favoured the experimental gaming group.

We must emphasize that there is no established taxonomy of game-based learning, which is still diverse in its outcomes and is certainly understudied as a means of providing knowledge about fiscal policy. A further direction might create different game design options for targeting different kinds of learning styles, as well as to increase the game's competitiveness and personalization by including the participants' knowledge and motivation.

References

1. PISA 2018 Results Volume III: What School Life Means for Students' Lives, PISA, OECD Publishing, Paris (2019)
2. Statistics Denmark. Average marks for all groups. Updated. https://www.dst.dk/da/Statistik/nyheder-analyser-publ/bagtal/2018/2018-06-26-karaktergennemsnittet-stiger-for-alle-gru pper-af-studenter. Accessed 07 July 2022
3. Verhoeven, L., Snow, C.E. (Eds.): Literacy and Motivation: Reading Engagement in Individuals and Groups. Routledge, Abingdon (2001)
4. Wigfield, A., Guthrie, J.T.: Engagement and motivation in reading. Handb. Read. Res. 3, 403–422 (2000)
5. Anastasiadis, T., Lampropoulos, G., Siakas, K.: Digital game-based learning and serious games in education. Int. J. Adv. Sci. Res. Eng. 4(12), 139–144 (2018)
6. Taspinar, B., Schmidt, W., Schuhbauer, H.: Gamification in education: a board game approach to knowledge acquisition. Procedia Comput. Sci. 99, 101–116 (2016)

7. Petersen, M.S., Hansen, N.L.S., Jakobsen, G., Bjørner, T.: Increasing reading engagement for danish gymnasium students: the hosier and his daughter as a serious game. In: Brooks, E.I., Brooks, A., Sylla, C., Møller, A.K. (eds.) Design, Learning, and Innovation. DLI 2020. LNICS, Social Informatics and Telecommunications Engineering, vol. 366, pp. 187–197. Springer, Cham (2021). https://doi.org/10.1007/978-3-030-78448-5_13

8. Bjørner, T.: How can a serious game be designed to provide engagement with and awareness of the plastic crisis as part of UN's SDGs. In: Proceedings of the Conference on Information Technology for Social Good, pp. 157–162, September 2021

9. Karakoç, B., Eryılmaz, K., Turan Özpolat, E., Yıldırım, İ: The effect of game-based learning on student achievement: a meta-analysis study. Technol. Knowl. Learn. **27**, 207–222 (2022)

10. Jabbar, A.I., Felicia, P.: Gameplay engagement and learning in game-based learning: a systematic review. Rev. Educ. Res. **85**(4), 740–779 (2015)

11. Derboven, J., Zaman, B., Geerts, D., De Grooff, D.: Playing educational math games at home: the monkey tales case. Entertain. Comput. **16**, 1–14 (2016)

12. Clark, D.B., Tanner-Smith, E.E., Killingsworth, S.S.: Digital games, design, and learning: a systematic review and meta-analysis. Rev. Educ. Res. **86**(1), 79–122 (2016)

13. Noroozi, O., Dehghanzadeh, H., Talaee, E.: A systematic review on the impacts of game-based learning on argumentation skills. Entertain. Comput. **35**, 100369 (2020)

14. Ritterfeld, U., Cody, M., Vorderer, P. (Eds.): Serious Games: Mechanics and Effects. Routledge, New York (2009)

15. Djaouti, D., Alvarez, J., Jessel, J.-P., Rampnoux, O.: Origins of serious games. In: Ma, M., Oikonomou, A., Jain, L.C. (eds.) Serious Games and Edutainment Applications, pp. 25–43. Springer, London (2011). https://doi.org/10.1007/978-1-4471-2161-9_3

16. Freitas De, S.: Learning in Immersive worlds A review of gamebased learning Prepared for the JISC e-Learning Programme, JISC eLearning Innov, vol. 3 (2006)

17. Plass, J.L., Homer, B.D., Kinzer, C.K.: Foundations of game based learning. Educ. Psychol. **50**(4), 258–283 (2015)

18. Zhonggen, Y.: A meta-analysis of use of serious games in education over a decade. Int. J. Comput. Games Technol. **2019**, 1–8 (2019)

19. Arnab, S., et al.: Mapping learning and game mechanics for serious games analysis. Br. J. Edu. Technol. **46**(2), 391–411 (2015)

20. Naumann, J.: A model of online reading engagement: linking engagement, navigation, and performance in digital reading. Comput. Hum. Behav. **53**, 263–277 (2015)

21. Cassar, A.G., Jang, E.E.: Investigating the effects of a game-based approach in teaching word recognition and spelling to students with reading disabilities and attention deficits. Aust. J. Learn. Difficulties **15**(2), 193–211 (2010)

22. Rueda, R., O'Neil, H.F., Son, E.: The role of motivation, affect, and engagement in simulation/game environments: a proposed model. In: O'Neil, H.F., Baker, E.L., Perez, R. (eds.) Using games and simulations for teaching and assessment, pp. 230–253. Routledge, New York and London (2016)

23. Pasalic, A., Andersen, N.H., Carlsen, C.S., Karlsson, E.Å., Berthold, M., Bjørner, T.: How to increase boys' engagement in reading mandatory poems in the gymnasium: homer's the odyssey as transmedia storytelling with the cyclopeia narrative as a computer game. In: Guidi, B., Ricci, L., Calafate, C., Gaggi, O., Marquez-Barja, J. (eds.) Smart Objects and Technologies for Social Good. GOODTECHS 2017. LNICS, Social Informatics and Telecommunications Engineering, vol. 233, pp. 216–225. Springer, Cham (2018). https://doi.org/10.1007/978-3-319-76111-4_22

24. Petersen, M.S., Jakobsen, G.S., Hendriksen, D.B., Hansen, N.L.S., Bjørner, T.: Can a serious game be designed to increase engagement in a mandatory postmodern novella at Danish gymnasiums? In: de Rosa, F., Marfisi Schottman, I., Baalsrud Hauge, J., Bellotti, F., Dondio,

P., Romero, M. (eds.) GALA 2021. LNCS, vol. 13134, pp. 57–67. Springer, Cham (2021). https://doi.org/10.1007/978-3-030-92182-8_6

25. Guthrie, J.T., Wigfield, A., You, W.: Instructional contexts for engagement and achievement in reading. In: Christenson, S., Reschly, A., Wylie, C. (eds.) Handbook of Research on Student Engagement, pp. 601–634. Springer, Boston, MA (2012). https://doi.org/10.1007/978-1-4614-2018-7_29

26. Wouters, P., van Nimwegen, C., van Oostendorp, H., van der Spek, E.D.: A meta-analysis of the cognitive and motivational effects of serious games. J. Educ. Psychol. **105**(2), 249–265 (2013)

27. Schønau-Fog, H., Bjørner, T.: Sure, i would like to continue a method for mapping the experience of engagement in video games. Bull. Sci. Technol. Soc. **32**(5), 405–412 (2012)

28. Raybourn, E.M.: A new paradigm for serious games: transmedia learning for more effective training and education. J. Comput. Sci. **5**(3), 471–481 (2014)

29. Roozeboom, M.B., Visschedijk, G., Oprins, E.: The effectiveness of three serious games measuring generic learning features. Br. J. Edu. Technol. **48**(1), 83–100 (2015)

30. Garcia, I., Pacheco, C., Méndez, F., Calvo-Manzano, J.A.: The effects of game-based learning in the acquisition of soft skills on undergraduate software engineering courses: a systematic literature review. Comput. Appl. Eng. Educ. **28**(5), 1327–1354 (2020)

31. O'Brien, H.L., Cairns, P., Hall, M.: A practical approach to measuring user engagement with the refined user engagement scale (UES) and new UES short form. Int. J. Hum. Comput Stud. **112**, 28–39 (2018)

32. Bjørner, T.: Data collection. In: Bjørner, T. (ed.) Qualitative Methods for Consumer Research: The Value of the Qualitative Approach in Theory and Practice. Hans Reitzel,Copenhagen (2015)

33. Bjørner, T.: Data analysis and findings. In: Bjørner, T. (ed.) Qualitative Methods for Consumer Research: The Value of the Qualitative Approach in Theory and Practice. Hans Reitzel, Copenhagen (2015)

34. MacPhail, C., Khoza, N., Abler, L., Ranganathan, M.: Process guidelines for establishing intercoder reliability in qualitative studies. Qual. Res. **16**(2), 198–212 (2016)

35. Chang, C.C., Liang, C., Chou, P.N., Lin, G.Y.: Is game-based learning better in flow experience and various types of cognitive load than non-game-based learning? Perspective from multimedia and media richness. Comput. Hum. Behav. **71**, 218–227 (2017)

36. Sousa, M.: Serious board games: modding existing games for collaborative ideation processes. Int. J. Serious Games **8**(2), 129–146 (2021)

37. Bjørner, T., Hansen, L.G., Valimaa, M., Sørensen, J.U., Dobre, M.: Design and evaluation of a serious game to supplement pupils' understanding of molecular structures in chemistry. In: Fletcher, B., Ma, M., Göbel, S., Baalsrud Hauge, J., Marsh, T. (eds.) Serious Games. JCSG 2021. LNCS, vol. 12945. Springer, Cham (2021). https://doi.org/10.1007/978-3-030-88272-3_19

38. Molin, G.: The role of the teacher in game-based learning: a review and outlook. In: Ma, M., Oikonomou, A. (eds.) Serious Games and Edutainment Applications, pp. 649–674. Springer, Cham (2017). https://doi.org/10.1007/978-3-319-51645-5_28

39. Bjoerner, T., Hansen, C.B.S.: Designing an educational game: design principles from a holistic perspective. Int. J. Learn. **17**(10), 279–290 (2011)

40. Bjørner, T., Sum, A.J., Ludvigsen, R.K., Bouquin, N.L., Larsen, F.D., Kampel, U.: Making homework fun: the effect of game-based learning on reading engagement. In: Proceedings of the 2022 ACM Conference on Information Technology for Social Good, pp. 353–359 (2022)

Decolonizing the Imagination: Designing a Futures Literacy Workshop

Cecilia Björkén-Nyberg$^{(\boxtimes)}$ (ID) and Maya Hoveskog (ID)

Halmstad University, Kristian IV:s väg 3, 301 18 Halmstad, Sweden
{cecilia.bjorken-nyberg,maya.hoveskog}@hh.se

Abstract. This article explores the potential of narratives and creative writing as tools for imagining possible futures within the pedagogical framework of futures literacy. We share our experiences of a transdisciplinary pre-study on future mobility situated at the intersection of business model innovation, narrative theory and pedagogy. The pre-study results show that it is difficult not to repeat present and past patterns when anticipating the future. A great challenge is therefore to decolonize the imagination when imagining possible futures scenarios. Based on the insights from the pre-study, we propose a futures literacy (FL) workshop as a structured learning process that combines an open-minded imagining of possible futures with the creation of strategic scenarios. Designed for students and practitioners within a transformative learning environment, the proposed FL workshop is process-oriented and has a focus on anticipation and exploration of limitless futures. Furthermore, it is argued that the workshop has the potential for facilitating agency in the process of business model innovation towards innovative organizational value logics. This paper provides hands-on details for a particular way of improving the capacity of students and practitioners for imagining the future differently and pluralistically. A key argument in the paper is that competence in narrative technique is required in designing, performing and analyzing the workshop activities.

Keywords: Futures literacy · Business model innovation process · Narrative technique · Anticipation · Creative writing · Rigorous imagining · Transformative learning

1 Introduction

To speculate about the future has always fascinated human beings. On a very basic level it is a means of survival and of making necessary plans for action in the near future. On a more sophisticated level, speculative thinking is connected to worldmaking and to our urge to place ourselves in new and unfamiliar contexts. As the output within the genre of speculative fiction shows, the representational potential of such worldmaking is enormous. However, due to our inability to sever the future from the present and the present from the past, it is virtually impossible to conjure up a completely new world

E. Brooks et al. (Eds.): DLI 2022, LNICST 493, pp. 168–181, 2023.
https://doi.org/10.1007/978-3-031-31392-9_13

[20]. So, when we perceive a world to be new, it is because familiar features have been rearranged in fresh ways that open up innovative perspectives.

For anyone who wishes to become futures literate, the connection between the future and the present is acknowledged as a prerequisite for imagining and for action. In fact, the main argument within a Futures Literacy (FL) context is that the future is used actively in the present [27–29]. Similarly, UNESCO [18] defines FL as "a capability" and "the skill that allows people to better understand the role that the future plays in what they see and do." Moreover, since, according to UNESCO, all people are capable of imagining, FL is closely associated with democratic values and is therefore comparable to both traditional forms of literacy and to digital literacy. Thus, FL is very clearly inscribed within a pedagogical framework [21].

This paper discusses FL in a business model context (BM). For a firm which aims to anticipate and act upon the future by innovating its business model, FL is a key capability that holds the potential for managers to go beyond their own cognitive perceptions and worldviews to embrace new ones. At present, the most commonly used approach for firms to orient themselves towards the future is aligned with optimizing their efforts to be able to reach a predetermined strategic goal. As Poli [32] explains, in this form of active orientation towards the future, the efforts are optimized towards a pre-supposed known future, and all choices are rational in relation to the costs and benefits to materialize this future. However, great challenges and trends such as digitalization, bring about a number of wicked problems, great transformation and uncertainty, which make this optimization strategy irrelevant. Therefore, rather than optimizing towards the future, managers should develop "the ability to aspire as an opening of possibilities" … for different ways of being and becoming" [32:5]. At present, however, as Sharma et al. [37] state, managers feel poorly equipped to do that.

In this article we will be sharing our experiences of working with creative writing as a tool for imagining possible futures within the pedagogical framework of FL. In a pre-study we asked two classes of senior high school students in southern Sweden to imagine what the world would be like in the year 2035 and then to compose short stories on the theme of mobility. The focus of the activity was to discern emerging trends in modes of transportation for people and goods as well as in digital user solutions. While this paper will discuss these trends, the actual implementation of them in the process of a company's business model innovation is a topic to be explored in a future study.

The pre-study is situated at the intersection of business model innovation, narrative theory and pedagogy. The advantage of this transdisciplinary approach is that patterns and methods in a given discipline are challenged when studied through the lens of another discipline. Introducing FL pedagogy within business model innovation (BMI), for example, may reveal that an optimization approach needs to be replaced by more process-oriented thinking. Conversely, within narrative studies the emphasis on action and "rigorous imagining" [27, 28] associated with FL may call for innovative ways of employing traditional narrative terminology (e.g. point of view) in order to design strategies for the future.

The results of our pre-study show that it is difficult not to repeat present and past patterns when anticipating the future. A great challenge is therefore to decolonize the imagination when imagining possible future scenarios. At the same time, though, and from a FL perspective, it is crucial to be able to distinguish a possible future which may generate innovative stories that are also of strategic importance and may inform the business model innovation process for companies. So, the aim of this study is to investigate how a structured learning process that combines an open-minded imagining of possible futures with the creation of strategic scenarios can be designed, and, more specifically, how this learning process may inform the process of BMI within a FL framework. These issues are addressed in our paper. We begin by introducing key ideas and terms related to FL generally which are then fitted into a BMI framework of organizational value logics [23]. Based on this theoretical foundation, we move on to present the main conclusions from the pre-study and end by proposing a more well-structured design for a futures literacy workshop. While an additional step will be to explore how the results of the proposed workshop can inform the creation of innovative BMIs, this is a topic beyond the scope of the present paper.

2 Theoretical Background: Futures Literacy and Business Model Innovation

What is so titillating about the future is that it cannot be known. No matter how sophisticated our calculations are, they are bound to be overthrown by uncertain parameters. This is because the world is never stable but in constant change and not even the present is completed although we may think so. FL is founded on this ontological premise of uncertainty and openness. According to Poli [32:4], accepting the "categorical openness" of hidden or emergent parameters is an essential component of FL. By contrast, the optimization approach is all about minimizing uncertainty in relation to the future. It is built on the assumption that the future can be known, that the sum of resources is stable [17, 28] and that costs and benefits can be calculated accordingly [32]. Considering uncertainty as an enemy to be conquered rather than a potential to be embraced does not only close down possible ways of knowing and doing but may actually have serious consequences [17, 32]. A case in point is ecological optimization where calculated disasters can lead to a management of fear [32] and to a suppression of possible futures scenarios.

Optimization is inscribed in a colonizing discourse. Making detailed calculations is a means of mastering the unknown. Miller [28:24–25] writes that "the idea is to impose our will on the future – imagining, if 'all goes well', that we can 'colonise' tomorrow so that it conforms to our desires and expectations". Similarly, Facer [17] sees optimization metaphorically in terms of territorial conquest and of defeating a hostile other. Such a defense strategy reduces the number of unfamiliar factors; yet, since we are governed by the principle of minimal departure (PMD) [35, 36] in imagining the future, it results in mere repetition of what is already known, Thus, by projecting present patterns onto emergent worlds, rather than open up vistas we close them down. What is needed – to avoid falling into the PMD trap – is a pedagogical approach that "copes with disorienting dilemmas" [21:2]. One challenge is to make sure that the narrative of growth is not simply replaced by a narrative of disaster since these narratives are just two contrasting facets of optimization [17]. The educator's role should therefore be to steer students away from the optimization discourse altogether to help them explore a variety of possible futures [32].

Thus, the ontological grounding of FL in worldmaking as an incomplete process has clear epistemological implications. Facer [17:64], for instance, declaring that "futurity is embedded at the heart of the educational process" advocates a "pedagogy of the present" which "might be understood as a process of becoming open to the excess and abundance of possibilities of creating new worlds" [17:70]. A central idea in this pedagogy is that of the "thick present" which is "neither past nor future... but its own distinctive time and space in which anticipatory practices and lived experiences combine and mingle, changing both the past and the future" [17:71]. A similar position is taken by Miller [28:25] whose "exploratory futures" are aspects in the present which, due to their emergent character, break with our ingrained patterns of thought. It is neither a matter of making predictions nor of finding smart solutions but of "'seeing' the present differently". Implementing an exploratory futures method within the framework of FL is a "balancing act" [28:25] that calls for "rigorous imagining" [27, 28]. Through several steps of "rigorous" choices to be made and questions to be answered, a large number of possible futures are narrowed down to a selection of possibility space stories that may be of strategic significance.

When designing for such "transformative learning" [21:2], anticipation is a key phenomenon. Since the future does not exist in the present, our only means of coming in contact with it is through anticipation, which "becomes a collective way of stepping into the future, of trying to transform one's own future or the future of the collective before it occurs" [9:42–43 in 32:6]. However, as has been pointed out above, anticipating the future is not merely an imaginary and speculative rambling; it is just as much a means of making sense of the present "through active systems and processes" [29:19]. These systems and processes need to be carefully designed and scaffolded in order to translate imagined future scenarios into present action.

Within a FL framework, imagining future worlds is closely associated with creating narratives. In fact, as Liveley et al. [24] state, the two activities cannot be separated. The Futures Literacy through Narrative (FLiNT) project focuses on collaborative and performative ways of composing stories. The FLiNT project, based in the UK, is a network of people from different sectors: policy makers, academics and practitioners. The purpose is to engage in anticipatory futures practices to "envisag[e] uncertain futures and communicate those possible futures in impactful ways" [24:2]. A narrative kit consisting of performative, interactive and intersubjective tools has therefore been designed within the project. A case in point is a character-based collaborative storytelling activity where participants first compose their own characters individually and then interact in the creation of a possible future world. The added value of the collaborative approach is that the participants have to engage in negotiation in the worldmaking process. Moreover, they can speak and act both through their characters and through their own personal perspectives. Performing through these "hybrid subjectivities", a "slippage" [24:5] is created between character and participant, between observer and hybrid participant and between participant and characters.

In this context Goodman's [20] worldmaking theory is of great significance. This theory is based on the idea that "worldmaking as we know it always starts from worlds already on hand; the making is a remaking" [20:6]. Consequently, when we perceive the world as new, we are only seeing a recreated version of the old world. Familiar features may be decomposed, weighted, or ordered differently, deleted supplemented or deformed. The way we perceive the world thus depends on the frames used and these frames "seem to belong less to what is described than to systems of description" [20:2]. In the FLiNT collaborative workshop, the participants are challenged in their ordinary ways of seeing the world by being exposed to worlds imagined through the frames of other participants. Thus, these participants stand a better chance of avoiding the PMD trap than writers of individually composed speculative stories do.

This shows that we need other people's perspectives "for the completion of our 'narratable selves'" [13 in 23:2]. Another vital element in the FLiNT project activities is "storyknowing" [33], that is gaining knowledge about the world through situated, relational and embodied forms of learning. What makes the FLiNT project practices special within FL is that they are so firmly grounded in theories pertaining to narrative theory: "Being futures literate, then, should arguably include a suite of skills and competencies drawn from the world of literary criticism to help expose the mechanisms and heuristics which we draw upon in making sense of the possible worlds that the future represents" [24:4]. Expertise in narrative technique is particularly valuable for generating "possible futures which do not merely re-present ... the priorities and concerns of the present" [24:4], in other words, for avoiding PMD. This applies also to the BMI field where the optimization tradition is still strong despite established techniques for working with storytelling, scenario-making and "antenarratives" [7, 25, 31]. However, as will be discussed below, more process-oriented and explorative approaches that fit into a FL framework start to emerge.

Business models (BMs) represent the organizational logics, and are seen as models that simplify the complex reality of the firm [14, 22, 38]. They constitute a key factor in contributing to companies' viability, and as such, they are descriptions of how firms define and achieve success over time [39]. BMs are, on the one hand, seen in terms of outcomes and market devices for value creation, delivery, and capture, and, on the other, in terms of a process perspective through which a new or innovated BM is created, namely BMI. Laasch [23:408] emphasizes the key role of the incremental, ongoing process of BMI and defines it as an "ongoing construction and reconstruction process of organizational becoming, rather than an exceptional event." This notion is in line with Nailer and Buttriss' [30:671] view of "business model as *practiced*", characterized by continuous change over time, pushed by the dynamic interactions between various actors anticipating and realizing value.

Laasch [23] explores how the BM value logics manifests itself in three key states (cognition, artefacts and activities) and suggests a conceptual model for how the integration of those three states drives the ongoing BMI process and the stepwise materialization of the new BM. In other words, as Laasch [23] reveals, value logics are in essence programs of action and agency – they are embodied in people's cognition, embedded into artefacts that together shape and enact activities for BMI.

To unpack Laasch's [23] key concepts, the first state – *value logics as cognition* – relates to the fact that BMs are simply models, simplifications of reality, BMs are namely the mental images (or cognitive configurations) which are in the minds of, for example, managers or entrepreneurs [1, 15]. Those mental images support anticipation, sensemaking, legitimization and decision-making processes when it comes to BMI in the form of mental shortcuts or simplified stories [14, 16, 26]. The mental images of the organizational value logic are realized in material or textual-visual *artefacts* such as populated visual BM representations of a BM described in, for example, stories, business plans, power point presentations and on websites. Those artefacts can be seen from the BM perspective as an outcome. However, such artefacts are also a cornerstone in the BM as a process since they shape cognition and activities [16]. The third state – *value logics as activities* – relates to the operational activities of the firm [11], for example, in terms of what kind of bundled products and services it offers in order to create and deliver value to its target customers. Another example of this state is what tools and processes are used in order to undertake the BMI process. The dynamics between those three states continuously influence each other to "constructing and reconstructing a firm's value logics, which in turn manifests and remanifests through potentially altered cognition, artefacts and, activities" (23:408).

Arguably, since the possible future BMs are the result of anticipation, exploration, experimentation, decisions, actions and efforts that firms make today, there is not one ultimate future BM but rather a limitless number of possible futures and future BMs of organizational being and becoming. Additionally, Nailer and Buttriss [30] emphasize the value anticipated and realized as a key causal mechanism which continuously drives the BMI process over time. This makes anticipation an important ingredient in this process of BMI and emphasizes the interactivity of value and its time dimension.

As described above, the process perspective foregrounds the exploration and experimentation process for the creation and development of new BMs [8, 19, 34]. As Breuer et al. [8] and Bocken et al. [5] stress, it is essential to better understand the emergent, continuous nature of the process of BMI and especially how the exploration and experimentation process influences the dynamics between the three value logics states (cognition, artefacts and activities) towards action. Likewise, Miller [27] advocates an increasing importance of experimentation and non-predictive imagining. As such, Laasch's [23] model may be said to be related to an anticipatory approach. Interestingly, this model is founded on the idea that BMs are modified in ways that are similar to Goodman's [20] worldmaking theory. When Goodman [20] writes about decomposing, reweighting, reordering, deletion, supplementation and deformation, Laasch [23:408] mentions "revision," "extension", "evolution" and "transformation". For both it is a remaking of something that already exists; it is a matter of using a different "frame" to use Goodman's [20] terminology and, as argued above, it is this change of perspective that is so important for challenging ingrained ways of seeing and for avoiding optimization scenarios and PMD.

In Laasch's [23] model – as in FL – there is a strong emphasis on transformative learning. Moreover, the nexus of transformation, embodiment and interactivity is reminiscent of the character-based FLiNT workshops: "These business models co-exist, interrelate and flexibly transform one into another. To understand business models, their becoming and change, it is thus necessary to not only understand a value logic or its individual states, but also the dynamics that interrelate them" [23:409]. While Laasch's [23] model is inscribed in an actor-network context, which means that the interrelation may take place between human as well as non-human actors, the FLiNT approach is specifically designed to generate interaction between human participants. However, the characters may be considered artefacts in the sense that they are created to make the slippage felt between themselves and the participant enacting them.

3   A Creative Writing Pre-study on Future Mobility

Our research process was divided into two phases. In the first phase, which took place from late autumn 2020 to late spring 2021, we designed a creative storytelling activity on the theme of future mobility at a senior high school in southern Sweden. We worked with two classes, each consisting of 27 students aged 16–17. The motivation for including this particular age group in our study was that their worldviews and perceptions in relation to the theme of future mobility have not previously been explored [12].

Our main interest was to find out how young people think about the future, the environment and mobility. The students were thus asked to create brief speculative scenarios of approximately 800 words set in the year 2035 and relating to the theme of mobility. A similar approach through the creation of "antenarratives" [6] has become established within organization and management studies. Antenarratives are short, fragmented stories in the making; hence, they lack the narrative stability and linearity of completed stories. In order to fit the activity as seamlessly as possible into the daily work at school, we had several meetings with two teachers from the senior high school. These teachers were to frame the theme of future mobility by providing inspirational material that they thought suitable for the students. Practical classroom details were specified and a selection of fictive and non-fictive genres (short story, diary, video, new article/report) suggested in a power point presentation.

In the first stage the students were asked to generate and share ideas about the theme of future mobility in groups; in the second stage they could choose whether they wanted to work individually, in pairs or in groups. A broad interpretation of the theme of future mobility was encouraged and included technical innovations of vehicles, short- and long-distance commuting, tourism, transportation of goods and migration as a result of climate change. With the aim to concretize the theme, the teachers put together an inspirational package consisting of for example multimodal material about future vehicles, digital innovations, the imaginary city of Notterdam and the lives of young refugees in Sweden.

As stated above, when planning the student activity, we were mainly inspired by previous studies made within organization and management studies foregrounding the treatment of time and place. This perspective was combined with a narratological focus and the two converged in the use of the *chronotope* [2], a term originally used within literary studies but now prevalent also within the field of organization and management [7]. The pre-study had not been consciously framed within FL. However, as we found out later, the general design of the activity may be said to be roughly in line with the first of the three levels (awareness, discovery and choice) in Miller's [27] method of the hybrid strategic scenario (HSS) for developing FL. This method, which is an example of "rigorous imagining", is hybrid in the sense that it is both sequential and non-hierarchical; the three levels are equally important but need to be dealt with in the set order. At the first level participants join in group discussions to make their implicit assumptions about the future surface and become explicit. Another purpose for this level is to raise an awareness about the complexity of the temporal dimension: change happens *over* time while the present is situated *in* time [27:347]. A technique for structuring thinking at this level is to ask the participants to construct stories based on five main criteria: 1) the type or purpose of the story, 2) the temporal and chronological frame and time-span, 3) the point of view (micro or macro level or a mix of the two), 4) the main protagonists (decision makers) and their interrelations and 5) rules and causal relationships for the action. The students were introduced to parameters similar to Miller's [27] first two criteria: the purpose of the story was strategic imagining related to the theme of mobility and the temporal aspect was made clear since the time horizon was the year 2035. While a strict adherence to all five criteria would most likely have yielded more consistent stories, a too rigorous system might have had a dampening effect on the students' inspiration.

In the second phase of the pre-study, we interpreted and analyzed the student stories on the theme of future mobility in the year 2035. Being aware of the multi-layered and ambiguous character of stories in general [3], we started to classify the student stories both in terms of form (genre, temporal dimension, modal form) and content (mode of transport, ownership or sharing, travel distance, elements of the business model, attitudes towards sustainability and technology and the senses activated in relation to technology). We also mapped companies, technologies and characters mentioned in the stories. However, this detailed analytical grid failed to capture features that criteria 3–5 in Miller's [27] level 1 HSS method are meant to concretize. As for the third criteria, for instance, we had used traditional categorization for point of view (first or third person) rather than a micro/macro perspective. Interestingly, however, we had noticed that most of the stories were set in everyday family situations (micro) far removed from decisions made on a macro level. Thus, the shift in point of view suggested in Miller's [27] HSS method was of crucial importance for uncovering the pattern we had discerned without being able to categorize it in a meaningful way. The question is, though, whether we should explicitly have raised an awareness in the students of all five story criteria in Miller's [27] level 1 HSS method and risked confusion or whether for this particular age group, it would have been sufficient to have included Miller's [27] parameters in our analytical model.

We found that the material used in class for introducing the theme of future mobility to the students had a great impact on the stories produced. For example, the hyperloop, which was included in the inspirational material as an example of a future vehicle, was frequently represented in the stories and often within the context of time efficiency without any obvious reason. In the student stories, generally, there is a strong emphasis on measurement in terms of time and space and little exploration of places and landscapes without a clear optimization purpose. The narratives of disaster dealing with the consequences of climate change, are different in this respect, though. These stories contain descriptions of damaged nature and, as such, function as a contrast to the narrative of growth but within the optimization context [17]. Technological and digital solutions are often added as an external feature and are superimposed on everyday patterns that are easily recognizable as our own present ones. The impression is that artefacts in the form of vehicles and digital tools impact cognition mainly to reinforce ingrained patterns of thought while the more complex role of artefacts in Laasch's [23] model is missing.

As a result, the PMD is clearly manifest in the student stories and this phenomenon is further reinforced by the choice of genre. As observed above, the genres in the inspirational material given to the students include, in addition to the short story, the semifictional diary form as well as the non-fictional news report. Analyzing the stories, we were little surprised to find that the non-fictional texts were not multi-layered in the sense in which Facer [17] defines the "thick present". As for the diaries, while the first-person perspective adds emotional depth, it fails to invite "disorienting dilemmas" [21:2] due to an absence of conflicting views of other possible futures. The diary entries are completed by the experiencing "I" and the same mono-imaginary approach is evident also in the short stories irrespective of being composed in the first or the third person.

4   Designing a Futures Literacies Workshop

Based on our insights from the creative storytelling activity in the pre-study, we suggest in this paper a futures literacies workshop which builds on the work from Liveley et al. [24] within the FLiNT project as well as on Miller [27]. The workshop is designed as a structured learning process that combines an open-minded imagining of possible futures with the creation of strategic scenarios which can inform the BMI process. The participants in the workshop can be students from different educational levels as well as industry and public sector representatives. The greater the diversity of actors the better.

The workshop is designed for approximately 20 participants. We start by dividing them into groups of five. First the participants work individually developing fully realized characters, fictional human beings, with the help of a facilitator with expertise in narrative theory and creative writing. The facilitator's function here is to raise an awareness about the chronological frame for the characters and the network of relations in which the characters are to exist. This first step is thus in accordance with the awareness-raising level in Miller's [27:348] model presented above for "shifting both values and expectations from tacit to explicit – all of which builds the capacity of people, teams and leaders to respond and innovate". It is also in keeping with the initial state of the FLiNT approach [24] in which the participants construct their characters individually.

In the second step, the students continue working in their groups. Their task is to collaboratively devise a possible world setting in which all characters can be brought together on a given future date. This step is intended to "develop a space for imagining possible futures" [27:352]. In Laasch's [23:411] terminology, this activity is a form of "process of translation", which corresponds to what Liveley et al. [24:4] describes as "an act of negotiation, creating a performative setting in which different subjectivities, emotions and modes of knowing are brought together to envisage a possible future". In this way, the participants perform their agency of sculpturing and constructing the world or, with reference to Laasch [23], contribute to the emergence of an actor-network. During this stage, the facilitator has the crucial role of asking questions directly to the characters about their worldviews so that participants may engage in the activity and "step outside the boundaries of the self-up-to-this-point" [24:5]. In other words, the participants are to be teased out of their normative thinking to avoid the PMD. In Miller's

[27] terminology, this is the "discovery" level informed by "rigorous imagining", where participants move beyond the PMD to be able to explore a plurality of possible futures. To facilitate such exploration is especially important as the pre-study showed that the students were restricted in their imagining due to the PMD.

In the third step all the groups meet in a joint class discussion where the members of each group share their experiences of being in a possible world with other characters. This activity is followed by a discussion exercise suggested by Miller [27] in which the participants are asked to discuss good and bad aspects in the created world, what features a preferred from a particular actor's/firm's point of view and what similarities and differences between the future worlds and the present worlds may be found. This shared activity is informed by Miller's [27] last stage of choice.

As has been described above, we have been inspired by Laasch [23], Miller [27] and Liveley et al. [24] in designing the FL workshop but have taken the liberty to combine features of these three frameworks in new ways. We realized, for example, that for the sake of clarity, Miller's [27] model needs to be somewhat simplified and some details have therefore been removed to make it more flexible and suitable for a greater variety of contexts. As a result, the "rigorous imagining" element is a little less "rigorous" in our modified version than in the original. We find the strong performative character of the Liveley et al. [24] approach appealing and believe that the situated, relational and embodied learning process it is founded on will have a stimulating effect on the anticipatory activities of imagining. Thus, the element of performativity is more foregrounded in our model of combined frameworks than it is in either Laasch [23] or Miller [27] individually.

We believe that the proposed workshop, with its strong focus on performativity, will be more useful for setting the stage for anticipating future possible worlds than the inspirational material of the kind used in the pre-study proved to be. We therefore suggest an additional workshop step in which participants compose exploratory and anticipatory stories about possible worlds subsequent to having engaged in the performative process. At this stage the participants are likely to be in a better position to decolonize their imagination and minimize the influence of the PMD in imagining the future by creating artefacts of narration in line with Laasch's [23] strong focus on the role of artefacts for the process of BMI. In creating these artefacts of future possible worlds, the participants will have the chance to draw on such factors as gesture, tone of voice and other embodied and multimodal forms of representation experienced during the workshop. These stories may be produced individually, in pairs or groups in the mode(s) chosen by the participant(s).

On the whole, this workshop approach allows us to explore whether we imagine the future differently when doing so through the eyes of another imaginary person and what new and previously hidden insights into worldmaking such collaboratively developed characters and contexts may reveal. Applying the FLiNT approach is not merely a matter of shifting perspectives but of creating "hybrid subjectivities" and a creative "slippage" [24:5] both within a participant and between participants. To move intuitively between the use of a first-person and third-person pronoun, between a present and a future self is an anticipatory activity that facilitates agency.

In line with Laasch [23], characters with different cognitive configurations that envision different value logics must be created so that new perspectives for driving BMI can be found. The proposed workshop has the potential to do so and to serve as a "change actant" [4:96]. As Laasch [23:411] states, the value logics are "programs of action" and agency requiring a process of translation; the suggested FL workshop provides one element in this process. Callon [10:60] explains that if there are actors with different logics, they will start a process of translation – an "interdefinition of actors" attempting to convince each other into adopting their respective logics. This definition aligns well with the character-based shared storytelling [33] feature of the FL workshop, which is connected to agency and emphasizes the role of relational experience. The outcome of our proposed FL workshop has the potential for inducing the process of translation, especially since it offers an encounter with non-business-model actors with divergent logics (e.g. students from different educational levels), if used as is suggested in this article. Furthermore, the FL workshop provides an opportunity to grasp scenarios in an accessible and impactful futures output which may engage diverse groups of actors in creating possible futures through audio-visual artefacts [24]. Thus, in line with Laasch [23], those artefacts may develop agency in creating and changing organizational value logics which may be useful in the early phases of BMI.

5   Conclusions

In this paper we have used the FL framework as an umbrella structure for business model innovation, narrative theory and pedagogy in order to promote a transformative learning environment not only for students but also for practitioners. One great advantage of this approach is that students within different disciplines and practitioners may engage in collaborative learning that opens up new ways of seeing the world. In the near future we plan to launch the workshop outline presented here with students from the Master's Program in Industrial Management and Innovation. The next step we envisage is to include students with competence in narrative theory. We believe that such a combination of student perspectives sets the stage for transformative learning processes [21].

This paper makes several contributions to prior research. When it comes to BMI, it aligns with Sharma et al. [37] and their cocreating forward approach. The suggested FL workshop gives students and practitioners a more process-oriented approach with focus on anticipation and exploration of limitless futures instead of optimizing scenarios based on the past and the present. Furthermore, in line with Laasch [23], the suggested FL workshop holds the potential for agency in the BMI process towards innovative organizational value logics. This agency can support the anticipation and realization of value as discussed by Nailer and Buttriss [30].

When it comes to narrative studies, this paper shows that competence in narrative technique is required outside the field of literary studies. Imagining possible futures is a difficult task for participants without proper knowledge of such aspects as point of view, setting and characterization. Conversely, for literature students who are mainly used to applying their skills when analyzing already completed fictional worlds, exploring possible futures in the making provides an added value: the effect of a particular narrative tool is made evident and thus the worldmaking process is concretized. Hence, the theory of narration is understood through a practice of narration. Moreover, to work with imagining based on a theme like future mobility within a BMI context gives a sense of purpose and direction to the process of narration and worldmaking. Exploring possible futures becomes a means for action and doing in the present.

As for pedagogy, this paper provides hands-on details for a particular way of how to improve the capacity of students and practitioners for imagining the future differently and pluralistically. This approach is in line with Miller [27] who also advocates a need for developing a better capacity for more imaginative storytelling decoupled from the planning of the future in a probabilistic manner associated with making calculations about the unknown.

While the present article presents one way of decolonizing the imagination through a futures literacy workshop, it only outlines the beginning of the journey. In the present study, we have explored anticipatory futures through the creation of narratives within a senior high school context, and based on this work, we have designed a workshop setup. Our next step will be to study the implementation of this approach in a business context during the early phases of BMI. Future research can test the FL workshop in different classroom settings and in multistakeholder workshops involving students from different programs and educational levels as well as practitioners and policy makers. In our opinion, it is vital that the practitioners and policymakers are involved already from the start including the stage of creating narratives and then throughout the whole process. This approach will give significant insights not only into how to further develop the workshop by, for example, including roleplay and joint reading of created narratives, but also into understanding how the FL workshop may contribute to learning and capacity building. Additionally, a longitudinal study can be made to follow up the role of the FL workshop and its future output; as a non-explicitly-business-model-related artefact it will be interesting to explore how effective it is for changing the business model of a firm. In conclusion, it will be of great interest as a means of revealing why and how and in what context artefacts develop agency.

References

1. Baden-Fuller, C., Mangematin, V.: Business models: a challenging agenda. Strateg. Organ. **11**(4), 418–427 (203). https://doi.org/10.1177/1476127013510112
2. Bakhtin, M.M.: The Dialogic Imagination. University of Texas Press (1981)
3. Bell, J.S.: Narrative inquiry: more than just telling stories. TESOL Q. **36**(2), 207–213 (2002). https://doi.org/10.2307/3588331
4. Bengtsson, F., Ågerfalk, P.J.: Information technology as a change actant in sustainability innovation: insights from Uppsala. J. Strateg. Inf. Syst. **20**(1), 96–112 (2011). https://doi.org/10.1016/j.jsis.2010.09.007
5. Bocken, N., Miller, K., Weissbrod, I., Holgado, M., Evans, S.: Business model experimentation for circularity: driving sustainability in a large international clothing retailer. Econ. Policy Energy Environ. **1**, 85–122 (2017). https://doi.org/10.3280/EFE2017-001006
6. Boje, D.: Narrative Methods for Organizational & Communication Research. Sage, London (2001)
7. Boje, D., Jørgensen, K.M.: A 'storytelling science' approach making the eco-business modeling turn. J. Bus. Models **8**(3), 9–26 (2020). https://doi.org/10.5278/jbm.v8i3.3454
8. Breuer, H., Fichter, K., Lüdeke-Freund, F.: Requirements for sustainability-oriented business model development. In: 6th International Leuphana Conference on Entrepreneurship, pp. 14–15. Lüneburg, Germany (2016)

9. Bryant, R., Knight, D.M.: The Anthropology of the Future. Cambridge University Press, Cambridge (2019)
10. Callon, M.: Some elements of a sociology of translation: domestication of the scallops and the fishermen of saint Brieuc Bay. Sociol. Rev. **32**(1suppl), 196–233 (1984). https://doi.org/10.1111/j.1467-954X.1984.tb00113.x
11. Casadesus-Masanell, R., Ricart, J.E.: From strategy to business models and onto tactics. Long Range Plan. **43**(2), 195–215 (2010). https://doi.org/10.1016/j.lrp.2010.01.004
12. Casadó, R.G., Golightly, D., Laing, K., Palacin, R., Todd, L.: Children, young people and mobility as a service: opportunities and barriers for future mobility. Transp. Res. Interdiscip. Perspect. **4**, 100107 (2020). https://doi.org/10.1016/j.trip.2020.100107
13. Cavarero, A.: Relating narratives: storytelling and selfhood, P. A. Kottman, trans. Routledge (2000)
14. Chesbrough, H., Rosenbloom, R.S.: The role of the business model in capturing value from innovation: evidence from Xerox corporation's technology spin-off companies. Ind. Corp. Chang. **11**(3), 529–555 (2002). https://doi.org/10.1093/icc/11.3.529
15. Demil, B., Lecocq, X.: Crafting an innovative business model in an established company: the role of artifacts. Bus. Models Model. Adv. Strateg. Manag. **33**, 31–58 (2015). https://doi.org/10.1108/S0742-332220150000033003
16. Doganova, L., Eyquem-Renault, M.: What do business models do?: Innovation devices in technology entrepreneurship. Res. Policy **38**(10), 1559–1570 (2009). https://doi.org/10.1016/j.respol.2009.08.002
17. Facer, K.: Using the future in education. In: Noddings, N., Lees, H. (eds.) The Palgrave International Handbook of Alternative Education, pp. 63–78. Palgrave Macmillan (2016)
18. Futures Literacy, UNESCO, UNESCO (2021). https://en.unesco.org/futuresliteracy. Accessed 28 July 2022
19. Geissdoerfer, M., Bocken, N., Hultink, E.J.: Design thinking to enhance the sustainable business modelling process – a workshop based on a value mapping process. J. Clean. Prod. **135**, 1218–1232 (2016). https://doi.org/10.1016/j.jclepro.2016.07.020
20. Goodman, N.: Ways of Worldmaking. Hacket Publishing, Indianapolis (1978)
21. Häggström, M., Schmidt, C.: To belong, participate and act!: an educational perspective. Futures **132**, article 102813 (2021). https://doi.org/10.1016/j.futures.2021.102813
22. Johnson, M.W.: Seizing the White Space: Business Model Innovation for Transformative Growth and Renewal. Harvard Business Press, Boston, Massachusetts (2010)
23. Laasch, O.: An actor-network perspective on business models: how being responsible led to incremental but pervasive change. Long Range Plan. **52**(3), 406–426 (2019). https://doi.org/10.1016/j.lrp.2018.04.002
24. Liveley, G., Slocombe, W., Spiers, E.: Futures literacy through narrative. Futures **125**, 1–9 (2021). https://doi.org/10.1016/j.futures.2020.102663
25. Lund, M.: Innovating a business model for services with storytelling. In: Emmanouilidis, C., Taisch, M., Kiritsis, D. (eds.) APMS 2012. IAICT, vol. 397, pp. 677–684. Springer, Heidelberg (2013). https://doi.org/10.1007/978-3-642-40352-1_85
26. Magretta, J.: Why business models matter. Harv. Bus. Rev. **80**(5), 86–92 (2002)
27. Miller, R.: Futures literacy: a hybrid strategic scenario method. Futures **39**(4), 341–362 (2007). https://doi.org/10.1016/j.futures.2006.12.001
28. Miller, R.: Futures literacy: embracing complexity and using the future. Ethos **10**, 23–28 (2011)
29. Miller, R.: Sensing and making-sense of futures literacy: towards a futures literacy framework (FLF). In: Miller, R. (ed.) Transforming the Future: Anticipation in the 21st Century, pp. 15–50. Routledge (2018)

30. Nailer, C., Buttriss, G.: Processes of business model evolution through the mechanism of anticipation and realisation of value. Ind. Mark. Manag. **91**, 671–685 (2020). https://doi.org/10.1016/j.indmarman.2019.04.009

31. Palo, T.: Interactive nature of business models: narrative approach. In: 31st IMP Conference, pp. 25–29. Kolding, Denmark (2015). https://eprints.lancs.ac.uk/id/eprint/75761

32. Poli, R.: The challenges of futures literacy. Futures **132**, article 102800 (2021). https://doi.org/10.1016/j.futures.2021.102800

33. Reason, M., Heinemeyer, C.: Storytelling, story-retelling, storyknowing: towards a participatory practice of storytelling. Res. Drama Educ. **21**(4), 558–573 (2016). https://doi.org/10.1080/13569783.2016.1220247

34. Roome, N., Louche, C.: Journeying toward business models for sustainability: a conceptual model found inside the black box of organisational transformation. Organ. Environ. **29**(1), 11–35 (2016). https://doi.org/10.1177/1086026615595084

35. Ryan, M.-L.: Fiction, non-factuals, and the principle of minimal departure. Poetics **9**, 403–422 (1980). https://doi.org/10.1016/0304-422X(80)90030-3

36. Ryan, M.-L.: Possible Worlds, Artificial Intelligence, and Narrative Theory. Indiana University Press, Bloomington (1991)

37. Sharma, G., Greco, A., Grewatsch, S., Bansal, P.: Cocreating forward: How researchers and managers can address problems together. AMLE **21**(3), 350–368 (2022). https://doi.org/10.5465/amle.2021.0233

38. Teece, D.J.: Business models, business strategy and innovation. Long Range Plan. **43**(2–3), 172–194 (2010). https://doi.org/10.1016/j.lrp.2009.07.003

39. Upward, A., Jones, P.: An ontology for strongly sustainable business models: defining an enterprise framework compatible with natural and social science. Organ. Environ. **29**(1), 97–123 (2016). https://doi.org/10.1177/1086026615592933

Author Index

E. Brooks et al. (Eds.): DLI 2022, LNICST 493, p. 183, 2023.
https://doi.org/10.1007/978-3-031-31392-9

Printed in the United States
by Baker & Taylor Publisher Services